THE MEITHEIS

THE MEITHEIS

A PEOPLE OF MANIPUR THEIR SOCIAL STRUCTURE, CUSTOMS, LANGUAGE AND RELIGIOUS PRACTICES

T. C. HODSON

INTRODUCTION BY

CHARLES J. LYALL

GYAN

Published by

Gyan Publishing House
5, Ansari Road
Daryaganj, New Delhi-110002
Phone: 011-47034999, 9811692060
E-mail: books@gyanbooks.com

Distribution Network
gyanbooks.com
India, USA, Canada, UK, Australia

ISBN: 978-93-6780-316-5 (HB)

First Published, 1908

2nd Impression 2025

Printed at: Gyan Press, Delhi.

THE MEITHEIS
Author: T. C. HODSON, Introduction by CHARLES J. LYALL

THE MEITHEIS

Frontispiece

RĀS COSTUME.

See p. 16

THE MEITHEIS

BY

T. C. HODSON

LATE ASSISTANT POLITICAL AGENT IN MANIPUR AND
SUPERINTENDENT OF THE STATE
FELLOW OF THE ROYAL ANTHROPOLOGICAL INSTITUTE

WITH AN INTRODUCTION

BY

SIR CHARLES J. LYALL

K.C.S.I., C.I.E., LL.D., M.A.

(Published under the orders of the Government of Eastern Bengal and Assam)

ILLUSTRATED

LONDON

DAVID NUTT

57, 59, LONG ACRE

1908

PREFACE.

THE AUTHOR desires to offer his sincere gratitude to those whose help has enabled him to complete this monograph. The chromo-lithographic illustrations are the work of Mr. W. Griggs, and have been prepared by him from designs (based on actual photographs) by Mr. Fred Andrews, Head of the Department of Arts and Crafts at the Battersea Polytechnic, and formerly Principal of the Art School, Lahore, and by Miss Theodora Hodson, of the Slade School of Fine Art, University of London, University College. The coloured illustrations of the Folk-Tale, "Khamba and Thoibi," are reproductions in three-colour process by Messrs. John Swain and Sons, Ltd., of pictures painted by Bhudro Singh, a Manipuri artist.

Last but not least, the copious Index is the work of Mrs. Eileen Mitchell, whose labours are most gratefully acknowledged.

EAST LONDON COLLEGE,
UNIVERSITY OF LONDON,
1908.

TABLE OF CONTENTS.

SECTION I.

PAGES

Habitat—Appearance—Geographical Distribution—Origin—Affinities—Dress—Tattooing—Ornaments—Weapons . 1—21

SECTION II.

Occupation—Houses—Villages—Furniture—Manufactures—Implements and Utensils—Agriculture—Crops—Fishing—Hunting—Food and Drink—Games . . . . 22—57

SECTION III.

LAWS AND CUSTOMS.

Political Organisation—Internal Structure—Marriage Rules Inheritance—Adoption—Tenure of Land and Laws regarding Land—Laws regarding other property—Decision of Disputes—War—Head-hunting . . . . . . 58—94

SECTION IV.

RELIGION.

Nature of Popular Beliefs—The Worship of Ancestors—Religious Rites and Ceremonies—Sacrifices—Priesthood—Nature Worship—Ceremonies attending Birth—Naming—Toga Virilis—Marriage—Death and Disposal of the Dead—Festivities, Domestic and Tribal—Genna . . 95—119

SECTION V.

Traditions—Superstitions and Folk-Tales . . . . . 120—154

SECTION VI.

Language and Meithei Grammar . . . . 155—181

APPENDICES . . . . 182—211

INDEX . . . . 213—227

LIST OF ILLUSTRATIONS.

TO FACE PAGE

Rās Costume . . . . *Frontispiece*

Map 1

Meithei Leisābi 14

Girl weaving 27

Polo in Manipur 48

Hī-yāng-tā-na-ba 53

Meithei Wrestlers 72

The Kohima Stone 92

Nātch Ghar and Temple of Govindji 102

The Nōngshā and Kangla 124

Nūmit Kāppa 128

Khamba and Thoibi—

The Dance before the King 134

Capture of the Wild Bull 143

The Torture by the Elephant 147

Thoibi tricks Kōngyamba 150

The Tiger Hunt 154

LIST OF AUTHORITIES AND WORKS CONSULTED.

Avebury, Lord . . . Origin of Civilisation and Primitive Condition of Man, 6th edition.

Brown, Dr. R. . . . Annual Report on the Munnipore Political Agency for 1868–1869. Selections from the Records of the Government of India, Foreign Department, No. lxxviii. Statistical Account of Manipur, 1874.

Butler, Major . . . Travels and Adventures in Assam.

Colquhoun, H. A., I.C.S. . MS. Notes.

Cox, Captain H. . . . The Burmhan Empire.

Crawley, E. . . . . The Mystic Rose.

Damant, G. H. . . . Journal of the Asiatic Society of Bengal, vol. xliv., Part I., 173; vol. xlvi., Part I., 36. Journal of the Royal Asiatic Society, new series, vol. xii., 228.

Davis, A. W. . . . Census of Assam, 1891, vol. i.

Elias, Ney . . . . History of the Shans.

Frazer, J. G. . . . The Golden Bough.

Gait, E. A. . . . . The Census of Assam, 1891, vol. i. History of Assam.

Grierson, Dr. G. A., C.I.E. . Report of the Linguistic Survey of India, vols. ii. and iii.

Grimwood, Mrs. E. . . My Three Years in Manipur.

Gurdon, Major P. R. T. . The Khasis.

Harrison, Miss Jane . . Prolegomena to Greek Religion.

Hodgson, B. H. . . . Journal of the Asiatic Society of Bengal, vol. xviii., 451.

Hodson, T. C. . . . Journal of the Society of Arts, vol. liii., 545. Journal of the Anthropological Institute, vol. xxxvi, 92.

Hunter, Sir W. W., K.C.S.I. History of the Indian Empire. Statistical Account of Assam.

Jevons, F. B. . . . Plutarch's Romane Questions. Introduction to the History of Religion.

Johnstone, Major-General Sir J., K.C.S.I.	My Experiences in the Naga Hills and Manipur.
Keene, A. H.	History of India.
Lewin, Colonel T.	The Hill Tracts of Chittagong.
Lyall, Sir A., G.C.B.	Asiatic Studies.
Lyall, Sir C., K.C.S.I.	Journal of the Society of Arts, vol. li., 618.
McCulloch, Major W.	Account of the Valley of Munnipore and of the Hill Tribes. Selections from the Records of the Government of India, Foreign Department, No. XXVIII.
Mackenzie, Sir A., K.C.S.I.	North-East Frontier of Bengal.
McLennan, J. F.	Primitive Marriage. The Patriarchal Theory. Studies in Ancient History.
MacMahon, General A. R.	Far Cathay and Farther India.
Maine, Sir H. S., K.C.S.I.	Ancient Law. Early Law and Custom.
Pemberton, Captain R. B.	Report on the North-East Frontier of India.
Robertson Smith, W.	Marriage and Kinship in Early Arabia.
Romania	Vol. xxxvi., No. 141, 36.
Sangermano, Father	The Burmese Empire.
Scott and Hardiman	Gazetteer of Upper Burma, vol. i., Part I.
Snodgrass, Major	Narrative of the First Burmese War.
Symes, Lieut.-Col. M.	The Embassy to Ava.
Tylor, E. B.	Primitive Culture. Anthropology.
Waddell, Colonel L. A., C.B., C.I.E.	Journal of the Asiatic Society of Bengal, vol. lxix.
Watt, Sir G., K.C.S.I.	Journal of the Society of Arts, vol. liii., 562.
Westermarck, E.	History of Human Marriage.
Wilson, H. H.	History of the First Burmese War.

The translation of the Ningthaurōl or Meithei Chronicles, of which much use has been made, is by Babu Nithor Nath Banerji. They have also been translated by Babu Umes Chandra Ghose, but the latter work has been lost.

INTRODUCTION.

A RECENT writer on the tribes of the Brahmaputra Valley * has asserted in forcible language that, "unfortunately for science, no steps are being taken to record the rare vestiges of prehistoric society which still survive here, but which are now being rapidly swept away by advancing civilization. . . . This unique mass of material which is available for solving important problems, lying at the very base of civilization and culture, is being allowed to disappear unrecorded. This regrettable fact has been repeatedly represented during the past few years, without practically any result."

The complaint is unjust; the bibliographies appended to the series of Ethnographical Monographs, of which the present volume is one, will show that there exists a large mass of materials dealing with a considerable proportion of the Indo-Chinese tribes of Assam. It is true that some of the most important of these are "buried away" in Gazetteers, Census reports, and contributions to the Journals of learned societies. But those who make it their business to investigate anthropological problems may surely be expected to search among such obvious sources for the information they desire. In India Gazetteers and Census reports are the appointed places for recording the results of inquiries into the characters and institutions of the various elements of the population. Such literature is scarcely likely to command a wide circulation in

* Lieut.-Col. L. A. Waddell, in the *Journal of the Asiatic Society of Bengal*, Part III., 1900.

any country, and writers who deal with it are necessarily confined to the means open to them of perpetuating the results of their investigations in the official publications of the Government. Nor is it true that "no steps have been taken" since 1872, when Col. Dalton's *Descriptive Ethnology of Bengal* was published, to extend our knowledge of these tribes. In 1881 Sir Charles Elliott, shortly after assuming the government of the Province, issued instructions for the compilation, not only of grammars, vocabularies, and phrase-books of the languages of all the leading tribes of Assam, but also of records of their customs and institutions. The result is a series of works dealing with the tribal languages of which the Province is justly proud, and records of customs and usages which, though doubtless capable of further extension (which they are now receiving), are of great anthropological value. The linguistic work done is indeed the principal fruit of the orders of 1881; but this is by no means, as Lieut.-Col. Waddell asserts, "of secondary importance." Without an understanding of the language of a tribe there can be no adequate investigation of its institutions; the speech is the expression of the mind of the people who speak it, the measure of their culture and outlook upon the world around them. It is, moreover, more especially in Assam, with its vast diversity of ethnic stocks, the only safe index to the affinities of a tribe with its neighbours, and, in the almost complete absence of historic record or remembered tradition, to the migrations which have brought the various units to their present sites.

So far as concerns the subject of the present monograph, the Meitheis or dominant race of Manipur, Lieut.-Col. Waddell is least of all justified in his complaint of insufficiency of record. We first became well acquainted with the Meitheis in the Burma war of 1824–26. On the conclusion of hostilities, the inhabitants of the reconstituted State of Manipur (which had been overrun and annexed by the Burmese, and recovered its independence as the result of our operations,) were carefully described by Captain R. B. Pemberton in his excellent *Report on the Eastern Frontier of British India*, printed at Calcutta in 1835. A dictionary of English and Manipuri, compiled by Captain Gordon of the Manipur Levy, was published in 1837. But the most exhaustive presentment of the State and its peoples is contained in the *Account of the Valley of Munnipore, and of the Hill Tribes, with a comparative vocabulary of the Munnipore and other languages*, by Major William McCulloch, printed at Calcutta in 1859. Major, afterwards Lieut.-Col., McCulloch was a man of culture and literary ability, and his work (of which Lieut.-Col. Waddell makes no mention in his brief notice of the Meitheis *) has ever since its publication been the chief authority on its subject. Col. McCulloch, who was the son of the well-known political economist Dr. J. R. McCulloch, was born in 1816, and went to Manipur as Assistant Political Agent in 1840; he became Political Agent in 1845, and held that post, with a year's intermission, until 1867. In this long period of twenty-seven years he acquired a most intimate knowledge of the State and its inhabitants; he married a Manipuri lady, of the family of Raja Nar Singh; and he exercised supreme authority over the Kuki tribes subject to the State, who inhabit the hills to the south and west of the valley of Manipur. After his retirement he settled at Shillong, where I enjoyed the privilege of his acquaintance, and died there, in his seventieth year, in 1885.

Colonel McCulloch's account of Manipur is not unknown even to British anthropologists. It is referred to by Mr. J. F. McLennan in his work on *Primitive Marriage*, and has been cited by Lord Avebury in his book on *The Origin of Civilization and the Primitive Condition of Man*. He was succeeded as Political Agent by Dr. R. Brown, who was the author of a *Statistical Account of Manipur*, printed by Government at

* Pp. 60–61.

Calcutta in 1874. This work incorporates most of McCulloch's information, with useful additions by Dr. Brown himself. It is an accessible book, and was widely distributed by Government on its publication; Lieut.-Col. Waddell does not mention it. Another contribution to the ethnography and history of the State was made by Mr. G. H. Damant of the Indian Civil Service, whose papers were published in the Journals of the Asiatic Society of Bengal and the Royal Asiatic Society.* Mr. Damant was greatly interested in the archaic literature of Manipur, and in the problem of the relation of the various Indo-Chinese races one to another. He met his death at Khonoma in the Naga Hills in 1879. The terrible events of 1891, which brought the little State prominently before the British public, led to a fresh development of descriptive literature in the books of Sir James Johnstone (for several years Political Agent in Manipur) and Mrs. Grimwood. These are not important contributions to scientific ethnography, but they —especially the former—contain interesting information as to the characteristics of the people.

It will thus be seen that the Manipuris have received no small share of attention in the past, and that the interest shown in them by investigators compares favourably with that aroused by the inhabitants of many other more accessible parts of India.

The author of the present monograph has wisely taken as his basis the accounts of Colonel McCulloch and Dr. Brown, and has noted where they need supplementing and completing, and the changes which have occurred during the past half-century. From his practical acquaintance with the administration of the State and its subject tribes, and his intimate knowledge of the Manipuri (as well as of the Thado Kuki) language, he has been able greatly to enlarge the field of our information; and the latter half of the book, dealing with the

* See the Bibliography.

traditions, folk-lore, and folk-tales of the Meitheis, and with their linguistic affinities, will be found to contain a mass of new and interesting matter.

It was my fortune to visit Manipur only once (in February, 1888) during my service in Assam, and I am thus acquainted with the subject chiefly by hearsay. But I have always taken a lively interest in this singular oasis of comparative civilization and organized society, set in the midst of a congeries of barbarous peoples, over whom its rulers exercise an authority which, if scarcely approaching the settled polity of more advanced communities, is at least in the direction of peace and order. The valley of Manipur in several respects resembles in miniature its neighbour, that of the Irawadi. In both the civilized people who occupy the central settled and organized region are nearly akin to the wild folk who inhabit the hills which enclose the alluvial plain. But while Burma has accepted the mild and gentle religion of Buddha, and thus profoundly modified the original animistic cult, Manipur has been taken into the pale of Hinduism, and has imposed upon itself burdensome restrictions of caste and ritual from which its greater neighbour is happily free. In both countries, however, the older religious ideas still survive beneath the surface of the philosophical systems borrowed from India, and in reality sway to a large extent the lives and sentiments of the people. The State has recently, after sixteen years of British administration, been committed to the government of the Prince who was chosen to fill the vacant throne after the events of 1891; and it is greatly to be hoped that its future may be happy and prosperous, and that it may exercise an increasing influence in winning to civilization the wilder tribes which recognize its authority.

C. J. LYALL.

May, 1908.

From a Picture by BHUDRO SINGH.

KHAMBA AND THOIBI

(THOIBI TRICKS KONGYAMBA.)

p. 150

ASSAM SHOWING AREA OCCUPIED BY THE MEITHEIS

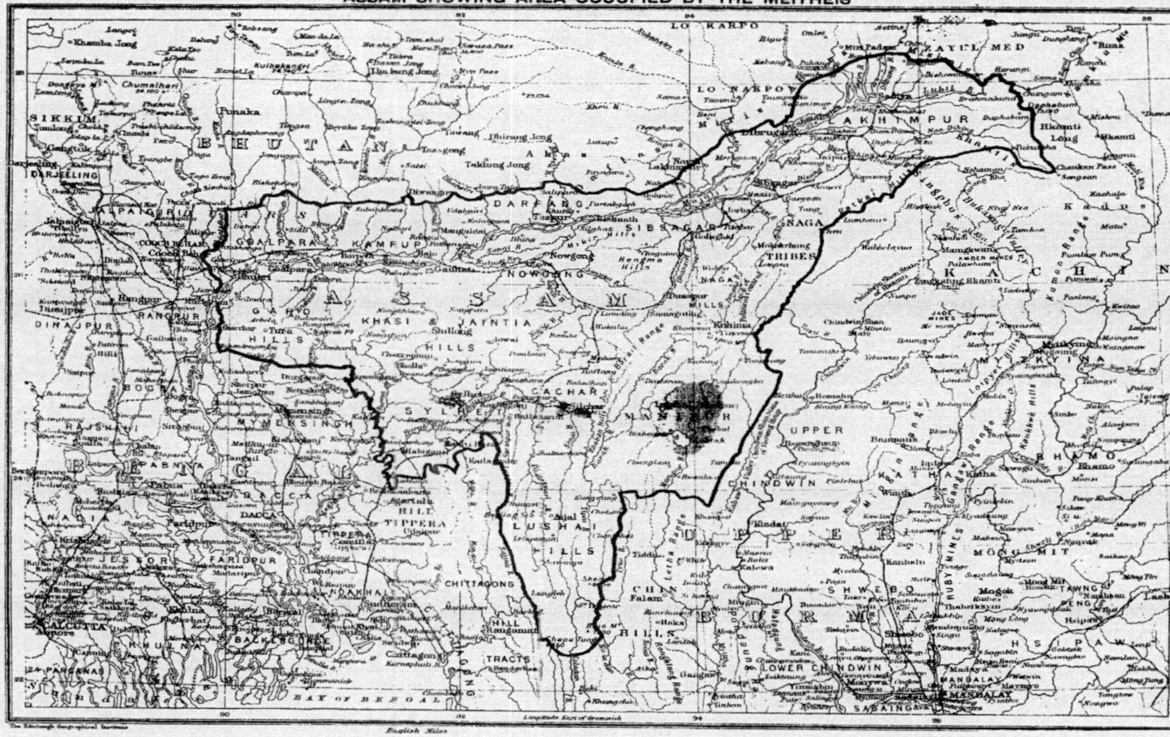

THE MEITHEIS

SECTION I.

HABITAT.

THE Native State of Manipur lies between Latitude 23° 50′ and 25° 30′ North and Longitude 93° 10′ and 94° 30′ East, and consists of about 7000 square miles of hill territory, and of 1000 square miles of level country forming the broad valley, to which the Manipuris have given the name Meithei Leipāk, or the broad land of the Meitheis. On the west its frontiers march with those of the British District of Cachar up to a point in the hills near which is the Naga village Maolong, from which the boundary line follows the river Barāk and then traverses the hills to Mao, where a natural frontier line begins again. There is a small piece undemarcated at the corner on which is situated the village of Jessami. The frontier touches Upper Burma and passes along the western edge of the Kubo Valley, for so long the subject of contention between Manipur and Burma. On the south the confines of the State touch the Chin Hills on the east and the Lushai Hills on the west. The Burmese call it Kathē, the Assamese Meklē, while, according to Colonel McCulloch, the Bengali name for the State is Moglai.*

Within the area of the State there is an immense variety of climate and scenery, which is only equalled by the variety of the types of mankind whose habits form the subject of these monographs. Tea is indigenous in the hills, and before unwise greed ruined it, the trade in tea seed was profitable alike to the State and to the traders. Rubber, too, grows in natural profusion in the hills. The teak timber in the State represents a

* *Cf.* Pemberton, *Report on Eastern Frontier*, pp. 19, 20; McCulloch, *Account of Munnipore*, p. 1.

natural wealth whose limitations are as yet unascertained. In the Nātch Ghar are beams of teak of enormous length and girth —from trees in the forests of the State. For the lover of sport the valley is a veritable Paradise. In the cold weather the numerous lakes and jheels are covered with wild duck, teal, geese, snipe, and in the hills woodcock and rare pheasants are to be found. The eastern edges of the Logtāk lake afford a home to the brow-antlered deer, while the fastnesses and thickets of the lofty mountain peaks shelter the timid *serao*. Of mightier game there is the tiger, a rare visitor to the byres of the plainsmen; now and then a leopard ravages the cattle, and up to the British occupation elephants were caught in the valley. Many are the tales that are told of the strange deaths of unhappy persons who have seen a *lairel* or python, while in the swamps of the Logtāk is found the King cobra (*Ophiophagus oelaps* or *tānglei* in the vernacular). The Russell's viper is found in the valley, but deadly though it is, the villagers often fear it but little, and I have seen a man break one in two with a dexterous twist.

The census returns of 1901 show a population of 284,465 in the State, of whom 180,960 are inhabitants of the valley and 103,505 hill tribesmen. It is impossible to make any deductions as to the increase or decrease of the population, for there are grounds for holding that the census of 1881 did not cover the same area, and was not conducted on the same careful lines as that of 1901. The census papers of 1891 were destroyed in the émeute of that year.

APPEARANCE.

Dr. Brown says that, "Although the general facial characteristics of the Munniporie are of the Mongolian type, there is a great diversity of feature among them, some of them showing a regularity approaching the Aryan type. Among both men and women the stature is very various, differing about as much as is found among Europeans. Some of them are very good-looking and fair. It is not uncommon to meet with girls with brownish-black hair, brown eyes, fair complexions, straight noses, and rosy cheeks. The Munnipories are decidedly a

	Tribe.	Sub-tribe.	District of birth.	Personal name.	Age	Height.	Height sitting.	Outspread arms.	Weight in pounds.	Cephalic length.	Cephalic breadth.	Min. frontal breadth.	Maximum bizygomatic breadth.	Bigonial breadth.	Nasal height.	Nasal width.	Nasal projection.	Naso-molar breadth.	Bimolar breadth.	Vertex to nasal notch.	Vertex to chin.	Left humerus.	Left radius.	L. mid. finger to middle of patella.	Left calf girth.	Colour. Breast { c = covered. s = semi-covd.	Colour. Face.	Colour. Iris.	Remarks.
439	Mitai or Manipuri		Manipur	Ning Tao-ba	45	1665				184	140	97	130		46	36	28	112	102	106	224				35			3	ear pierced, not tattooed.
440	"		"	Chengo	38	1658																							
441	"		"	Ebai	40	1595				185	143	104	133		45	35		108	96	103	216				33			1	"
442	"		Sibsagar	Kunjo	35	1656				186	135	99	136		45	38		118	97	90	206				32			4	"
443	"		Manipur	Mele	40	1705				188	136	109	138		50	38		124	105	104	226				32			3	"
444	"		"	Nildhar Sing	50	1595				185	143	104	133		45	35		108	96	103	216				33			4	"
445	"		Sibsagar	Hiru Chandra Sing	35	1656				186	135	99	136		45	38		118	97	90	206				32			2	"
446	"		Manipur	Chengo Sing	40	1705				188	136	109	138		50	38		124	105	104	226				32			3	"
447	"		Sylhet	Muktah Sing	40	1658				193	144	102	137		52	38		121	100	97	221				35			4	"
448	"		Nowgong	Mele Sing	29	1640				182	144	105	132		48	36		112	99	113	228				33			3	"
449	"		"	Lasan Sing	30	1634				186	140	93	121		51	37		107	92	113	220				32			4	"
450	"		Dibrugarh	Gopal Sing	26	1585				177	141	97	128		44	37		106	94	118	230				33			2	"
451	"		Sylhet	Kunje Sing	28	1638				185	146	104	142		47	38		120	105	113	225				33			2	"
452	"		Sibsagar	Benu Sing	27	1595				180	152	101	133		48	35		108	102	97	211				32			2	"
453	"		Manipur	Ebai Sing	40	1583				181	143	99	130		44	35		118	101	105	226				33			1	"
				Average ...		1640				184	141	100	133		47	36		114	99	105	220				33			3	

Journal of the Asiatic Society of Bengal, vol. lxix. (1900), part iii., pp. 114–115. Article: "The Tribes of the Brahmaputra Valley." Colonel L. A. Waddell, M.B., LL.D.

[*To face page* 3.

muscular race, some of the men particularly so; they are generally spare in habit of body, and fat people are rare. They have good chests and well-formed limbs. The men wear their hair, which is coarse and black, long, and combed back from the forehead, which is occasionally shaved; the hair is gathered into a coil behind. Moustaches are uncommon, so much so that a man with a moustache invariably is nicknamed *khoi-haoba*, although a man with a thick straight moustache will be seen. They have no beards, or very rudimentary ones. Boys' heads are generally shaved, leaving only a straggling quantity of hair at the back. The hair of the females is worn in three different ways, according to age. When quite young, up to the age of about ten, the front part of the head is shaved, the back part, from about the level of the ears round the head, being allowed to grow loose behind. The next fashion is that for unmarried girls, and is very peculiar: the hair behind, from about the middle of each ear round, is allowed to grow long, is combed back and tied in a knot or left loose. In front of this the hair is combed forwards, and cut equally so as to reach over the forehead an inch or so above the eyebrow. In front of and over each ear is a lock of hair about two inches broad, and reaching down to the angle of the jaw. In married women the hair is allowed to grow long, and is combed back from the forehead, Bengallee fashion, and tied in a knot behind, leaving a few inches dependent from the knot. All who can afford the luxury wear a chignon, which, as with the Bengallees, is incorporated with the knot of back hair." * The men are not heavy, though averaging about five feet seven. The women are four inches shorter than the men. Colonel L. A. Waddell, LL.D., C.B., C.I.E., has kindly permitted the publication of the anthropometrical data in the accompanying table.

The Lois very closely resemble the Meitheis, and are to all intents and purposes indistinguishable from their over-lords. Indeed, it is remarkable to observe how much the individuality of such people as the Meitheis, the Lois, the hill people, and even the Gurkhas, depends on differences of clothing and coiffure. In the case of the Lois, who are either earlier settlers or the direct descendants of Meitheis banished to Loi villages

* *Op. cit.*, pp. 28 and 29.

as a punishment, this phenomenon is intelligible, for the infusion of true Meithei blood into Loi families by mixed marriages is undeniable.

The Panggan or Muhammedan settlers are distinct from the Meithei, as is reasonable to expect, although it has been noted that many of the Muhammedan inhabitants of Sylhet and Cachar resemble the hill type.* The Panggans are believed to have originated from Cachar as prisoners of war taken by Meitheis.

GEOGRAPHICAL DISTRIBUTION.

Historical circumstances account for the rather wide geographical distribution of the Meitheis. There are colonies in Burma which owe their origin to the disastrous raids which, made by way of reprisal for the invasions of Burma by the forces of Manipur in the beginning of the eighteenth century, culminated in the great depopulation of the country in 1819, when the Burmese soldiery took with them into captivity enormous numbers of Manipuris of all ages and of both sexes. Political events have conduced to the growth of settlements of Manipuris in Cachar, Sylhet and Dacca, while in Bengal and in the United Provinces there are small colonies of Manipuris who have left their country for their country's good. These settlements, whether at Nadia, where the sentiment of religious attachment to the Guru of the Royal Family binds them together, or in Cachar where they originally settled to form a bulwark against the forays of Kukis, keep aloof from the people around them, whom they regard, sometimes without injustice, as their inferiors in culture and civilization.

ORIGIN.

The Chronicles of the State of Manipur open with an "authoritative" account of the origin of the Royal Family to which interest of an uncommon kind attaches because

* Sir Charles Lyall, K.C.S.I., *Society of Arts Journal*, No. 2637, vol. li. p. 618.

these documents are now for the first time available for the student.

"By the end of the Dapar Jug and beginning of the Kali Jug (year 3435), Enoog Howba Chonoo, the wife of Babroobahan gave birth to a son called Pākhangba. He used to assume the form of Gods by the day, and by the night he used to be a man."

Around the personage of Pākhangba legends have grown up which declare him to have had the power of changing his shape into that of a snake, and his death, which alone proved his humanity, was due to the accidental infliction of a wound by his son, who saw his father in the house at night and killed him all unwittingly with a spear. To this accidental parricide the Manipuris attribute the frequency of parricide at the early part of the eighteenth century. But there are current other versions of the origin of the *Ningthaja* or Royal clan, and from one of these I take the following genealogy. "The Brahma dev (The creating God of the Universe) had sprung out from the Navel lotus of Narayan (the Protecting God of the Universe), Marichi Muni (a Hindu sage) was born from the limbs of Brahmadev. Marichi's son, Kosshop Muni (a Hindu Saint); Kosshop Muni's son, Surja (Sun); Surja's son, Shaborna Muni; Shaborna's son, Indoo Muni; Indoo Muni's son, Chitra Ketoo; Chitra Ketoo's son, Chitradhaja; Chitradhaja's son, Chitrabija; Chitrabija's son, Chitra Sarba; Chitra Sarba's son, Chitra Rat; Chitra Rat's son, Chitra Vanoo. Chitra Vanoo had no son, only a daughter named Chitranggada; Chitranggada's son, Babrubahan; Babrubahan's son, Sooprabahoo; Sooprabahoo's son, Pākhangba (Jobista). The Jobista or Pākhangba was the first ruling King of Manipur."

Such tales are obviously tainted by the influence of Hinduism, and the appearance of non-Hindu names seems to mark the beginning of native legend. Among the Manipuris, at the time when Colonel McCulloch wrote his remarkable account of the valley, there were extant legends which induced him to believe that "From the most credible traditions, the valley appears originally to have been occupied by several tribes, the principal of which were named Koomul, Looang, Moirang, and Meithei, all of whom came from different directions. For a time the

Koomul appears to have been the most powerful, and after its declension, the Moirang tribe. But by degrees the Meithei subdued the whole, and the name Meithei has become applicable to all. Since their conversion to Hindooism, the Meitheis have claimed for themselves a Hindoo descent. This claim, in his report of the Eastern Frontier, Captain Pemberton rejects, and says, 'we may safely conclude them to be descendants from a Tartar Colony from China.' For this conclusion I can see no reason, and think there is far more ground to conclude them to be descendants of the surrounding hill tribes. The languages spoken by these tribes are in their pristine state: I conceive then, that in their spoken language, an indication of the descent of the Munniporees might be found. Tradition brings the Moirang tribe from the South, the direction of the Kookies, the Koomul from the East, the direction of the Murrings, and the Meithei and Looang from the North-west, the direction of the Koupooees. The languages of the Murrings, Kookies, and Koupooees, are all very similar, and as the Koomul, etc., the offshoots of these tribes were, as before said, at different periods the dominant tribes in the valley, it might be expected that the present language of the people, united under the name of Meithei, would have a very apparent likeness to these languages, and such is the case. All these tribes have also traditions amongst themselves that the Munniporees are offshoots from them. These traditions then, and the composite nature of the language, appear to me to afford more reason for supposing the Munniporees to be descended from the surrounding hill tribes than from a Tartar Colony from China. Besides the stories of their ancestors, which at times the Munniporees relate amongst themselves, show, that up to a very recent period, they retained all the customs of hill people of the present day. Their superstition, too, has preserved relics, which alone would have led to the suspicion of an originally close connection between them and Nagas. The ceremony denominated *Phumbānkāba*, or 'ascending the throne,' is performed in Naga dress, both by the Rajah and Ranee, and the *Yim Chau*, or 'great house,' the original residence of the Meithei Chief, is, though he does not now reside in it, still kept up, and is made in the Naga fashion." *

* *Op. cit.*, p. 4. *Cf.* Pemberton, *Report on Eastern Frontier*, p. 36.

This careful opinion drew the consent of Dr. Brown, who adorned it with some interesting speculations. "Should it be a correct view that the valley of Munnipore was at no very distant period almost covered entirely by water, the origin of the Munnipories from the surrounding hill tribes is the proper and only conclusion to be arrived at. I think it probable that when only a small part of the valley skirting the hills was capable of cultivation, the hillmen bordering it used to descend and cultivate the little land there then was, returning to their homes in the hills after reaping their harvests: as, however, land increased, some few of them settled permanently in the plain, gradually increasing in numbers. The various tribes thus settling in different parts of the valley would in time come into contact, and after a struggle for supremacy, amalgamate. That this is what actually did take place is borne out by the traditions of Munnipore. The above account is by no means accepted as correct by the upper classes of Munnipories, who deny their origin from the hill tribes surrounding the valley, although, when asked to account for themselves otherwise, they have no plausible story to offer. They can merely say that they always belonged to the valley and have always been a separate race. The theory that the valley was once covered with water, although supported by their own traditions, they utterly ignore. A small section of them, however, go a step further than this, and, as alluded to by McCulloch, actually claim for themselves a Western and Hindoo descent. This idea is quite untenable, and rests upon a very slender foundation, or rather on none whatever. The name 'Munnipore' is thus accounted for by the Munnipories, who quote the Mahabārat in confirmation of its accuracy. They say the name is from Muni, a jewel; this jewel was formerly in the possession of the Rajas of the country ages ago. The country was at one time named Mahindrapore, but on a Raja, by name Bubra Baha, coming into possession of the jewel (which formerly belonged to a Nag Raja or Serpent King) and the guddee, he changed the name to Munnipore. According to the Mahabarat, however, the name Munnipore was in existence before the birth of Bubra Baha, and Mahindrapore or Mahindrapahar, was the name of a high hill,* situated but a short

* Vernacular: Nongmai-Ching (*nong* = sun or day; *mai* = (?) facing;

distance to the east of the capital. With regard to the Naga dress, said in the foregoing quotation from McCulloch to be worn by the Raja on ascending the throne, it is stoutly denied, by a section, at least, of the Munnipories, that it has anything to do with the Nagas, but is an ancient Munniporie costume. Besides being worn as above by the Raja on ascending the throne, during the various games hereafter to be described, as the boat races, this dress is worn by the chief competitors as well as by the Raja, who attends the races, steering his own boat in this dress. If really originally a Naga costume, it has little or no affinity now with what is worn by them." *

Major-General Sir James Johnstone, K.C.S.I., lends the weight of his long and interesting experience in Manipur to the belief that "There can be little doubt that some time or other the Naga tribes to the north made one of their chiefs Rajah of Manipur, and that his family, while, like the Manchus in China and other conquerors, adopting the civilization of the country, retained some of their old customs. This is shown in the curious practice at the installation of a Rajah, when he and the Ranee appear in Naga costume; also that he always has in his palace a house built like a Naga's, and wherever he goes he is attended by two or three Manipuris with Naga arms and accoutrements. I once told a Manipuri what I thought on the subject, and he was greatly struck by it and admitted the force of what I said." †

Photographs of the *kangla* or Coronation Hall show that the front beams of the roof have crossed and carved ends which are distinctly reminiscent of the decorations of the houses of the Khullakpas of Naga villages. It may be observed that the *sang-kai punsiba* or hut in the Naga style, to which Major-General Johnstone makes reference, means the long-lived hut and granary (*sang* = hut, *kai* = granary, *punsiba* = late dying = long lived).

The Lois, a title applied to the inhabitants of a number of

ching = hill), probably the hill that faces the sun. The great annual *rainpuja* takes place on this hill, which is intimately connected with other magical rites.—T. C. H.

* *Op. cit.*, pp. 27 and 28.

† *Experiences in Manipur*, pp. 82, 83. See also p. 97. *Cf.* Lyall, *Asiatic Studies*, vol. i. p. 96.

villages which are some distance from Imphāl, and which are and have for long been in subjection to the Meitheis, are of various origin. Sengmai, a village on the Manipur-Kohima cart road about nine miles from Imphāl, is said to have moved there from the south. Fayeng Loi, however, preserves a tradition that they once occupied the site of the Kōnung or Fort from which they were driven out by Pākhungba, which means the rise of the Meithei power. Andro Loi, a village in the vicinity of Fayeng, claims the same origin. The villagers of Chairel, situated on the Imphāl river not far from Shuganu, declare that they once occupied the slopes of Nongmaiching. The Lois in the south-east of the valley at Kokching, who live by iron-smelting, were once under the rule of the Heirōk King, whose dominions stretched from Kokching to the Imphāl river. McCulloch * states, that the appointment of an official with the style and title of Budhiraj to govern Kokching dates from the reign of Gharib Nawaz. The village of Susakameng is said to be inhabited by the descendants of Chinese who came to Manipur in the reign of Khāgenba. The villages on the Logtāk, Thānga and Iting, are known to have had their origin, as had Shuganu, on the banks of the Imphāl river, as penal settlements to which all classes of offenders were sent. From the Chronicles it would appear that the Loi villages possess considerable antiquity, for it is stated that they were founded by Airaba, whose reign is dated about 1000 A.D., that is, in the period before history of any real authenticity begins.

Khāgenba seems to have been the first monarch to make use of the Loi villages as places of detention for prisoners, for he is said to have sent captives, taken on a raid against Nagas probably in the neighbourhood of Marām in the north, to Shuganu in the year 1645 A.D. Ten years later his successor, Khul Chaoba, transported a number of Manipuris, who, under the leadership of the Angōm Ningthou, had raised the standard of rebellion against him, to Eharai Loi. In the same year this king seems to have had trouble with other Loi villages, for he is recorded as having sent expeditions against Andro, Kameng Chīkhōng (salt well), and Yaripōk, all of which are capable of identification as extant in modern days. The religious changes

* *Op. cit.*, p. 14.

introduced by Gharib Nawaz were the occasion of wholesale deportations to Loi villages, and from that time onward the Chronicles constantly make mention of deportation to a Loi village as a punishment. In spite of, or perhaps because of, this not very auspicious origin the Loi villages are among the most prosperous villages in the State, for the reason that, untrammelled by caste prejudices, they are able and allowed to practise industries which are denied to the Meitheis, whom, however, to the neglect of their temporal advantages, they are anxious to follow into the respectability of Hinduism. On the occasion of the recent census many of them seized the opportunity to declare themselves Hindus, a proceeding which greatly shocked the Meitheis.

AFFINITIES.

The group name "Meithei" has been derived from *mi* = man and *thei* = separate, while in a footnote to a contribution of immense value to the Asiatic Society of Bengal in 1853, Brian Houghton Hodgson expressed the view that "in the 'Moitay' of Manipur we have the combined appellations of the Siamese Tai and the Kochin Chinese 'Moy.' In other words, the Manipurian tribe, called Cossiahs by the Bengalis, belong to the Moi section of the great tribe called Tai by themselves and Shan vel Syan by the Burmese, the sectional name being also foreign and equivalent to the native." * Of course, the Manipuris are totally distinct from the Khasis,† and while Shan influence has exerted as great an influence over the culture as over the politics of Manipur, it is difficult, especially on linguistic grounds, to group the Meitheis with the Tai races when the structure and vocabulary of the Meithei language alike agree with those of the Tibeto-Burman races, a conclusion which rests on evidence very largely provided by Brian Hodgson himself.

* J. A. S. B., vol. xxii. (1853), pp. 14, 15.

† Consult monograph on "Khasis," by Major P. R. T. Gurdon, I.A., who deals with the linguistic affinities of the Khasis very thoroughly: also consult vol. ii. of the *Report of the Linguistic Survey of India*. Mon-Khmer and Tai Families.

The researches of the Linguistic Survey of India enable us to take a comprehensive view of the relationship of the Meithei language to the languages spoken by the hill tribes both in the State and beyond it. Dr. Grierson gives it a place in the Tibeto-Burman group of languages and defines the position of the Kuki Chin group to which it belongs, in the following words:—"The Kuki Chin languages are closely connected with all the surrounding groups of the Tibeto Burman family, the Bodo and Naga languages to the north, Kachin to the east, and Burmese to the east and south. More particularly they form a link which connects Burmese with the Bodo and Naga languages, having, especially in the north, many relations with the Kachin dialects, which in their turn, form another chain between Tibetan and Burmese." * In another passage he insists on the close connection between Kachin and the Kuki Chin languages, especially Meithei which he considers to be the link between the two groups.†

The remarks which I shall have to make when dealing with the hill tribes in Manipur need not be here anticipated, but their effect, cumulative and sustained, is to show that two hundred years ago in internal organization, in religion, in habits and manners, the Meitheis were as the hill people now are. The successive waves of foreign invasion, Shan, Burmese, English, Hindu, have each left permanent marks on the civilization of the people so that they have passed finally away from the stage of relatively primitive culture into one of comparative civilization, but their ultimate homogeneity with the Nagas and Kukis of the hills is undoubted, and in my opinion needs no further insistence.

The annals of Manipur leave it impossible to doubt that at an earlier period the intercourse between the Meitheis and the Naga tribes was coloured by considerable intimacy which may explain, if it does not altogether justify, the legend that at one time the Manipuris used to marry Naga girls from the great village of Marâm. In a passage in the narrative of the reign of the reformer Gharib Nawaz, we find mention of an invitation to all the Naga chiefs. "The ministers and Sirdars of Manipur received the Naga Chiefs continuously, and made friendship

* *Op. cit.*, vol. iii., part iii., p. 6. † *Loc. cit.*, p. 14.

and intimacy with them. The Raja entertained the Naga chiefs with good feasts and wine."

Whether the real nature of the connection between the Manipuris and the hill tribes will ever be traced is doubtful, because it is obscured by the lack of historical material, the place of which cannot be entirely taken by comparative ethnology. Among the hill tribes in Manipur we find the same system of exogamic divisions, even the same names for the divisions, a phenomenon which is in my opinion capable of a very simple explanation. This topic will be discussed when dealing with the hill tribes. A speculative writer, like McLennan,* may found on such facts an elaborate theory of the growth of early human society, but here is it not due rather to community or identity of origin than to contact and chance connection?

In discussing the origin of the Loi communities I found it necessary to set in array facts which clearly show that they are for the most part of the same origin as their Meithei masters. Unfortunately it is not within my power to add very much to Dr. Grierson's remarks on the paucity of linguistic evidence as regards the affinities of these minor groups. "None of these dialects has been returned for the survey, and they have probably all disappeared. The vocabularies published by Major McCulloch show that they cannot belong to the Kuki Chin group. But it has proved impossible to class them as belonging to any other group. There is apparently some connection with the Naga languages, especially with the eastern sub-group. But the materials available are not sufficient for a definite statement. The question must therefore be left open. But in order

* *Primitive Marriage*, pp. 109–111. Among many of the hill tribes are current legends which, differing in details, invariably agree in declaring the Manipuris to be the descendants of the youngest of three brothers and therefore the most favoured. These legends are fortified by allusions to such differences as the superiority of the Manipuris in the matter of the clothing and their greater cleanliness. All that these *ex post facto* stories prove is that the hill tribes recognize their relationship with the Manipuris who, on their side, are for the most part content to acquiesce tacitly in the claim which they cannot explicitly deny. Such a legend as that which explains the ignorance of writing among the hill tribes, is found in many places with just enough variation to adjust it to local peculiarities. *Cf.* Dr. Tylor (*Anthropology*, p. 377): "What the poet relates may be fiction, what he mentions is apt to be history."

to make it possible to compare the forms given by McCulloch with those occurring in other Tibeto-Burman languages, I have given them as an appendix to the Meithei list, because this language has, to a considerable extent, influenced the vocabulary of the Lui dialects." * It is curious to observe that the names of the two principal Tableng villages, the members of which speak a language belonging to the south-eastern sub-group of Naga languages, are Wanching and Wakching, which happen also to be the names of villages in the south of Manipur.

While the advance of Meithei has obliterated the dialectical distinction of the Lois of Sengmai, Andro and Chairel, their religious customs have suffered less modification, as will be seen in the section on religious beliefs and practices. In anticipation of these results I venture to say that we may regard the Lois as in much the state as the Meitheis were when coerced into the smooth paths of Hinduism.

DRESS.

Colonel McCulloch describes the dress of the Manipuris in the following terms: "The men dress in the same way as they do in Hindustan; but as a people the Munniporees far surpass the people to the west in the cleanliness of their garments. . . . Unless permitted by the Raja, various articles of dress and ornament cannot be worn, and permission to wear any of these articles is much coveted. Persons of high rank are permitted to have carried before them a red woollen cloth; of a less rank, a green woollen cloth; and of a less still, a cloth of cotton manufacture. These they use as rugs to sit on, and it is only for such use they are prized; as articles of dress they may be used by any who can afford to buy them. The dress of the women is quite different from that worn by the women in the west. It consists of a striped cotton or silk cloth passed round the body under the armpits and over the breast, a jacket, and a sheet." † Dr. Brown, however, amplifies this account in the following passage: "The dress of the men does not differ materially from that of the Bengallee, and consists of the

* *Op. cit.*, vol. iii., part iii., p. 43.

† *Op. cit.*, p. 22.

dhotie, a *koorta*, or shirt, only occasionally worn, and a *chudder*, or sheet. In winter those who can afford it wear a quilted and padded coat, like that worn in the Punjab, generally having long uncomfortable sleeves and enormously high collars. Shoes are seldom worn. The *puggree* is shorter than that worn by Hindustanis, but is put on in the same manner. The dress of the women when of good quality is picturesque and pleasing. During the hot weather it consists of a piece of cloth open except at the bottom, where it is stitched together by the edges for a few inches; this is folded round the body, under the arm-pits and over the breast, and tucked in by the hand at the side of the body. In length it reaches the ground, but as this would be inconvenient in walking, it is hitched up about halfway to the knee, and tucked in again at the waist. This piece of cloth, called a '*fanek*,' is only wide enough to go one and a half times round the body; this gives enough room, however, for the legs in walking. The *fanek* is made in cotton and silk, and the only patterns are stripes of various colours and widths running across the material, the groundwork being of different colours. The commoner patterns are red with green stripes, green and black, blue with black and white stripes, yellow and brown, dark blue with green and white stripes, etc. At the top and bottom of the garment is a broad margin, on which geometrical figures or patterns of various kinds are sewn by hand with floss silk in various colours. Over the *fanek* is worn a white sheet,* which is folded in the usual native manner, the face, however, being left uncovered. In the cold season a short jacket with long sleeves is worn; this reaches below the bust over the *fanek*, and is worn tight-fitting. The material is usually velvet or satin, black, blue, or green being the favourite colours. The great drawback to this dress in a European's eyes is its tendency to spoil the figure: the whole weight of the *fanek* resting on the bust soon ruins the shape. Female children, until puberty, or near it, wear the *fanek* round the waist, the upper part of the body being bare."† It is necessary to add some particulars to the above accounts by noticing the peculiar costumes which custom permits or demands on certain occasions, by mentioning in some detail the sumptuary rules and regulations, and by

* In-na-phi. † *Op. cit.*, p. 29.

MEITHEI LEISĀBI.

(Unmarried Manipuri girl).

p. 14

giving some account of the periods at which, according to the annals of the State, changes in the attire of its people have been introduced.

The following sumptuary laws are recognized, and were enforced among the Manipuris by their own officials :—

The *Kameng chatpa dhoti* is a white silk *dhoti* with purple patterns of scrolls stamped on it by means of wooden blocks, which are said to have been introduced by the Chinese merchants who visited the State in the reign of Khāgenba, *circa* A.D. 1630. It may not be worn by persons of inferior rank, but Rajkumars may use it at their pleasure, a privilege which is now extended to sons-in-law of the Raja.

The *phi-ge-napu dhoti* is an orange-coloured *dhoti* which may be worn by the classes of persons mentioned above. Children, however, are permitted to wear it.

The *ju-gi mairi dhoti* is a red silk *dhoti* which may be worn in the presence of the Raja by persons who hold titles of office as members of the Chirāp, or by the favour of the Raja. On ordinary occasions it may be worn by anybody, but not in the presence of the Raja.

The *gulap machu dhoti*, or rose-coloured silk *dhoti*, of a pretty pink shade, may be worn only by the privileged persons who hold office or enjoy the royal favour, but it may be worn by any one else on ordinary occasions provided the Raja is not present. Children may wear it at pleasure.

Pagris with silk-patterned ends may be worn by descendants and relatives of the Raja and by those upon whom it is conferred as a mark of favour or distinction. *Pagris* with silk borders may not be worn in the presence of the Raja. Wrestlers and runners when performing in public wear a *pagri* with a projecting front, to which the name *lam khāng poāk* is given. The Raja's immediate servants, when in attendance at his meals or when accompanying him to worship or when massaging him, wear the *pagri* so as to cover the mouth. Ordinary persons at ordinary times are not allowed to come into the presence of the Raja with their *pagris* coiled in this fashion, nor are they permitted to twist it in rough coils when entering the royal presence.

Women are not allowed to wear *chadars* embroidered with

gold either in the presence of the Raja or elsewhere without permission. Descendants of the Raja are not bound by this restriction.

The national sports and games afford an opportunity for special and elaborate costumes. On the occasion of the great annual boat-races, in which in former days the Raja used to take part, the steersmen of the competing crews wear a *kameng chatpa dhoti* (see above), and to add to the dignity of the high-coiled *pagri* with fringed ends permitted to them, they wear feathers of the Argus pheasant or of the Humè's pheasant, with blossoms in long trailing coils of the blue orchid (*Vanda caerulea*). The wrestlers wear the *kameng chatpa dhoti* and the curious head-dress, which has a portion twisted up in front, in a manner which resembles the Marring coil. The costume of the polo players is more practical, and consists of a short jacket of dark velvet, worn even in hot weather, a *dhoti*, generally of white cotton, and quilted leggings of a stout and serviceable nature. The *pagri* is fastened in such a way as to protect the ears and side of the head from blows, and if not particularly picturesque, is at any rate of great use, for in the heat and fury of the game the players become excited, and some people think that if they cannot hit the ball, they may as well hit the man.

The religious festivals, such as the *Lai haraoba* (or making merry with the gods), are occasions when the sumptuary laws are a little relaxed, and women don their gayest apparel without let or hindrance. Those who have been selected to take a part in one of the religious dances wear a handsome costume which is as modest as it is also beautiful, and which is sanctioned by long custom for these occasions. Old women make a living by hiring out these costumes, for they cost too much for ordinary purses to buy outright, and the appreciation of their charm, which so many British officers have shown, adds to their cost. The head-gear is a small skull-cap of black cloth or velvet, with a narrow band of pearl trimming at the edge; sometimes they wear an ornamental branching spray of white imitation pearl beads on the cap. The jacket is close-fitting, and is of black cloth or velvet, with gold trimming about two inches deep on the sleeves, which do not reach down to the elbow. A white cloth is wound tightly round the waist from under the breasts just over the hips to give support. The petticoat is made of silk, either green or dark red, and at the bottom is a band of sequin ornamentation eighteen inches to two feet in depth. Over the shoulder and round the waist is fastened a decorative ornament, which I can only compare to a sabretasche with a shoulder-strap. On a groundwork of red silk or satin, they sew round, oval, or square pieces of glass silvered, set in gold and silver tinsel, with loose fringed ends of the same bright materials. Over the silk skirt they wear a top-skirt of white delicate muslin woven in the country, on which are sewn rows and rows of silver tinsel, till the whole is a mass of gorgeous splendour, reflecting the light in all directions, as the agile creatures whirl round and sink down in ecstatic worship of Radha Krishna, in whose honour they dance. The little lad who takes the part of Sri Krishna wears a handsome dress with a resplendent head-gear, adorned with peacocks' feathers and silver tinsel.

The first change in the matter of dress occurred, according to the Chronicles, in the reign of Chalumba, *circa* 1550, who is said to have "introduced the system of wearing *Dhuties* and decent clothing, coats made of wax cloth were also introduced during his time." It would be of extreme interest to know the precise nature of the presumably indecent clothing thus displaced. The *lūhup* (*lū* = head—not a Meithei word—*hūp* = *khūp*, to cover) or head dress was first brought into use by Khāgenba in about 1600, and the Chronicles note that it is used by men of rank at the time of the festivals. Khāgenba is also responsible for the adoption of the head gear known as *Lamkhang poak*. He was a zealous reformer in the matter of dress, for he also caused the people to take to the turban or *pagri*. The first mention of the *Kameng chatpa dhoti*, or royal *dhoti*, dates from the reign of Pikhomba, who ordered a man of the Potsangbom pannah to be beheaded for stealing one of these cloths, but its introduction is probably much earlier, as, according to tradition, it was first made in the country by Chinese, who are said to have visited Manipur in the reign of Khāgenba (*circa* 1630 A.D.), the inventor of a costume to which the name *ningkham furit* was given for the use of royalty and the ministers of state. The *faichareng*, a cap worn by ladies of high rank, is first mentioned in the year 1746, when the Rani, the wife of the Raja Pamheiba or Gharib Newaz, wore it at a dancing party given by the Chothe Nagas in their village. Since that date changes of costume are not mentioned in the Chronicles, but the approach of European civilization has given rise to the fashion of wearing cast-off clothes from England. The combination of two such excellent garments as the *dhoti* and the frock coat does not display the merits of either garment, but the "old clothes" corner of the Sena kaithel is always crowded, and in the early days of the British occupation a frock coat fetched in Manipur considerably more than it originally cost, while the competition for collars raised the price to about one rupee each. Free trade in these commodities has lowered the prices, but "Bilati" coats are worn by as many as can afford them, and the sale of old uniforms is making the fortunes of the enterprising traders who import them.

In dress the Lois are not distinguishable from Meitheis. The women wear the same costume. These remarks are also true of the Panggans, men and women, with the difference that the Panggan women wear *faneks*, which they fasten under the right breast, while Meithei women fasten this garment under the left breast. The colours of the *faneks* of Panggan women differ from those used by Manipuris, as, for instance, the green used by a Meithei will be darker, less glaring than the shade of green allowable to the Panggan.

TATTOOING.

The Manipuris do not tattoo, and there is no record of their having at any time practised this custom.

ORNAMENTS.

Dr. Brown * says that "The ornaments are earrings, necklets, and bracelets; ankle ornaments are never worn, or rings on the

* *Op. cit.*, pp. 29, 30.

toes. Nose ornaments are limited to a small piece of gold wire in the side of each nostril. The only ornaments which may be worn without restriction are earrings: these may be worn by any one. With regard to other ornaments of gold, permission for all but the upper classes to wear them must be obtained from the Raja. Ornaments of other metal than gold may be worn freely." The earrings worn by the men and by the majority of the women are of plain gold, generally a thin casing over a solid piece of lac. Men do not wear other ornaments, but the necklaces worn by the women of the upper classes are of tasteful, simple filigree designs manufactured by native goldsmiths, who prefer almost pure gold to work on, as their tools are not tempered for work on alloyed gold. The bracelets and necklaces are of chased and hammered patterns, while plain beads formed round a hollow nucleus of lac are common.

WEAPONS.

The universal weapon, used in all kinds of emergency and for every purpose, in the fields, in war and in the arts of a more peaceful nature, is the *dao*. But the more the people of Manipur have become acquainted with the tools and implements of western civilization, the more thoroughly have they accepted the specialization of tools which marks the progress of organized modern industry. The advent of the horse, the foreign animal [*să*, animal; *gol* or *kol*, foreign], added an arm to their military organization which eventually became famous in the wars of the dawn of British authority in Further India. The cavalry of Manipur, better known as the Cassay Horse,* fought both for and against us in the First Burmese War. Their weapon was

* Extract from Snodgrass's *Narrative of the First Burmese War*, pp. 85, 86: "Numbers of these unfortunate beings (captives of war) from Cassay, Arracan, and Assam are to be found in Ava; and even villages are to be met with on the Irrawaddy inhabited by mechanics, ironsmiths, and particular trades, whose features plainly indicate a foreign origin. The Munniporeans or people of Cassay, in particular, abound in great numbers, and they are much prized as clever workmen. Owing to their superior skill in the management of the horse, the Burmese Cavalry is almost exclusively composed of them; and they are distinguished by the national appellation of 'The Cassay Horse.'"

the *rāmbai* or dart, the use of which was due no doubt to the fact that shock tactics could not be successfully carried out with such light cavalry in any country in which they were called on to operate.

"It consists," as Dr. Brown says,* "of two parts—one, the outer, is formed of ten or twelve long quills of peacock feathers, which are bound together so as to form a narrow hollow cylinder. At one end is fastened a heavy pointed piece of iron; into the sheath thus formed a bamboo rod is placed, projecting outwards about five inches, and forming a handle; to this handle, to give a better hold, a piece of cord is attached; each horseman had two quivers full of these *arāmbas* fixed on either side of his saddle behind; in using them, the handle of the rod, which fitted the sheath with moderate firmness, was grasped firmly and the sheath flung, leaving the bamboo core in the hand; the heavy iron on the point made the *arāmba* fly true. In pursuing, the *arāmba* was thrown in front, and in retreating was useful in throwing behind and impeding the enemy." Spears, bows and arrows were also used as weapons of offence, and the introduction of firearms, while rendering them and the *arāmba* to a large extent obsolete, also gave scope to the ingenuity of Manipuri artisans, who manufactured rough matchlocks, and are known to have risen to the height of producing a breech-loading gun of iron, which Dr. Brown thus describes: † "The breech-loader above mentioned, which is still in existence, is of iron and about three feet long; the breech piece is separable from the gun and received the charge, its extremity being then inserted into the bore of the gun, a portion of barrel being cut out to admit of this; the movable breech piece fastened behind by a slot passing through the gun (see photograph).‡ The bullet weighed only a few ounces, the bore being small. The piece, carriage and all, was carried by two men. Nothing is known of the inventive genius who made this gun, except that he was a native of Munnipore: it is probably about a hundred years ago." Round shields, made of buffalo hide and studded with

* *Op. cit.*, pp. 55 and 56. † *Op. cit.*, p. 55.

‡ The photograph is not given in the book but may still be in existence among the archives of the Foreign Department of the Government of India.—T. C. H.

brass knobs, sufficiently thick and strong to turn a spear thrust, are carried, but mainly on ceremonial occasions only. Tradition asserts that from Chinese merchants who visited the State during the reign of Khăgenba, *circa* 1630, the Manipuris learnt the art of manufacturing gunpowder, an art which to this day is still practised by the Kukis, who probably derive their acquaintance with it from the Manipuris. The Chronicles state that Khăgenba, in 1627 A.D., "experimented to make big guns, and prepared one metal gun of big size."

There is a curious weapon of the form and on the principle of the bow, which is used as a catapult. The pellets of hardened clay travel with considerable force and with some accuracy.

SECTION II.

OCCUPATION.

In Manipur we find many forms of industry practised by the people who are mainly agriculturists. In every house the wife weaves the cotton cloths for her family and husband. There are goldsmiths whose art produces much that is of great beauty though simple, so that we can believe that, in the palmy days of old, before the great devastation of the country by the Burmese, the land was in enjoyment of such wealth and prosperity as are now impossible. Yet the misfortunes of the past do not altogether account for the decay in the finer arts. In the economic system competent observers like Colonel McCulloch find a cause of stagnation and decline. "In a country in which each family produces nearly all which it consumes, any advancement in the arts can scarcely be expected. But if without other impediments, improvement could take place, it would be repressed under a Government such as that of Munnipore. Under the operation of the *laloop,* a good artificer works along with a bad one, and receives no more thanks for his work than if it were as bad as that of his less skillful associate. He becomes disgusted, and his only aim is to amass quickly, by his superior intelligence, enough to purchase his release from work. This done, he thinks no more of his trade. Thus all are for ever at the rudiments and no progress is made. What cloths are made, are distinguished for strength more than for fineness, and the inventive faculties having no play, there is very little variety in pattern. Some little embroidery is practised, in which the same paucity of invention is more apparent. Their eating and drinking vessels, principally of bell metal, are substantial, but in shape vary little from those of the west. They have some dyes and have some taste in the arrangement of colours, but of drawing or painting they have no idea." *

* *Op. cit.*, pp. 33, 34.

The women hold a high and free position in Manipur, all the internal trade and exchange of the produce of the country being managed by them. The habit of the country is to have bazars at convenient spots by the road side, where a handful of women congregate at an early hour, whiling the time away with gossip and light work, and attending to a chance customer when one offers himself. Imphāl possesses the largest and most important of these bazars, to which the name Sena Kaithel * is given. It is said to have been founded by Mōngeanba in about 1580. It is close to the Pāt or Royal enclosure, and now consists of a number of embanked mounds which are allotted to the different trades, the cloth weavers being found in one place all together, and the dried-fish vendors gathering their savoury wares in another. According to Dr. Brown the manufactures of the people are of some extent, and will be described in a later passage. The women weave all the cloths, and all girls whose position is at all respectable learn to dance, for in Manipur the dancing profession is often a road to royal dignity and is not despised in any way as is the case in India. Parties of girls with a master in charge travel to Assam, Cachar, Sylhet, even as far as Calcutta, where they give public performances which are very attractive to the Manipuri exiles in those districts who, I am informed, consider themselves to be the real Manipuris, and the present inhabitants of the country to be of poor adulterate stock; a compliment which is reciprocated too often with acerbity. I have known Manipuris make a living by gambling with Gurkha sepoys during the Durga pujahs, for the sober and wily Manipuri is at the best of times more than a match in an encounter of wits for the Gurkha, and when the brave little man is excited by orgies of blood and ready, like the heroic but foolish Pandavas, to gamble his all, the astute Manipuri reaps a veritable golden harvest. But gambling and cockfighting are among the cardinal vices of the Manipuri, and are fruitful causes of crime sometimes even of a serious nature. More than one observer has denounced the Manipuri for useless economy of the truth which is contrasted with their admiration for truth as an abstract virtue. It must be remembered that for many years they occupied the difficult position of avoiding the

* Meaning Golden or Royal market-place.

attentions of British authority which they saw enveloping them, and at the same time of keeping themselves safe from the vengeance of the Burmese who remembered the part played by Manipur in the First Burmese war. Such a position does not make for the development of the manliest virtues, and to those who condone prevarication so long as it is capable of being decently regarded as diplomacy, no excuse need be made for the failing of the Manipuri in this matter. There is but ltitle serious crime among them. In the account given by Dr. Brown of the State in the year 1868, there is a table of the offences for which the prison population was confined, and it is interesting to compare it with the offences most common in Manipur at the present time. Dr. Brown states * that there were in the jail when he visited it 122 prisoners: Munnipories 110, hillmen 10, Munniporie Mussalmans 2. So far as numbers go, the average daily population of the jail with which I was acquainted, was about 100, and the number of hillmen, Mussalmans, etc., divided in not very different proportions. It is equally remarkable to study the offences which were then common in comparison with those now responsible for the inmates of the jail. Treason then accounted for sixteen, but it has practically disappeared from the list of offences. Coining sent seven prisoners then, but is now rare, and we have now, as then, a large number of persons imprisoned for theft, inclusive of cattle theft. Bribery was the cause of the detention in 1868 of five persons, and it is not by any means eradicated yet. Another offence which has ceased in altered circumstances to add to the jail population, is slave stealing and abetting desertion of slaves. Then, as now, the liberal employment of the prisoners on extramural labour seems to have conduced to the preservation of their health in spite of bad sanitary surroundings. In those days education cannot be said to have existed in Manipur, while now there are many primary schools and in Imphāl a fair secondary school, originally founded by the efforts of Colonel Johnstone, and, reconstituted in later years after the occupation of the State in 1891, is attended by a small but increasing number of scholars. The education of women cannot be said to have made equal progress, although it was hoped, not without reason, that, in a country like

* *Op. cit.*, p. 45.

Manipur where women hold such an important position in the economic activity of the State, the efforts to establish a good school for the daughters of the higher classes would have been attended with more success than has actually been the case. The failure is not improbably due to the rumour, started by malignity and disseminated by stupidity, that as soon as the girls had been satisfactorily taught to read, write, and speak English, they were to be shipped off to England where there was said to be a scarcity of marriageable women. The sole basis for this untoward myth lay in the fact that at that time among all the officers of Government, Civil and Military, then serving in Manipur, not one was married. Such rumours are constantly arising in Manipur, and derive their wide circulation through the agency of the bazars, where time hangs so heavy that such gossip is eagerly retailed and receives too often ready acceptance.

HOUSES.

Colonel McCulloch says that "the dwelling houses of the Munniporees are all of the same form, but those of the rich are larger and constructed of better materials than those of the poor, that is, the posts and beams of the former are of wood, whilst those of the latter are of bamboo. The walls of both are of reeds plastered with a mixture of earth and cow dung, and the roofs of all are thatched with grass. All the dwelling houses face to the eastward, in which direction they have a large open verandah. In this verandah the family sits during the day, and in it all the work of the household is carried on, except cooking, which is performed inside; in the south side of the verandah is the seat of honour. Here a mat or cloth is laid for the head of the family, upon which no one intrudes. Inside, the house is without partitions. The bed of the head of the family is placed in what is called the Luplengka, close to the wall on the south side about the middle. It is usually screened by mats. The daughters usually sleep on the north side. There are no windows in the houses, the only light admitted being by two doors, one opening into the open verandah, the other to the north, near the north-western corner of the house. The fireplace is on the floor towards the north-west corner. There is no chimney. The fuel used is generally dried reed jungle. This answers every purpose in the warm weather, but is a sorry substitute for wood in the colder months." *

The style of houses was introduced by a mythical king named Khooi Ningon, but in the reign of Khăgenba changes were made. Not many houses are built of brick, though the recent development of the manufacture of bricks may lead to an increase in their number. The temples, both private and public, are built of brick, and the walls of the *natch ghar* or dancing house which is built in the trabeated style with massive teak beams of enormous size and thickness, are also of the same material. The native bricks are long, wide and thin, possessing considerable durability, which is in part due to the liberal amount of genuine mortar and lime used on the walls.

The Chronicles state that in the reign of Khăgenba, which seems to have witnessed the inception of the development of civilization in Manipur, two brick-built walls called Hogaibi were erected. Colonel Johnstone † attributes the erection of these blocks to Chinese settlers, the remnants of a force of invaders which was nearly annihilated by the Manipuris. To this day, people going to the State office (which is close to the site of these pillars or walls), especially members of the Lairik Yengbam or writer caste, offer a devout salutation to the memory of Khăgenba. I may add that it has been put to me that Khăgenba may be resolved into *Khăgi-yen* (or *yăn*) *-ba*, the scatterer or slaughterer of the Chinese (*Khăgi* = Chinese).

VILLAGES.

The chief town in Manipur, known as Imphăl or the collection of houses (*Im* = *yum* = house, *phăl* = to gather or collect), is situated in the north of the valley and possesses some 30,000 inhabitants, but it is not a town: rather it is a gathering by simple accretion of small villages around the Păt or royal enclosure. An ordinary Manipuri village is a long straggling series of houses, each standing within its own enclosure with access to the river, on the bank of which it is built. It

* *Op. cit.*, pp. 20, 21. † *Op. cit.*, p. 80.

MEITHEI GIRL WEAVING.

From a photograph by Mr. A. Eleazar,
Indian Telegraph Department.

p. 27

possesses length without breadth. The villages are not surrounded by any rampart or fortification, and when, as has happened in the case of Imphāl, neighbouring villages grow and expand, there are no arbitrary boundaries, though custom recognizes them for purposes of administration. The limits of the original settlement are often known though now obliterated.

FURNITURE.

In a Manipuri house the most important article of furniture is the bed of the head of the family, a large wooden structure with four posts, which forms a conspicuous feature in the wedding processions. Then the chest, in which the family belongings are kept, generally an old wooden box with an iron lock at which the thieves of Manipur laugh. The eating and drinking vessels, the implements of spinning, the few tools if the owner happen to be a carpenter, a blacksmith, or a goldsmith, the jewellery of the wife and the universal *dao*, these constitute the ordinary furniture of the house. In the houses of the better class one may find stools or chairs of European design, perhaps a lamp or two, as likely as not borrowed from one of the public street lamps.

MANUFACTURES.

Nearly every housewife is capable of weaving all the cloths needed by her family, and the simple loom stands in the verandah of the house. These cloths are mainly intended for wear and not for decorative purposes, yet since the occupation of the State a trade in fancy and decorative cloths has sprung up. The Nagas, especially those to the north, often make large purchases of cloths in the Golden Bazar, both of ordinary white with red and blue stripes, and also the more special cloths of a dark-blue ground with figures of animals woven in red thread round the borders. There is reason to believe that in former times this industry was artificially supported, if not altogether created, by royal decrees punishing any Naga who failed to buy his cloths in the Sena Kaithel. The manufacture of silk cloths is entirely in the hands of the Lois, whose low social position permits them to practise many remunerative forms of employment which custom denies to the Meithei.

Dr. Brown gives a complete list of the manufactures then produced by the Manipuris, and as regards the cloths, states that "These are manufactured in cotton of various kinds, chiefly a coarse quality called 'Kess': these coarse cloths are purchased by the hill tribes chiefly: some, however, find their way into Cachar. Of late years finer qualities of cloth have been made from English yarns. In leather manufactures, I am told, there has been of late years a great improvement. Formerly tanning was a matter of great difficulty, and the results inferior. Now they use the bark of a tree (name unknown to me), which is found in plenty in the jungles; by this they make leather superior to any formerly known in the country; they also enamel the leather very nicely in black. The skins used are those of deer and calf, and the articles made, saddles, shoes, belts, pouches, etc., for the use of the troops. In clay only ordinary pots and water *ghurrahs* are made. Stone bowls are also to be found nicely made and polished: the stone is ordinary sandstone, artificially blackened.

The jewellery manufactured is of fair workmanship, but not distinguished by any special merit: rings, bracelets, necklets, are the articles chiefly made. A large number of brass and bell metal armlets are made which are disposed of to the hillmen.

In iron and steel are made *daos* of various kinds, spear and arrow heads, etc., etc. Firearms are not made in any form.

Carpentry.—The Munnipories have a great reputation as carpenters in the adjoining provinces of Cachar and Sylhet, especially for the better kinds of work: here good workmen are few, and are entirely monopolized by the Raja. The good carpenters there are, however, are capable of turning out first-rate work, and can imitate English work successfully. Shortly after my arrival in the country the Raja one day borrowed from me a revolving stereoscope which I had, and rather surprised me by showing me a few days afterwards a duplicate perfect in every way excepting the lenses, which, although they had a pair removed from an old stereoscope, they could not adjust properly. Since that time I have had two photographic cameras made by them, complete in every respect and serviceable, which would not show unfavourably when compared with the more common run of English goods.

Turning, etc.—Turning in wood and ivory * is common. They can also silver glass and electro-plate, make good serviceable locks, and can at a pinch repair and clean a clock.

Dyeing in a few colours is practised; a yellow dye is common, procured in the hills.

McCulloch in his account, says, "They have some taste in the arrangement of colours, but of drawing or painting they have no idea." There is at present in Munnipore the son of a Brahmin, a native of the country, about thirteen or fourteen years of age, who has what I would call a very remarkable knowledge of drawing and painting so far at least as copying goes. Some time ago, I gave a Lactrope to a Munniporie, and he astonished me a good deal by showing me some copies of the figures so beautifully and correctly drawn and coloured, that it required a close examination of original and copy to detect the difference. I am informed that this lad is engaged in drawing some original comic slides, which I have not yet seen." †

It is sad to notice the decay in native art which follows almost instantaneously on the withdrawal of the artificial atmosphere of royal patronage, but the phenomenon is neither rare nor inexplicable. At a period much earlier than that of the passage above quoted art and manufactures in Manipur seem to have been in a much more healthy state than in the later years of independence. The first blow to Manipur as a centre of artistic and industrial activity was dealt by the Burmese, whose repeated invasions of the country depopulated it, and who kept in captivity all or nearly all the famous silversmiths of Manipur. To the excellence of Manipuri art and manufacture, testimony is borne by several observers. In the treaty concluded in 1762 with Governor Verelst, mention is made of the following articles, products of the country: silk, iron, kupass, dammer, wood oil, wax, elephants' teeth, agar, sandal wood, camphor, black thread, red ditto, blue ditto, white ditto, black coss, Meklee cloths, Meklee gold rupees.‡

* I have seen some really exquisite ivory carving done by a Manipuri, who acquired his skill in a jail in Burma.—T. C. H.

† *Op. cit.*, p. 25.

‡ Pemberton, *Account of the North-Eastern Frontier of Bengal*, p. 42.

Colonel Johnstone, speaking with the sympathy of an ardent educationalist, says of the decline of native arts and industries in Manipur, that free trade has done much to injure the trade in cotton goods of local manufacture in India,* but it must in fairness be pointed out that until the revolution in taste has evicted the deeply ingrained religious and tabu beliefs of people like the Manipuris and the hill tribes, or until the manufacturer in Manchester has learnt to imitate native patterns, there will be a large and effective demand for the products of native looms.

Another matter in connection with the manufactures of the Manipuris; nearly all the real manufactures are now in the hands of the Loi communities, and while among the Manipuris we have weaving as a general industry with one or two families exercising special forms of this craft, they practise few other manufactures, and are carpenters, blacksmiths, jewellers, workers in brass, metal casters, bone setters and house builders. I may also add that the manufacture of wooden false teeth gives employment to one old gentleman, who has quite a large clientèle.

The Chronicles contain a passage describing the magnificence of the table equipage of King Khăgenba, who feasted off vessels of solid gold and sat on a chair of gold.

As in the days when Colonel McCulloch wrote, so even now, "the Loee population is exceedingly useful. Amongst them are the silk manufacturers, the smelters of iron, the distillers of spirits, the makers of earthen vessels for containing water or for cooking in, the cutters of posts and beams and canoes, manufacturers of salt, fishers, cutters of grass for the Raja's ponies, the payers of tribute in *Sel*, the coin of the country, etc." Dr. Brown goes into interesting details of the several industries above enumerated.† Of the silk manufacture he says that "the cultivation of silk which, if properly developed, would form a most important article for export, is unfortunately, much restricted. The silk culture is entirely in the hands of the Loee part of the population, and only five villages to the west and northwest of the valley close to the hills cultivate the worm. The fact of the Loee being the cultivator of silk is fatal to its extension, as by the custom of the country, which so much associates position or caste

* *Op. cit.*, p. 116. † *Op. cit.*, p. 25.

with the nature of the various employments pursued, any one wishing to engage in silk culture must lose his position and become a Loee; thus it is that the production of silk is on a very limited scale. The food of the silkworm is the mulberry, and the species is, I understand, common in Bengal, although the silk yielded is of a decidedly superior quality. About 300 persons are employed in the silk culture, and they pay for the privilege some 300 Rupees annually; they are for this payment excused from the operation of *lalloop*, or forced labour. The raw silk is disposed of by the above to a weaver class called 'Kubbo'—they having originally, it is said, emigrated from the Kubbo Valley in Upper Burmah. These weave it into various cloths, *dhoties*, *puggris*, *kummerbunds*, dresses for the women, etc. A small quantity only of silk cloths find their way into Cachar. The Burmese traders who frequent Munnipore, buy up greedily all the raw silk they can get; this speaks well for the quality of the silk, as the silkworm is plentiful in and near the Kubbo Valley." The trade with Burma is not nowadays of any importance, though the improvements which have been made in the alignment of the Palel-Tamu road through the hills should conduce to an extension of commercial intercourse.

Iron smelting is thus described by Captain Pemberton.* "Iron, the only metal yet ascertained to exist in Munnipore, is found in the form of titaniferous oxydulated ore, and is obtained principally from the beds of small streams south of Thobal, and the hills near Langatel; its presence in the latter is ascertained by the withered appearance of the grass growing above it, and in the former it is generally sought after the rainy season, when the soil has been washed away; an iron-headed spear is thrust into the ground, and the small particles adhering to it lead to the discovery of the bed in which they had been deposited; this employment of the spear furnished an accidental but very striking illustration of the magnetic property being acquired by iron, which is preserved in the same position for any length of time; the spear of the Munniporee and Naga is almost invariably thrust vertically into the ground when not in use, and the fact of its being so employed to ascertain the presence of the ore is a proof of the very high degree of magnetism or polarity it must

* *Op. cit.*, p. 27.

have attained. The loss produced by smelting the ore amounts to nearly 50 per cent., and the Munniporees are perfectly sensible of the difficulty of fusion increasing with the greater purity of the metal. The principal articles manufactured are such as would be thought of in the earliest stages of civilization—axes, hoes, and ploughshares for felling timber and preparing the ground for agricultural purposes, spear and arrow heads for self-defence or aggression and the destruction of game; and blades from one to two feet in length, which, firmly fixed in a wooden or metal handle under the name of *dao*, forms the inseparable companion of the Munniporee, Burma, Shan, and Singpho. With it he clears a passage for himself through the dense jungle that obstructs his path, notches the steep and slippery face of the hill he wishes to climb, and frequently owes the preservation of his life to the skill with which he wields it in the field." In Dr. Brown's time accident led to the discovery of a shallow deposit of iron ore at Kameng. I do not know for certain, but believe that limestone is used as a flux in the process of smelting. It seems reasonably certain that the comparative abundance of limestone outcrops in the valley, occurring at places many miles apart, is significant of the presence of this valuable mineral beneath the alluvial deposits of the valley. It is known that some of the limestone deposits were worked one hundred and fifty years ago.

Yu, or country spirit, is manufactured by several Loi villages, some of which are abandoning the industry in order thereby to qualify themselves for admission into the Hindu community. At Sengmai, which, from its position, is well known to Nagas coming from the north, there are stills which produce a liquor which is greatly appreciated by the Nagas, but which to an untrained palate tastes of candle grease and methylated spirit.

Chairel and Shuganu, both on the Imphal river, are the principal villages engaged in the pottery business, probably because suitable clay occurs in their vicinity and not elsewhere, just as in the hills the manufacture of pottery is confined to two Tangkhul villages near which are outcrops of clay. Here the clay is found in the bed of an old lake, between strata of worthless deposits. The girls knead it with their feet till it acquires the consistency of indiarubber. It is roughly fashioned by hand, then placed on a circular flat disk which is twirled by the thumb and forefinger of the free hand. A rough conventional pattern of cross lines is stamped on it with a piece of wood. The ovens are out in the open. The use of the wheel indicates that they have reached a higher standard of skill than the Nagas, who mould their vessels on a bamboo cylinder and work it into a rounded shape by hand. The pots made at these Loi villages are brought by boat to Imphāl and there sold.

I do not know that any Loi village is specially set apart for the work of cutting timber, but the village called Hiroi Lamgang, in the south of the valley not far from Shuganu, makes boats for the Raja. The villagers themselves assert that the name of their village means "boat-maker on dry land" (*hi* = boat, *loi* = to make, cf. Meithei root *loi* = to complete or to be completed, *lam* = ground, *gang* = *kang* = dry), but the presence of the root *Loi* which is used constantly in names of Loi villages, may mean that this is one of the Loi villages. Against this we have the fact that this village is not included in the lists of Loi villages, and that it is obviously more closely related in the mass of its customs to hill people than to Lois who are valuable as a link connecting the Meitheis with the hill tribes.

Dr. Brown records the following observations regarding the process of salt manufacture *:—"Nearly the whole of the salt consumed by the Munnipories is obtained from salt wells situated in the valley. A small quantity is occasionally imported in times of scarcity from Burmah.† The principal wells are situated at the foot of the hills to the north-east, about fourteen miles from the capital; they are four in number and are named Ningail, Chundrakong, Seekong (*Chī* = salt, *khong* = well), and Waikong; they all lie close together and are surrounded by villages wherein reside those engaged in the salt manufacture. Wells have been opened in other parts of the valley but the supply has not been remunerative. Of late years

* *Op. cit.*, p. 22.

† At the present time salt from Cheshire comes into Manipur, and its price regulates the price of local salt, a fact which affords an interesting lesson in Applied Political Economy. In addition to the Indian salt tax, this salt has to be re-melted by the dealers so as to give it the shape and appearance of the local salt.—T. C. H.

a road has been constructed between the salt wells and the capital; it is not finished but will be a good road for all weathers when it is so, and will have brick bridges. This is the only made road in the country outside the capital with the exception of that leading from the capital to the foot of the hills to join the Government hill road to Cachar.* Ningail has three wells, all contained in a somewhat elevated dell of small dimensions, surrounded by a low range of hills covered with grass and scrub. It is stated by the Munnipories that the situation of an underground salt spring is discovered by the presence of a peculiar mist seen hanging over the spot in the early morning. When the sinking of a well is determined on, large trunks of trees are prepared by hollowing out into cylinders which are sunk gradually until water is reached. In the Ningail wells the depth at which water is found is about 35 to 40 feet, and the wooden cylinders rest upon rock, the intervening stratum consisting chiefly of loose earth and boulders. In the oldest of the three wells at Ningail in which the cylinder has been sunk, it is said for about one hundred years, the wood has become entirely petrified throughout its whole substance, which is more than a foot thick. The others are only partially petrified, they being newer and the supply of water being less. The soil and vegetation surrounding the wells shows nothing peculiar, and there is no appearance of any deposit of salt on or near the surface. The water is drawn out by wicker baskets and emptied into large earthenware *ghurrahs* or hollowed out trunks of trees placed by the side of the wells, from whence it is carried in smaller vessels to the boiling down sheds situated some distance off. The water as it is drawn is quite clear, but from its being stored in mud tanks in the sheds it soon becomes very dirty; this could easily be avoided, but the Munnipories do not seem to object to the impurity, and it is positively relished by the hillmen. There are in Ningail three boiling down sheds nearly always fully employed. The salt water is evaporated in small earthenware dishes, shallow and saucer shaped. Before the water is poured into them they are lined with plantain leaves,

* The valley now possesses excellent internal communications, and the completion of the cart road *viâ* Kohima through the hills gives easy access to heavy traffic which in Dr. Brown's days was denied.—T. C. H.

to which the salt adheres, and the contents when the salt has filled the dish, are thus easily removed. The pans, about 100 in number in each shed, are placed over little holes, and underneath is the fire which is stoked at one end, the fuel used, as in the Sylhet lime kilns, being dry reeds. The attendants are constantly on the move supplying the pans with water, emptying them and filling them again. The Chundrakong salt wells—two in number—are much the same as the above, and somewhat similarly situated in a village to the north-west of Ningail. There is one peculiarity worth noting in Chundrakong, that is, the existence of a fresh-water well in close proximity to the salt ones; this well requires constant pumping to prevent its diluting the salt water in the other wells. It would appear from the existence of this fresh-water well that the very edge of the salt deposit at this place has been struck in sinking. The salt water here does not seem to have the same petrifying power as that of Ningail, and the same observation holds good with regard to the other wells. The other wells present no peculiar feature. Seekong has four wells, Waikong five; from this well a superior quality of salt is obtained, which is set aside for the Raja and his immediate retainers; it can, however, also be procured in the bazaars at a slight advance on the price of the commoner sort; it only differs from it in being cleaner. Ningail is the oldest of the wells, and has always given the greatest yield. The amount of salt manufactured varies according to season, the most being made in cold weather, when the water is at its strongest. About 150 maunds a month was the average last year (1867–8), of which more than half was furnished by Ningail alone. The effect of the earthquake of January, 1869, has been to increase the yield of salt water in the wells enormously; the water in the Ningail well after the earthquake rose six feet, and this rise has continued up to the present time undiminished. The effect of earthquake has been observed before, but not to such an extent or remaining for so long a time. The whole of the wells named above belong to the Raja, and are worked for his benefit. The men employed are, however, remunerated for their labour, and a certain proportion of salt is set aside for their benefit. The proportion that goes to the Raja is 30 per cent. of the quantity manufactured, the remaining 70 per cent. is divided among the workmen. The wells are under the charge of a *dewan* who resides in the capital and visits the wells occasionally. All the men employed in drawing and evaporating the water are Munnipories of the *Loee* caste or division, the lowest among the Munnipories. These work fifty at a time, and are changed every month. One man's *lalloop* or forced labour is six months in a year; but it is stated that no objection is made to this, as they are paid regularly for their labour. About 200 men are usually liable to this labour in Ningail alone; this year, on account of the great increase in the yield, more have been required. Besides the Munnipories, many coolies are required for carrying fuel, and these frequently change. Hillmen work for a short time in order to procure a payment in salt. I am assured none of the coolies are pressed, and that all are paid in salt for their labour. No attempt has at any time been made to reach the salt itself; were this possible I have no doubt that rock salt in large deposits would be found. As an experiment I evaporated 36 ounces of filtered water from Ningail, from which I procured 6 drams of pure salt free from smell and apparently quite pure. As before stated, the salt as manufactured is very impure from its being contaminated with mud, but this seems to be relished rather than otherwise. The salt is disposed of at the well to parties who retail it in the various bazaars; the wholesale price last year before the earthquake was about 6 rupees 4 annas a maund, a little above that in British territory; now, however, it is considerably less, as the greatly increased yield has caused a fall in the price, and salt has never been so cheap in the country before." In all essentials the salt is manufactured now in the way described by Dr. Brown. For earthen evaporating pans, iron *korais* of the same shape have been substituted, and are leased out by the State on payment of an annual charge.

There is a disagreement between Colonel McCulloch and Dr. Brown as to the exact position in society held by the Sel Lois or Lois who paid their revenue in *sel*, the bell-metal coinage of the country. The point is immaterial, and the industry has now ceased to exist, for British rupee coinage circulates in the country, although for some purposes *sel* are still used. Dr. Brown gives a clear account of the coinage. "The only coin proper to the country is of bell metal, and small in size, weighing only about 16 grains. This is coined by the Raja as required, goods or money being taken in exchange. The metal is obtained chiefly from Burmah, and consists of gongs, etc.: some of it is also procured from the British provinces. The process of coining is very primitive: the metal is first cast in little pellets: these are then softened by fire and placed on an anvil: one blow of the hammer flattens the pellet into an irregularly round figure; a punch with the word *Sri* cut on it is then driven on it by another blow, which completes the process. The market value of the *sel*, as it is called, varies: when rupees are plenty, then *sel* is cheap: when scarce, the opposite. The present value of the coin is 480 to one British or Burmese rupee, and its usual variation is said to be from 450 to 500. I have before me now eight varieties of *sel* coin, dating from the reign of Pakungba downwards. The coin shown me as Pakungba's is, the Munnipories say, the oldest in the country; it is a shield-shaped disk of bell metal, very thin, but of large size, measuring rather more than 3½ inches in diameter: it has no marks on it of any kind. In Khakamba's reign the coin is almost square, and has faint marks on it. McCulloch * credits Khakamba with first introducing bell-metal coinage, and figures the coin, which is round; the Munnipories, however, have shown me all the old coins they have, and I have adopted their nomenclature as regards the Raja, who issued it. Marangba coined of a round shape smaller than the above, and with well-raised characters; Keeyamba, of an irregular square form, with very indistinct characters; Paikomba, irregularly rounded and faintly marked; Charairomba, square and with the lettering distinct; Gurreeb Newaz, round, well-made coin, lettering very superior, the best finished of any of the coins. From Chingtungkomba downwards the coin has not altered much, and is much smaller than any of the above (about 1760 A.D. till the present time). There is no evidence whatever of there having been at any time a gold coinage in existence; but it is stated that Chourjeet Singh, about 1815, coined silver of a square form, and of the same value and weight as the British rupee. I have only been able to obtain one specimen of this coin. The British and Burmese

* *Op. cit.*, p. 37.

rupee, both representing the same value, circulate freely; also the smaller silver coins, as four-anna and two-anna pieces. About seven years ago an attempt was made by the then Agent to introduce copper coinage, and a large quantity was supplied by Government. The experiment totally failed, as the women in the bazaar positively refused to have anything to do with it, and the coin had to be returned. The bell-metal coin, in conjunction with rupees and smaller silver coins, are amply sufficient for the wants of the country, and I consider the attempt at introducing copper was unnecessary, as was indeed proved by the determined refusal of the women to accept it." *

Colonel McCulloch refers to the treaty into which Gourosham entered in the middle of the eighteenth century with the East India Company, in one of the articles of which mention is made of gold rupees which Colonel McCulloch regards as a mistake.† This is probable enough.

The Chronicles do not afford us any help in determining the nature of the coinage or the date when coins were first struck. It is curious to observe that while in England we change the direction in which the face of the sovereign looks, with each reign, in Manipur they changed the shape of the coin entirely.

Colonel Johnstone, in an interesting passage, records the trouble caused by the great fluctuations in the exchange between *sel* and rupees.‡ The cambists brought the rupee exchange down to 250, whereas its normal rate was, as Dr. Brown says, from 450 to 500, but Major Johnstone, as he then was, induced the Raja to make an issue of *sel* so that the usual ratio was established. Currency questions, as Mr. Gladstone once said, disturb the mind more than love, and by the abolition of *sel* and the introduction of the copper coinage of India the State has been free from anxiety of this nature.

It is impossible to overlook the ingenious speculations proffered by Colonel Sir Richard Temple in the *Indian Antiquary* § on the origin of the scale of value between the *sel* and the rupee as due to the system of reckoning 400 cowries to the anna, and to the identity of the *sel* of Manipur with the *dam* of Akbar and

* *Op. cit.*, pp. 47, 48.

† *Op. cit.*, p. 37. Cf. Pemberton, *op. cit.*, p. 42.

‡ *Op. cit.*, p. 123.

§ Vol. xxvii. pp. 169 *seq.*

of modern Nepal. In the first place, perhaps as a result of the disappearance of the *sel* coinage, the word *makhai* is not now used by natives to describe *sel*. In itself *makhai* means the half, from *khai-ba*, to divide; and the word *yāng khai* = fifty shows the same force in the second of its components. *Yāng* probably means one hundred, for we know the language has become denasalized, and the equation *chā* = *yāng* is phonetically permissible. The use of cowries has been completely forgotten.

IMPLEMENTS AND UTENSILS.

Mention has been made of the many uses to which the *dao* is put in Manipur, and it may therefore be classed not only as a weapon, but as an implement also of uncommon utility. The *khutlai*, or hand possessions (*khut* hand; *lai* or *nai*, to belong to or be possessed), vary according to the trade or occupation of the owner. Thus the agricultural implements will be described in the section appropriated for agriculture, while the implements of the several arts and industries of the country will be set forth in the section reserved for the manufactures. The household utensils consist of earthen pots manufactured for the most part by the Lois of Chairel and Shuganu, who also produce stone bowls, which they turn from the rough sandstone, which is blackened by lamp black and then wrought to a high polish. Brass, copper, and bell-metal cooking pots are in common use, but are imported from Cachar. Plates, both of metal and cheap earthenware, are found in many houses, for the withdrawal of the numerous sumptuary and economic restrictions which formed so conspicuous a part of the political system of a former day, has undoubtedly been the cause of a rise in the general taste of the community, so that articles, such as an umbrella, once the treasured token of royalty, or at least of royal favour, are now carried without fear of let or hindrance.

AGRICULTURE.

Captain Pemberton states that "The agricultural produce of the country consists principally of rice, which forms the staple article of food, and the fertility of the soil is so great that the crops generally prove most abundant; the innumerable streams which gush from the bases of the ranges surrounding the valley insure an adequate irrigation, even to the fields which are above the level of the general inundation, and it has sometimes happened that the whole population has been entirely subsisted by the produce of the lands so situated on the inclined planes at the foot of the hills, when from unusual drought there has been an entire failure of the crops in the central portions of the valley: rice has frequently been sold during the last year, when the country was only recovering from the devastating visitations of the Burmahs, at the rate of five maunds for a rupee, and the land now under cultivation is scarcely one-fourth of that which could be rendered available for the same purpose, were the population better proportioned to the extent of country it subsists upon. Tobacco, sugarcane, indigo, mustard, the different varieties of Dhal, and opium are also cultivated. . . . Almost all the garden produce of Europe is now found in the valley, such as peas, potatoes, the different varieties of greens and cabbages, carrots, radishes, beetroot and turnips, none of which were known until introduced by the European officers, who have been resident in the country since the late war. The potato and the pea particularly have proved so acceptable to the people, that they are now almost universally cultivated and exposed for sale in the different bazars of the country.

"Fruits do not appear to attain such perfection as the vegetables, though from the varieties which grow spontaneously in various parts of the valley we should infer that nothing but culture is required to render them as good as the latter. Apples, apricots, raspberries, strawberries, oranges, limes, pomegranates, guavas, mangoes, and jackfruit are all found within this mountain valley, but none attain to such flavour as might have been expected, from the total absence of care and skill in their cultivation; and we can hardly suppose that they would fail to prove as excellent as the pineapple were the same attention bestowed upon them that is shown in the culture of the latter." * Colonel McCulloch gives some interesting

* *Op. cit.*, pp. 29–31.

details of the methods of Manipuri agriculture.* "A branch of a tree crooked in this form  the end of which is faced with iron, forms the Munniporee plough. To this a buffalo is attached between a couple of shafts, thus . With this instrument the ground when dry is little more than scratched. The plough is held in one hand, and the buffalo, by means of a string passed through his nose, and a vocabulary he seems to understand, is guided by the other. Instead of the buffalo, two bullocks are sometimes attached to the plough, one on each side of a centre pole. The operation of scratching up the soil and preparing the field for the reception of the rice seed commences in February; and in May they sow what is called *poong hul*, or dry seed cast in dry ground. In June, the rains having set in, the field is brought by successive ploughings into a state of liquid mud, and in this the *pang phel* is cast. The seed for the *pang phel* is first quickened by being moistened with water and kept in a covered basket until it shoots. As this seed floats on the surface of the mud, it has to be carefully watched until it takes root, and three or four leaves have sprung up, in order to protect it from wild ducks and other birds. After this comes the *lingba* or transplanting. The seed for the plants which are destined to be transplanted are usually sown very close in plots carefully prepared for the purpose. When the transplanting season arrives, the plants are by washing divested of all earth attaching to them, and having been taken to the field, they are one by one separately inserted in the mud. For a time after transplanting they look as if they were all withered up, but they soon spring up and afford an excellent crop. If the ground has been carefully deprived of weeds before sowing the crop, weeding afterwards is not required. The only cultivation of any importance is rice. Not a particle of manure is placed on the ground, and yet year after year good crops are raised from the same spot. The yield has, of course, lessened from what it was, but its being so very considerable as it is evinces a very rich soil. The mainstay, however, of Munnipore is the crop raised at Thobal and its vicinity. There the river once, at least, in the year inundates the rice fields, giving them amazing fertility. About Thobal they weed

* *Op. cit.*, pp. 27, 28.

with a harrow, which, drawn by a buffalo over the rice field, uproots indiscriminately the weeds and the rice. The former die, but the rice plant takes root again and is not injured. When the rice begins to ripen, it has to be watched against the depredations of immense flights of birds. Deer and other wild animals also do a great deal of mischief, and against them precautions have to be taken. The rice having ripened is cut with a knife slightly curved at the top, and having a rough edge like a saw. As it is cut it is laid in handfuls on the ground, and when dry tied up in sheaves. These sheaves are carried to the part of the field most convenient for the purpose, and the rice beat from them on a large reed mat. After having been winnowed by means of fans, the rice is ready for the granary and removed to it. This sun-dried rice keeps very well in husk, but when cleared of the husk it can be kept for a very short time only. The straw is left lying in a pile around the place where the rice was beat out. Except as fuel, no use is made of it."

The yield is still high and the land shows no serious symptoms of exhaustion, and not only is there still a fair amount of land available for the extension of cultivation, but very large tracts could be made cultivable by well-planned and not necessarily very expensive drainage operations. One danger, however, exists, the possibility of fraud on the part of speculators who have at times in the past attempted to profit by the new revenue system to take out *pottahs* for land which they sublet for grazing purposes to the neighbouring villages at high rents. Undoubtedly custom recognizes that village rights to grazing and wood and grass-cutting extend over the waste lands adjoining the cultivated areas. The Chronicles contain mention of attempts to divert the course of rivers, and while some if not the greater number of them are due to the desire to provide courses for the boat races, in one or two cases they seem to have been destined to benefit the cultivators by furnishing irrigation channels.

The agricultural implements used by the Meitheis are the *kangpōt*, or sledge, the *langōl* or plough, the *ūkai anālba* or smooth harrow, the *phao intōk* or paddy spoon, the *humai* or fan used for winnowing the paddy, the *ūkai samjet* or toothed harrow, the *chairong* or paddy thrasher or flail, the *thânggōl* or sickle (lit. round *dao*), the *yōt* or spade, the *thāngchao* or large *dao*, and the *yeina phak* or threshing mat.

CROPS.

The staple of the valley is, as has been said, rice. Dr. Brown * says that "No fewer than seventeen varieties of rice are grown; these may be divided into early and late crops. The early crop ripens in three months and is ready for cutting in about September. Of late years a large quantity of the early sort has been sown. Of the early there are four varieties. The late crop ripens in six months, and is reaped in November. The great bulk of rice grown in the country is of the late varieties, which comprises thirteen kinds, chiefly distinguished by size of grain and colour. The finest of these are named Phourail, Yentik, and Loeening; these are white and of large grain—*dal*. Only two kinds of *dal* are grown, *khessaree* and *moongh*. English vegetables grow remarkably well, and I have a finer garden in Munnipore than I have ever had in India, the Punjab excepted. The pea of the country is of small size but of good quality; it resembles the English pea.

"Vegetable productions of the country . . . pulses as *dal*, *kalye*, etc., are grown, but not largely; pepper, onions, tobacco of good quality, sugarcane, potatoes of small size and inferior quality; wheat is grown in the cold season in small quantity. Fruits are scarce and few in number. Plantains of fair quality, pine apples, mangoes (some of large size and fair quality) are almost the only fruits procurable which would be relished by an European. A plum resembling an English variety is common, but as met with in the bazaars, is excessively bitter. That this is simply the result of bad culture, however, I have proved, as I have several plum trees in my compound which I pruned last cold weather, with the result that the fruit this season is perfectly sweet. McCulloch mentions in his account the existence of good oranges on a hill in or near the Logtāk Lake, but I have never seen any. Peaches grow, but of poor quality.

* *Op. cit.*, pp. 14, 15.

Apples grow on the slopes of the hills of fair appearance externally, but quite uneatable. Throughout the valley and the neighbouring hills the bramble and wild raspberry are common."

Dr. Brown's experience of the oranges of the islands of the Logtāk Lake is unfortunate, as, though not very plentiful, the fruit is sweet and of fair size. The rice fields are cropped once only in the year, and the winter cultivation is all or nearly all of the garden type. The cultivation of wheat has not proved a success, but there is every reason to believe that with due care rubber, tea, and in some spots perhaps jute might be profitably raised. The climate is favourable for the production of mulberry trees which form the food of the silkworms. The floral wealth of the country as a whole is famous. Sir George Watt, K.C.I.E., says that "probably no part of India had such varied and beautiful flora. On going into Manipur the first thing that struck the traveller was the enormous number of trees with which he was not familiar in other parts of India. Speaking from memory he believed that there were probably twenty species of the oak. Manipur was the home of the tea-plant. Another interesting fact about Manipur was that it was the home of the silkworm. He believed it highly probable that the real mulberry silk insect originated in Manipur and went from there into China. The whole of the typical plants of Sikkim were in Manipur, but at an altitude considerably below what they were in Sikkim. Then in the valley of Manipur, the peach, the pear and apple trees were cultivated which would be quite an impossibility in any other part of India at the same altitude."*

FISHING.

As a large portion of the valley is still under water, and as fish forms an article of food of the Meithei community, the gentle art gives employment to many people. At present the State enjoys a large revenue from the fisheries, but there is no monopoly in consequence of the wise policy of reserving a

* *Journal of the Society of Arts*, No. 2733, vol. liii., p 562.

number of *jheels* and *pāts* (lakes), which are open to the public at certain times of the year. The Logtāk, the great lake of the south end of the valley, is free, and the price of the produce of the private fisheries is regulated by the competition of the fishers of the Logtāk. There are varying methods in use in accordance with the needs and capabilities of the different localities. Weirs, fishing baskets, traps, spears, nets, are all used, and all show a high degree of suitability. The women fish with a square net suspended from a central pole by four strings at each corner, and dip the net well under the turbid waters of the edges of lakes or ditches, and slowly raise it till the catch rises above the surface of the water, when they smartly bring it out. Colonel McCulloch gives the following interesting particulars concerning the method of fishing employed by the fishermen on the Logtāk: "The Logtāk, the great resort of these aquatic birds, is covered with floating islands. Under these, amongst the roots of the vegetation of which they are formed, fish, in the cold weather, collect in great numbers, and are caught in the following manner: An island, having been cut into a manageable size, is pushed to a part of the lake where the water is not very deep, and where the bottom has been paved with stones. There it is fixed by means of long bamboo stakes; and when the fish have collected in sufficient quantity, a long strip sufficient to surround it is cut from some other of these floating masses of vegetation. With this the asylum of the fish is surrounded, and a row of stones being placed on the edge nearest the island, that edge sinks down to the prepared bottom, whilst the rest remains upright in the water, and thus forms a wall all round. The fish are now driven out of their sanctuary; if small they are taken in nets, if large they are speared by torchlight."* Pemberton† states that in the Logtāk there are "no less than twenty-six varieties, eighteen common to the rivers of Bengal and eight not found in any of them." Dr. Brown, in his account,‡ remarks that: "Of fish there is a considerable variety, and the supply is plentiful. River fish afford about thirteen different kinds. Of these the most important are the *goallee* of Bengal (called in Munnipore, '*Surreng*'), the *bao mash*, *gna raa*, the *Ranee*

* *Op. cit.*, pp. 30, 31. † *Op. cit.*, p. 25.
‡ *Op., cit.*, p. 21.

mash, surrong koibee, bagh mash, gna rel, the *vapeea, gna tel;* the rest are small and unimportant. The fish inhabiting the lakes and *jheels* are, it is said, of twenty-two kinds." The industry is largely in the hands of Lois, but affords employment to Manipuris, who speculate heavily. The policy of letting the fisheries by public auction is attractive to the sections of the community who have means, but it has on occasions given rise to a conflict of the interests of the fishery lessees and of the villages, many of which enjoy local rights over weirs and streams.

HUNTING.

The Manipuris are orthodox Hindus of a strait way, and are not hunters, but for the preservation of human and animal life from the depredations of leopards and tigers which at one time seem to have been fairly numerous in the valley, each village possesses an organization called the *keirup* (*kei* = tiger, *rup* = club or association) or tiger club, which is responsible to the authorities for the upkeep in proper order of nets and spears in sufficient quantity. As soon as authentic news of the whereabouts of a tiger is brought in by the *hui-rai* (*hui* = dog; *rai* = *nai*, to own or possess) or scouts, the *keirups* of the neighbouring villages proceed to the vicinity of the beast's lair, which they surround with the nets. Rockets and rough squibs are fired off in the jungle, and the infuriated creature rushes to his death by charging the line of nets. There is considerable danger in this method, but the Manipuri is full of courage and resource in emergencies. It will be remembered, and for the credit of the Manipuris should be placed on record, that about four years ago a small party of British officers went to a quarter of Imphāl to shoot a leopard which had taken up its abode in the compound of a house there. The wounded animal sprang on one of the party inflicting injuries which proved fatal, and a casual passer-by jumped to the rescue, snatching up a bamboo with which he belaboured the beast till it let go and ran away. It is hardly necessary to add that this required no small courage, because a wounded leopard is fierce and dangerous.

Bee hunting is practised by Manipuris, who, as noted by Colonel McCulloch,* "when they come upon a bee of this species (*koibi namthou*) catch him, and, having attached a thread to his body, let him loose. By means of the thread his flight is observed, and he can be followed to his nest. The spot is marked, and fire having been procured, the bees, otherwise so formidable, are easily destroyed. The spoil, consisting of comb filled with the young, is considered a *bonne bouche.*"

It is clear from the Chronicles that the Manipuris were in former times great hunters, and mention is made of the skill of King Pikhōmba with the bow and arrow. He is declared to have been able to shoot fish under water, and as more than one king bears the title *Til haiba*, or skilful archer, it may be believed that they were exceedingly clever in the use of the bow and arrow.

FOOD AND DRINK.

The Chronicles contain ample evidence of the change in the diet of the Meithei section of the population which is due to the introduction of Hinduism at the beginning of the eighteenth century. The earlier reigns seem to have been one long feast with hecatombs of fat cattle and oceans of spirituous drinks, even culminating on more than one instance in fatalities due to an excessive appreciation of the good cheer. They then lived like the wild Nagas of the hills, each tribe regarding only its special *tabus*, and each individual abstaining only from the private *tabus*. But the official adoption of Hinduism not only removed the ban against milk but created many prohibitions to which the new converts eagerly submitted. Animal flesh is forbidden, and all spirituous liquor or intoxicants are accursed. Fish is eaten, and is a common article of diet, so much so, that, as described above,† special care had to be taken to prevent any monopoly of fishery rights from unduly raising the price of this commodity. Rice forms the staple of food, and is boiled in the open air in earthenware pots, and, connoisseurs often have the rice cooked inside a hollow bamboo, and declare that the *ūtōng*

* *Op. cit.*, p. 33. † See p. 45.

chāk (*ū* = wood, *tōng* = to cook, *chāk* = cooked rice) or wood-cooked food, possesses a very delicate flavour. But in childhood the strict rules of Hinduism are not enforced, and old age has like relaxations, a fact which was noticed by Colonel McCulloch, who remarks, "Children up to ten or twelve years of age eat every sort of food without regard to the Hindoo notions of purity or impurity. And it is a common practice for old people to abandon altogether Hindoo observances." * Honey is eaten by many, who buy it from the hunters whose methods are described above. Children are said to eat the white ant and the grasshopper. †

Dried fish is imported in large quantities from Cachar, and has often been assumed to be the means of spreading cholera through the country, but in the absence of definite scientific investigations into the causation and distribution of that disease, this favourite dainty must be entitled to a verdict of "Not Proven."

Dr. Brown mentions ‡ that, "The Munnipories, both male and female, are inveterate chewers of *pān sooparee.* The whole of this is brought from the neighbouring district of Cachar, and forms a considerable trade. The betel-nut tree will not grow in Munnipore territory. Tobacco is used by all classes and ages, and the tobacco is used and smoked as in Bengal. I am informed that opium is not used by the Hindoo part of the population, neither is there any consumption whatever of Indian hemp or other intoxicating drugs." In recent years, the introduction of cigarette smoking has aroused vehement protests from the stricter kind of the orthodox, who elicited a formal condemnation of the habit from the wise men of the Chirāp. At about the time when the best intellects of Manipur were exercised by this problem, another matter of supreme interest occurred which drew public attention away from the misuse of cigarettes. *Horribile dictu,* a Manipuri was seen in the hills somewhere between Imphāl and Cachar, carrying a load slung on his back Naga fashion. He was warned not to do it again, but to use a yoke in future. These edicts produced little effect.

* *Op. cit.,* p. 17. † Brown: *op. cit.,* p. 21.
‡ *Op. cit.,* p. 33.

KHĂNG-JEI SĀ-NA-BA. POLO IN MANIPUR.

From a photograph by E. J. Mitchell, Esq.

p. 48

GAMES.

Physically a fine race, the Manipuris are devoted to sports and games. The principal game is foot hockey, or *khōng kāng-jei* (*khōng* = foot, *kāng* = ball or round object, *jei*, from root *chei* = to hit), which is played by every naked little boy on the waste lands surrounding the village. Armed with a slightly curved bamboo stick, they play keenly, and as time goes, some reach such a degree of proficiency that they are selected to play for the "Panna" in which they live, before the assembled crowds at Imphāl during the Durga Pujas. There are nine players a side, and the game comes to an end when one side obtains an agreed number of goals. The principal stroke is on the "nearside," as it gives protection to the legs from blows of an opponent's stick. A player may "collar" or trip an opponent, or may pick the ball up and run with it some way. Such runs are generally terminated by a piece of "gallery" play, the striker throwing the ball up in the air and hitting it. Jeers await the unskilful wretch who unsuccessfully attempts this stroke. In the reign of Khāgenba, *circa* 1600, the great and famous game of polo was introduced into Manipur. The ponies are strong, wiry little creatures rarely more than twelve hands in height, and are fed on grass, with now and then an allowance of paddy. The saddle is large, light, and peaked both in front and behind. The most curious feature about the saddle is the addition to it of a pair of leather flaps which project around the legs of the rider and afford some protection from a blow. These flaps are made of enamelled leather, and are fastened underneath the stirrup irons. The bit is a heavy mass of iron in two pieces which are jointed in the middle where the joint makes a huge knob. The reins, which are of cotton rope, are fastened through rings at either end of the bit, and the headstall carries a framework to which are attached little wool or cotton balls, the purpose of which is to excite the pony and to give it some scanty protection from blows. The saddle is girthed on in the ordinary way so far as I know. The player does not grip with his knees, but balances himself. The polo stick (*kāng hū*) consists of a long shaft of bamboo with a head of hard wood set on at an obtuse angle which is much greater than is usual among European players. This is necessitated by the fact that the most successful of their strokes are played on the near side, a result of their long practice as children playing hockey. Their fore-arm development is magnificent, and really out of proper proportion. The ball (*kăng drŭm*) is made of bamboo root. To describe the game is beyond the powers of any but an imaginative and practised pen, for, in respect of brilliance of play, constant excitement, rashness, courage, skill, and popular enthusiasm, there is no game to equal it. Every man in the huge gathering which sits in an orderly mass on the banks lining the polo ground, is a competent critic, and while the excellences of individuals meet with approving cheers of *yăm phă-i* or very good, Homeric laughter is the portion of the ambitious, but unskilful player who essays in vain some difficult stroke. Keenness is the order of the day, and the right of individual players to appear is jealously scrutinized, and there is a rule that no pony must be allowed to play which at any time during the preceding month has belonged to a representative of another "Panna." By a courteous evasion of difficulties they allow high officials to lend their ponies as they please, on the ground that they are officers, not of a part, but of the whole of the country. The rules of the game are not obvious, indeed, most observers declare that rules are conspicuous by their absence. Many things are permissible to them which the greater dangers of the game on the bigger ponies render impossible or too hazardous. An opponent's stick may be crooked in any position, and the rule about crossing is not in existence among them. Yet serious accidents are rare, partly as a result of the fact that the Manipuri is light in bone, and active, and the ponies up to the weight they have to carry. Once the ball crosses the back line, a goal is scored, and the ball is thrown in from the middle line, not along the ground, but in the air, so as to give occasion for the brilliant stroke of hitting it in mid-air. Reliefs are permitted, and constantly take the place of tired players. To prevent accidental damage, the players swathe their heads in their *pagris*, which are fastened under the chin, and wear padded and quilted leggings. It is customary for the losing side to provide rewards for the winners, and, if a man desire to gain reputation, he may arrange a game and provide these not expensive rewards for all the players, adding special prizes for any who have distinguished themselves in the game. Signal skill at the game was a sure road to royal favour in olden times.

A party of polo players went to Calcutta on the occasion of the visit of H.M. the King, when Prince of Wales, to India, and again to Delhi to perform before the multitudes which assembled there in 1901. There is evidence that the popularity in India of polo as an organized form of sport is in part attributable to the enthusiasm of British officers who saw that there were sporting possibilities latent in the game as played by Manipuri teams in Cachar and Calcutta.

After the races come sports, such as the *rāmbai hūnba* * or javelin throwing, "tossing the *caber*," in this case, a weighted *dhān* pounder, "putting the stone," high kicking, sword play, and spear play with shield and plumes, which distinctly remind one of a Naga warrior's dress. The Mussulman section of the population contributes acrobats and contortionists, and there is always a troupe of low, sometimes very low, comedians, whose jests afford supreme delight to the crowd. But many of the best known performers have either left the country or gone to the majority, and the art of javelin throwing, long one of the special features of the annual sports, is in jeopardy of extinction, for as yet no successor worthy of the name has arisen to take the place of old Bedām Singh, the Nestor, when I knew him, of modern Manipuri polo players, whose fund of reminiscence of the good old days was ever at the disposal of those who loved the royal game and were in sympathy with the departed splendours of the country.

Hardly less enthusiasm is aroused among the Manipuris themselves by the boat-races which, to other eyes, seem to lack that sporting interest which is the great charm of polo in its home. Yet the clean crowds, all well behaved and orderly, present a picturesque sight, for among the men who are dressed in spotless white, are groups of women in bright attire, and on the banks of the river of Imphāl the waving beauty of clumps of feathery bamboo, hiding or partly revealing the houses behind, gives an air of placidity to the scene. The six

* See page 20, *supra*.

Pannas or Revenue divisions of the country send in a boat each, and, according to custom, the Pannas compete in a fixed order—Ahalup *versus* Nahārup, and Khābum *versus* Laipham, Hitak-phanba *versus* Pōtsangba. Dr. Brown says,* "The boat-races occupy three days in September, and take place on the moat which surrounds on three sides the Raja's enclosure.† This ditch is about 25 or 30 yards broad, and at the season when the boat-races come off, contains plenty of water. This festival is the most important held in Munnipore, and great preparations are made for it; stands are erected on both sides of the moat, the one for the Raja being of considerable size and height. The women occupy stands on the opposite side of the moat. The boats used in the races are two in number, one of great length, and hollowed out of a single tree. The rowers number about seventy men, each with a short paddle. Besides the rowers are several men attending to the steering, and urging on the crew. One of these stands in the front of the boat, and, leaning on his paddle, encourages the efforts of the men by stamping violently with his right foot at intervals. The race itself differs from most boat-races, in the fact that here the great object is for one boat to foul the other and bore it into the bank, so that one side of the boat is disabled, the men not being able to use their paddles. The boats are thus always close together until at the finish, when the race is usually won by a foot or two only. The distance paddled is about quarter of a mile. Each race is rowed twice whichever wins, and the results are carried on from year to year. As in the *Lumchel,* the competitors are men belonging to different *punnahs.* There are no rewards for the races, they being rowed merely for the honour of the thing. The Raja in his boat, which is like the others, but ornamented with a carved deer's head and horns gilt at the prow, accompanies the race; the Raja on the chief day steering his own boat in the dress formerly alluded to. McCulloch, in his account, mentions that the boat-race is not a fair race, but a struggle between the rowers on either side, in which those who can deal the hardest blows, are usually the victors. That

* *Op. cit.*, p. 36, 37.

† This moat was drained in the early years of the British occupation, and the boat-races now take place on the Imphāl river

HĪ YĀNG TĀ-NA-BA. Manipuris wearing the special costume for Boat racing.

p. 53

fights occasionally happen is correct, but they arise from accidental causes and are really not a premeditated part of the performance. While the boats are paddling down to the starting-place, a good deal of chaffing, flinging of weeds, water etc., between the rival boats takes place, but all seems to be conducted in a good-humoured manner." Neither of these authorities refers to a curious custom connected with the boat-races, by which the steersman of the losing boat becomes the slave of the steersman of the victorious crew, to whom the statutory fine of fifty rupees has to be paid for release.

Dr. Brown gives the following account of the Lamchel or foot race (*lam* = distance, and *chel* = to run).* "This Lumchel is a competition between the different 'Punnahs' or classes among the Munniporie population. Brahmins, as also the lowest class of Munnipories, the Looees, are not allowed to compete, but Mussulmans may.† The distance run by the competitors is a straight course from the brick bridge formerly mentioned‡ to the inside of the Raja's enclosure; the distance is under half a mile. The first part of the races consists of trials of speed by two Punnahs at a time; the winners in these races run again when all have had their trial, and the first man in of the whole wins the race of the year. The first man receives as his reward, sundry presents, and is excused from all forced labour or *lalloop* for the rest of his life; he becomes a hanger-on about the Raja usually after his victory. Old winners are allowed to run again for the honour of the thing; when they win more than once, they get presents. The first in at the preliminary races between the Punnahs are allowed three months' exemption from *lalloop*. These races cause great competition, and for months before they

* *Op. cit.*, pp. 35–37.

† The prohibition against the Brahmins and the Lois in this matter is probably due to the fact that the division of the country and its population into the six Pannas, dates from a period antecedent to the advent of Hinduism, when the Lois were simply the conquered earlier inhabitants of the country, and therefore excluded from participation in the festivals of their conquerors. The Mussalmans came into the country at an early period, about the middle of the sixteenth century, and the great period of internal organization and development in the history of Manipur is the reign of Khăgenba (1588–1652, A.D.), to whom the introduction of polo and the boat-races are due.—T. C. H.

‡ Over the Nambol river.—T. C. H.

come off, various lanky-looking men, with a scanty proportion of clothing, may be seen, morning and evening, trotting along the roads, getting themselves into training for the important event. The Raja is always present at these and the other games, seated in a sort of gateway which bounds the straight road along which the races are run.

"*The Wrestling.*—After the races there is an exhibition of wrestling; this presents nothing very peculiar; the only thing that need be mentioned regarding it is a curious custom which prevails. The victor over the wrestler who competes with him, before salaaming to the Raja, leaps up in the air, alighting on his left foot; as he descends he gives his right buttock a resounding slap with his right hand; having thus asserted his superior skill, he makes his salaam in the usual manner.

"*Hockey matches after the boat-races.*—On each of the three days devoted to the boat-races important hockey matches take place. Immediately after the races an adjournment takes place to the hockey ground, close by, and the game is at once commenced; the play being much better than can be witnessed at any other time. The ground at that time not being in good condition, many falls take place, which are not allowed, however, to interrupt the sport. The scoring is carried on from year to year also in this case, and many sporting gentlemen may be seen in various parts of the field carefully marking the results with pieces of pebble. The excitement and interest manifested in the result is very great."

The dances of the country are four in number. *Rās, maribok jagoi, khubeiscisakpa,* and *sanjoiba.* In the first three, girls take part, while the last is performed by boys alone. The peculiar costume described above * is worn by the girls who appear in the *rās,* eminently a dance of sacred origin. In the dance called *maribokjagoi,* or the dance of the four corners, only four performers are required, and in the *khubeiseisakpa* or the singing with the clapping of hands, the girls keep up an accompaniment to the music with vigorous hand-clapping. They wear the ordinary *fanek* for this last. The boys who dance the *sanjoiba,* wear a remarkable head dress of peacocks' feathers. The dances and costumes are very picturesque, but the noisy

* Page 16, 17.

drums on which quite a disproportionate amount of energy is expended, the clanging cymbals, the nasal singing, produce a cumulative effect which soon becomes tiresome. The game known to the Manipuris as *kāng sā-na-ba* or playing the *kāng*, is the local variant of the widely played game described by Captain Lewin under the name of *konyon*.* Colonel McCulloch thus describes it: † "The amusement in its season most enjoyed is *kāngsānaba*, a game as peculiar to Munnipore as that of hockey on horseback. It is played only in the spring, the players being generally young women and girls, with usually a sprinkling of men on each side. The game seems to cause great excitement, and there is great emulation between the sides. The *kang* is the seed of a creeper: it is nearly circular, about an inch and a half in diameter, and about three quarters of an inch thick.‡ It is placed on the ground upright, at one time with its broadside towards the party by whom it is to be struck, at another edge wise. When the *kang* is placed with its broadside to the party, it is to be pitched at with an ivory disk, when it is placed edgewise, it is to be struck by the disk propelled on its flat side along the surface of the ground by the force of the middle finger of the right hand acting off the forefinger of the left. A good player can propel the disk in this way with great force and precision. The side having most hits wins. The whole is closed by a feast at the expense of the losers."

The wandering minstrel of Manipur is a familiar feature, especially in the villages outside the Capital. Ignorant for the most part of the art of writing, they recite, to the accompaniment of the *pena* or fiddle, ballads, some of which are of local origin, while others are products of Hindu piety. As remarked by Colonel McCulloch, § "Some of the language used in their songs is quite different from that commonly spoken. The same is the case in their writings; but the meaning of the songs is known to most, whereas the writings are intelligible only to the initiated. Amongst the hill tribes there is the same

* Lewin, *Hill Tracts of Chittagong*, p. 40.
† *Op. cit.*, p. 26.
‡ *Kāng* means anything round, as *kāng drūm*, polo ball.—T. C. H.
§ *Op. cit.*, p. 27.

difference between the common language and that in their songs. The singers of the adventures of Khamba and Thoibee accompany their song with the notes of the *pena,* the solitary musical instrument of Munnipore, a sort of fiddle, with one string of horsehair, the body of which is formed of the shell of a cocoanut. On the bow of the fiddle is a row of little bells which jingle in harmony with the air." The sad tale of the distressful loves of Khamba and Thoibee,* though localized at Moirang, the home of the inveterate enemies of Meithei hegemony, is supremely popular. The story of the adventures of Ching Thang Kōmba, when wandering in exile from the attacks of the Burmese, is sure of a welcome, for the Manipuris have the historical sense more distinctly developed than most, and love to hear of the former greatness of their country. A ballad like that of *Nūmit kāppa* † serves as a change to the monotony of sadness produced by the recital of the sufferings and trials of Dhananjai, the Hindu Saint and ascetic. The group of listeners know the right times for mirth and tears, and never fail at the psychological moment, for most of them have heard the tale scores of times before, and take their time from the bard. *Wāri tābas* or parties to listen to these stories are very popular, and the rewards earned by the minstrel are often solid enough.

Pigeon fighting and gambling attract them to a fatal degree, and many are the edicts passed against these sports. Card playing is in great vogue, and the games played are a kind of "Beggar my neighbour" and a hybrid variant of whist. Neither of them are of native origin. Riddles, as noted by Colonel McCulloch, "are a fertile source of amusement. They appear usually far fetched, and sometimes not over-delicate." ‡

Dr. Brown mentions the game of *kekere ke sanaba,*§ which he says is "only played by the women: in it a number of them join hands dancing round in a circle and chanting the praises of Raja Chingtung Komba in his fights with Nagas to the north."

In the Chronicles in a passage of the date 1746 occurs the following mention of a game which is still played on occasions: "The Raja had the pleasure to witness a performance of

* See p. 165 *seq.*

† See p. 125.

‡ *Op. cit.*, p. 26.

§ *Op. cit.*, p. 34.

khangjing sānaba in the moonlight night. *Khangjing sānaba* is a kind of play, generally used to play in the night time when the moon is clear, by males and females of the country. A long piece of bamboo green suitable for the purpose, placed in the middle part, when a party of males, say a dozen or more in number, will catch the same by the one end, and a party of the female sex of the same number will hold the bamboo by the other end, then both party will pull that bamboo with all their might until one of the party is defeated." It is likely enough that this pastime, to which the name *thaurichingba* or rope-pulling is applied,* is modelled on the ceremonial rite common among certain of the hill tribes.

The musical instruments of the Meitheis are numerous, but not very elaborate. The drums are of five patterns, differing in length and shape. The horn is used by minstrels who precede the Raja when he is travelling, and they are accompanied by performers on the conchshell and castanets. The stringed instruments range from a very simple type to the modern violin, which is an importation from Calcutta. In essentials they are identical, consisting of a sounding-box and a frame on which the vibrating strings are fastened. Some are played with a bow and others with the bare fingers. Cymbals and a triangle are also used. It will be observed that the horn is not a reed instrument proper, and that, while the principle of the vibrating reed is perfectly understood in the hills, it is not employed for caste reasons by the Meitheis.

* *Assam Census Report*, 1891, vol. i. p. 244. The Tang Khuls have a crop festival of which the rope-pulling ceremony forms a part.

SECTION III.

LAWS AND CUSTOMS.

POLITICAL ORGANIZATION.

THE country was divided into six *pannas*, *Ahālūp* (the club of the old men), *Nahārūp* (the club of the young men), *Laipham* (abode of the gods), *Khābum* (belonging to *Khāba* or bitter, from *khāba*), *Hitakphānba* (gatherer of tobacco), and *Pōtsangba* (watchmen). The earliest mention of these associations occurs in the reign of Kòirengba, A.D. 1510, and it is clear that at that time they were already military associations, and on the complete organization of the *lāl-lūp* (war club or militia), which took place in the reign of Pamheiba, they became what for some time they had been in fact, constituent parts of the militia of the country. *Ahālūp* and *Nahārūp* seem to have been the first two to be established, and, on the creation of the *Laipham* and *Khābam* divisions, precedence was assigned to these latter over the older bodies. The precise reason for this is obscure, but may be connected with the difficulties which Pamheiba, a great reformer, experienced in introducing Hinduism as the formal religion of the State.

It is now almost impossible to tell the precise conditions of membership in these associations before the period of the Burmese invasions, because the devastation of the country and its repeated depopulation completely disturbed the internal organization of the state, and the system described by Colonel McCulloch and other observers was the creation of Gambhir Singh at the comparatively recent period subsequent to the treaty of Yandabo in 1826. Nevertheless, it seems probable that the ancient model was closely followed, and that the basis of it was personal, not territorial, a feature which is due to the fact that such a system only became possible after the hegemony of the Ningthajā * clan had been finally settled. One difficulty remains. The Moirang tribe preserved a very fair amount of independence up to the advent of British authority, and from the Chronicles it is evident that their subjugation in the great battle of A.D. 1431 failed to suppress completely a sense of separateness which their remote habitation and comparative homogeneity enhanced as time progressed, and as the difficulties of their rulers increased. As will be seen later, the Moirangs have not shared in the progress and development of the civilization of the country to quite the same extent as the other tribes.

Primarily, as has been said, the *lāl-lūp* was a military organization, but in the piping times of peace it was made to play a part in the economic life of the country. Indeed, the change which came over it was completed by the introduction of modern weapons, which involved the employment of trained soldiery. Gambhir Singh, who raised and commanded the Manipur levy which operated with success against the Burmese in the campaigns of 1824–26, maintained the levy as a separate organization, though adhering to the principle which formed the pristine base of the earlier *lāl-lūp*, namely, of so many days' service and a grant of land. The members of the levy were called *lāl-mī*, or men of war, and formed a separate division or section of the community.

The centre of the State was the Rāja, and, while he himself took no direct part in the administration of the State, except on formal occasions, when he presided at Durbars, or meetings of the high officers, all was made to serve his interests. His sons held important offices, the eldest bearing the title of *Jubrāj*, the next that of *Senapati*, then came the *Kotwāl*, or head of the police, then such officers as the *Sagol Hanjaba*, or master of the horse, the *Sāmū Hanjaba*, or master of the elephants, the *Dolaroi Hanjaba*, or master of the doolies. All these officers had seats on the *Chirāp*, the chief judicial body in the State, but it was not necessary that they should be members of the royal family. The office of *Awā purel*, or foreign minister, seems to have been first created by Chandra Kirti Singh, and to

* See "Internal Structure," p. 73.

be associated with the military rather than the civil organization. To secure the due and efficient working of the *lāl-lūp*, the six Pannas were minutely subdivided, the total number of divisions reaching the high figure of 107, exclusive of the military divisions or regiments and the Loi and Nāga villages. The persons liable to duty under the *lāl-lūp* system were the Meitheis, the Brahmins, and the Musalmans, who are called Pang-gans. Nāgas and Lois are subject to much heavier duty, and with them work the *Keis*, or slave communities. Each of the 107 subdivisions possessed a number of officials, some of whom held *ex officio* seats on the *Chirāp*, thus bringing the judicial and the executive organizations into touch in a manner which may offend strict theorists, but which was in close harmony with the ideas of the people themselves. Some of the *lāl-lūp* officials were village officers, while others belonged to the central organization. Thus, to take an example at random, the *Thūmjao Rūngba*, or overseers of the salt wells, were four in number, and investigated all cases arising out of the salt revenue. One of them was a village officer, while the three others remained in Imphāl, only visiting the salt wells occasionally. Nearly all the divisions possessed an office known as the *lāl-lūp chingba* ("puller of the *lāl-lūp*"), who seems to have been the active intermediary between the officers at the capital and the men in the villages. Now the Loi, Nāga, and Kei villages were all framed on the well-known system, with village officers possessing the same titles as are now found among the hill tribes, *khūl-lākpa, lūp-lākpa*, but with a large number of additional functionaries, some of whom are clearly religious, others again being executive. Taking, as an example, the case of Chairen, the village which turns out earthen pots, we find that the head of the village is called the *Ningthou*, or king. Next to him in rank is the *senapati*, or commander-in-chief. The *khūl-lākpa* and the *lūp-lākpa* follow him in precedence, then came the *khūnja-hanba* (elder of the village), a functionary whose duties are not defined. The next officer, the *Yūpalpa* (the manager of the *yū* or beer, brewed from rice), was a sort of gauger who tasted the brew each year, and was responsible for the entertainment of strangers, performing duties which, in some Kuki villages, are entrusted to the king or chief. The *pākhan-lākpa* (*lākpa* of the young unmarried men) is the man who looked after the young men's club, for the custom of keeping the young men in one dormitory is known to have been at no distant date common among the Loi communities. The *Nahārakpa* is the ruler of the lads who are still younger than the *pākhans*, the fully fledged but unmarried men, and his sphere of authority extended over the lads in the same manner as did that of the *Pākhanlākpa* over their immediate elders. The remaining officers, the *Telloi Hanjaba*, the *Telloi Hidang*, the *Hinaoba*, the *Hirūba*, the *Lao mī rākpa*, the *Lao mī hidang*, seem to have been responsible for the work of the villagers in making and repairing boats, and in cultivating the fields.

The officers in one of the greater divisions, such as the *Khābam Sanglen*, or the great house of the *Khāba*, were men of considerable importance, and the three principal officers, the *Lākpa*, the *Sanglen lākpa*, and the *Dewān*, held *ex officio* seats on the *Chirāp*, the chief judicial authority in the country.

The *lālmī*, or military organization was organized on somewhat different lines. The central organization consisted of the *Bijaya Garot*, presided over by the *Senapati*, who, as we have seen, was often, if not generally, a member of the royal family. The majors commanding the regiments, and the *Awā puren* major (responsible as has been noted for the management of relations with Burma) together with 11 subordinate officers, composed the Bijaya Garot which had thus 20 members in all. There were eight companies which were settled in a number of villages, and were controlled by their own officers who bore the titles of officers, commissioned and non-commissioned, of the Native Indian Army. The majors, or officers commanding, were members of the central organization. Then there were other sepoy villages organized on similar lines, but which were not quite so closely connected with the central "staff" as the eight regiments and their "company" villages.

The Brahmin community was liable to *lāllūp*, and from the *guru* at the top of the list of officers to the private priests of the Mahārāja at the end of the list there were in all some 32 grades of appointments.

The definition of *lāllūp* as given to me by an experienced authority is the duty of appearing at the king's office (*loisang*) ten days, and doing the proper work of the grade to which the person belonged. For the following thirty days he remained at home. If a man did not come to his *lāllūp*, he forfeited one rupee, and for this sum a substitute was hired. The following is the vernacular statement: "*Ningthou-gi loi-sang-dā (amāsung office-dā) nūmit tarānī kāduna lāllūpki thobak toururaga nūmit kūnthrāni mayūmdā leijei. Lāllūp kādraduna mi aduna tōkla-badi lāllūp amādā rūpā amā lou-ba haonei, asīnā mahūt mi neknei.*" *Khundin* is a branch of the *lāllūp*, and consists of the duty of seeing that the men liable to *lāllūp* are regular in attendance, and covers cases of illness where a substitute is provided. *Lāllūp kāgadaba lei-ba adubu khudin kaoaji. Mi adugi karigumba thobāk leiba amādi anā ayek leiraduna lāllūp kāraroidaba leirabadi haijarabasung, mihūt pīrabasung, khūndin nūmitta kārakada-ba lāllūp chingba, machāhalna chingba kāduna khangnaba haonei.*

Chingjin-langpōn thou kai haibadi. There was special duty to be performed in the months of Asin or Bhadra [or in Manipuri the months of Langpon or Mera]. The absentee made a bargain for substituting a man who received the sum of four rupees. Connected with this is the *Paimilang panthou kai*, which extended for three months and according to which the substitute received six rupees. *Mayūmdā kūmbana thā anī loisangdā (amasung office-dā) sarucargi nūmit khuding thobāk toujei, mī adūna kāroi hairaga, mi amādā chingjinlangpōn haiba tougē haiba, asīmadā rūpā marī wāsā sai. Matōmdi Lang-ponthā Mera thā.*

The last regulation mentioned is the *Akā akum thing ba.* This referred to any special work. In cases where the men of any area found that the work imposed on them was beyond their powers it was possible to call in men from the whole area till the work was finished. *Lam amādā thobāk achaoba khūn amā anīdūna ngamdaba thobāk thōklabadi, lam adugi mi makhai lāllūp kāduna thobāk loidriba makhai touagē lāllūpti lam amāram-dagi mīna (hun kotli) lai.*

Colonel McCulloch gives the following description of the *lāllūp* of his day: * "This population is composed of different classes. The principal is the Meithei, next the Phoongnai, after

* *Op cit.*, pp. 11–13.

whom the Teng-kul, the Ayokpa, the Kei, the Loee, and the Mussulman. The Meithei population is divided into four parts called, 'Punnahs,' which are designated in the order of their superiority, 'Kaphum,' 'Lai phum,' 'Ahulloop,' and 'Nihaloop.' The Punnahs perform *lalloop* or service for ten days in rotation, thus bringing every male in the country above sixteen years of age on duty, ten days in forty. This service is due to the State; none are remunerated for it. The head of each family or tribe furnishes the proper persons for the different services required of that tribe. The immediate family of the 'Peepa,' or head of the tribe, is not called upon to perform any heavy duty. Its post is near the Raja, acting as '*Ningthau selba*' or personal attendants. The family next in seniority has a heavy duty to perform in the '*Laikai.*' The third has the '*Lal mee,*' and the fourth the '*Sungsa roi.*' The *lalloop* of the second and fourth families works generally in unison. Their chief duty is to make houses and bridges for which they cut and bring the materials. The *lālmēē* was in former times the soldier of Munnipore, but since the raising of the troops before mentioned in the time of the Raja Gumbeer Sing, the *lālmēē's* duties have become civil. Of the families after the fourth the places are not fixed, some are *khoot naïba* or artificers, as goldsmiths, blacksmiths, carpenters, workers in brass and bell metal, etc., who all have their *lalloop* in which they perform any work in their respective lines they may be called upon to do; some again attend to the Raja's elephants, some to his ponies, etc. The Brahmins even have the *lalloop,* during which they cook for the Raja and their idol Govindjee. In fact, excepting the lowest description of service, there is scarcely any which is not performed by some part of the Meithei population. The heads of the Punnahs and all the officers required in connection with them are appointed by the Raja from amongst his favourites, and generally without reference to their origin. The appointment to office exempts the holder's immediate family from the performance of any heavy duty, and, if above a certain rank, entitles his heirs to the distinction of bearing silver spears, and being horsemen in attendance on the Raja, distinctions, however, not nowadays much coveted. A fixed allowance is not attached to any office. Some officers are entitled to *loee-il,* that is to a follower or followers, who perform any work they may be set to. The *locee-ils* dislike this, and usually compound with those they should attend for a sum of money, which having paid they remain at their homes. Individuals belonging to any *lalloop* who are anxious to remain at home, can do so by paying the chief officers. Sick people even have to pay if they miss their *lalloop*. These monies are the perquisites of the officers and form the chief emoluments of office. A few high officers have Naga villages given to them. Until lately the privilege of '*yim tinaba*' was given to officers of high rank—that is, the family or tribe from which he sprang or any other made over to him by the Raja, had to serve him; thus if he was building a house all the tribe assisted, and if his wife went abroad, the wives of the tribe attended her. This was a most distasteful custom and was done away with by Debindro Singh. The Phoongnai is divided into Hitakphalba and Potsungba. The Hitakphalba is called from his having to attend to the Raja's *hooka*. The Potsungba spreads the cloth for sitting on. The duties engrafted on these are too many to enumerate. Of the Tengkul the chief duty is gardening. They sometimes also hew stones and make vessels of that material. Both the Phoongnai and the Tengkul were originally slaves of the Raja. On a change taking place in the rulers of the country it was formerly the custom to seize the slaves of those who had held office and to divide them amongst the adherents of the new ruler. This practice when the changes of rulers became so very frequent, as it latterly did, was found to entail upon individuals more hardship than the worth of the slave. Slaves, therefore, when seized were not distributed amongst adherents but made to work for the Raja under the name of Ayokpa.* Their principal work is gardening. They used to be recruited by children of free men by slaves, but this is now discontinued.

"The particular duty of the Kei (originally slaves of the Raja) was to provide and pound the rice for the Raja's household. Formerly they were sufficient for this purpose, but they are not so now, and in consequence what is called a *Kei-roi-thau*, has been fixed upon the residents with certain exemptions of all places but the Capital. This *Kei-roi-thau* or 'work of Keis,' †

* *Ayokpa* means "maintained."

† And Lois.—T. C. H.

is not confined only to the supply of rice, but may be said to embrace any work or the supply of any article the Raja chooses, and is from this arbitrariness most oppressive."

Reference may be made to one point which more properly belongs to the section on the rules regulating the tenure of land. The liability to *lāllūp* commenced as soon as a man reached the age of seventeen, when he also became entitled to cultivate one *puri* of land with the tax in kind exacted by the Raja.

To give this sketch of the economic system of Manipur a reasonable degree of completeness, it has been necessary to refer to the foreign elements in the State, the Brahmins, the Muhammedans, the Nagas and the Lois. The historical circumstances which account for the presence of these distinct groups need not be set forth at any length, but it will suffice to say that the Lois, who in fact comprise several distinct villages which till a recent date had even kept up a separate dialect in each, are said both by the Meitheis and by their own traditions to be the descendants of the *autochthons* of the country, who were dispossessed of their fertile lands by the tribes of the Meithei confederacy.

The *Chirāp* consisted of the following persons: The Jubrāj (eldest son or heir apparent of the Raja), the Angōm Ningthou with whom the Raja was closely connected by marriage, the Wāngkhairakpa or lakpa (overseer) of the Northern quarter, the Khurai-rakpa or lakpa of tho Khurai, the Mantri (confidential minister), Jaisagun lakpa (functions not clear), Pukhrumba (title of honour), Nōngthōnba (title of honour), Laipham lakpa or lakpa of the Panna Laipham, Ahallup lakpa or lakpa of the Panna Ahallup, Khābam lakpa or lakpa of the Panna Khābam, Nahārup lakpa or lakpa of the Panna Nahārup, Luang Ningthou or King of the Luangs, Moirang Ningthou or King of the Moirangs, Katum (functions unknown), Phungnai Sang Lakpa or lakpa or the Phungnai House, the four dewans of the four Pannas, and the sanglen lakpas of the four Meithei Pannas.*

In the Pannas *Ahallup* and *Laifam* were fifteen officials of

* Ahallup or Aharup, Nahārup, Laifam, and Khābum. The two "*Phungnai*" Pannas, Hidākphāmba and Pōtsangba, are inferior classes. Cf. McCulloch, *op. cit.*, pp. 11, 12, and Brown, *op. cit.*, pp. 38, 39. Their duties are to provide for the Royal Household. See below, p. 67.

"Khullakpa" rank, who seem to have been regarded as eligible for seats in the Chirāp. Their titles are Laipham Sangguba Sanglakpa, Ahal-lup Sangguba Sanglakpa, Lairik-yengba Sanglakpa, Lairik-yengba Hanchaba, Khetri Hanchaba, Thāngsu-Hanba, Tensu-Hanba, Lālmī-Rakpa, Endren-Lakpa, Laipham-Puren, Ahallup-Puren, Khanton-Lakpa, Irak-Lakpa, Nakap-Lakpa, Phamthokcha. Similarly in the lower grade of officials ranking together as holders of *phams* of "Luplakpa rank," but, equally with the above, Chirāp-*pāmbom* or eligible for seats in the Chirāp, were the Pukhrun Hidang, Laipham Sanglen Hidang, Ahallup Sanglen Hidang, Thangsu Hidang, Tensu Hidang, Lalmi Hidang, Endren Hidang, Irak Hidang, Khundang Hidang, Nakon Hidang, Lairen Lakpa, Phamtokcha Hidang, and Lairen Hidang. Corresponding to these functionaries there were in the Khullakpa grade of officials in the Pannas *Khābam* and *Nahārup* as eligible for seats on the Chirāp, the following: Khābam Sangguba Sanglakpa, Nahārup Sangguba Sang-lakpa, Changam Ningthou, Umu Khullakpa, Singsu Hanba, Kekre Hanba, Huidru Hanba, Khābam Puren, Nahārup Puren, Laikhu Rakpa, Pallum Puren, Huirai Hanba, Khābam Konsa Hanba, and Nahārup Kōnsā Hanba. Of Luplakpa rank, in these two Pannas there were Wāngkhai Hidang, Jaisagun Hidang, Nōngthōn Hidang, Umu Hidang, Singsu Hidang, Kekre Hidang, Nakappa Hidang, Laikhu Hidang, Pallum Hidang, Huirai Hidang, and Sanglen Hidang. There were thus fifty-three persons eligible for seats on the Chirāp, in addition to the twenty-four *ex officio* members.

It is curious to note the division of offices between the Pannas. Why do we find officers as the head of the House of the Clerks (Lairik yengba sanglakpa), the chief maker of *daos* (Thāngsu Hanba), the chief arrow maker (Ten-su Hanba), in Pannas Ahallup and Laifam, and not in Pannas Nahārup and Khābam? Why, again, should Pannas Nahārup and Khābam include the chief of the scouts (Huirai rakpa) and the chief brass worker (Kōnsā Hanba), to the exclusion of these officials from the lists of Pannas Ahallup and Laifam?

The internal organization of the Pannas is no less complicated. The four principal Pannas were divided into two departments each, Sanglen and Sangguba, to each of which were attached officials whose titles are given in the following lists:—

SANGLEN.

Laipham lakpa	Naharakpa
Dewan	Phammi Ahal
Sanglen lakpa	Phammi Nahã
Sanggoiba Hanjaba	Singsuba Ahal, 4
Sanggoiba Hidang	Singsuba Nahã, 4
Pākhan lakpa	Kuarangba, 4

SANGGUBA.

Lairen lakpa	Nahārakpa
Sangguba hanjaba	Singsuba Ahal, 2
Sanggoiba Hidang	Singsuba Nahā, 2
Pākhan lakpa	

The officers in Department Sanglen were in the service of the Raja, while Sangguba officials worked for the Rāni.

The Phungnai "class" was divided into two Pannas, *Hidāk-phānba* * or persons who attend to the *huka,* and *Pōtsangba* or persons who act as watchmen. Each of these divisions is subdivided into *sanglen* or servants of the Raja, and *Laima-nai* or servants of the Rani. There are officers in each group whose titles resemble those given to the Panna officers above, with the addition of a class called Chabon, whose rank is not very high. There is also attached a class called Thong-loi-sang, which belongs to the Phungnai class but is not subdivided between the Raja and Rānī, though it has its complement of officers. We then come to a real servant class, the Panam Ningthou semba, whose duty it is to keep Royalty in all the apparatus for polo. The officers attached to this group are in seven grades, Sellungba ahal, Sellungba nahā, Pākhan-lakpa, Nahārakpa, Yāphī ahal, Yāphī Nahā, Sennakhal. The next group, entitled Laima Semba, are servants of the Rāni, with six grades of officers. Then we have the Anam Sang class, who serve both Raja and Rāni and are employed in work of a judicial nature, probably as messengers and clerks. The domestic servants of the Royal Household belong to Divisions Feida and Sangairen, and have their officers. We now come into touch with officials engaged in the administration of the country, and the following classes, Kairungba yairek sang, Kairungba maroi, Chongkhanba, Lourungsang, Phaorungba, Thumjao rungba and Hiruhinaoba, deal with the Royal granaries, storehouses, fields and cultivation, salt wells, and fisheries. The

* *Hidāk* = medicine, magical properties. Tobacco. *nong mei hidāk* (*hitāk*) = gunpowder.—T. C. H.

Arāngba have to see that the Royal Household is kept properly supplied with oil, fat, and cooking pots. The Sagonsang take charge of the horses, but when a horse or pony in their charge falls ill, the animal is in the charge of the Wāngmanai class, who belong either to the *Khumanthem* (meaning those who soothe the Khuman, or the *Sagonsem* (groom) *sagei*. The Thānggang sāba provide *daos*, and Gārisang, Sāmūsang, Sallungsang departments each have their officers, and are charged with the care of carts, elephants, and cattle belonging to the Raja. The Liman Sang department is in charge of minor work at Royal granaries.

The Thāngja pānnaba mainly look after iron smelting and the manufacture of iron implements. The Patchā Loisang are responsible for the safety and comfort of the Raja and Rāni when touring in the country, and are divided into fifteen grades of officers whose titles are rather unusual. The chief is the Bebosta, then the Ningthem porohit, the Patchā Hanba, Achromba, Achramba, Achan khulel, Achan khuba, Kairungba, Sellungba, Apampa, Salai Hanba, Takhen Hanba, Mayang Hanba, Kabo Hanba, Angōm Hanba. The next two classes, Dulai-paba and Dolai-roi, are in the first place *doolie* bearers, and are further employed as judicial messengers and *lictors*. The Urungba Loisang is charged with the duty of providing wood, bamboo, creepers, and such materials. The Yumjilloi have to keep State buildings in repair. The duties of the Maifengba class are probably of the same nature as those of the two preceding classes. The Usāba department is in charge of heavy carpentry work. The Hijaba bangmai provide cut bamboos of all sizes. The Paijasuba fasten up the creepers which are used in domestic architecture. The duty allotted to the Nandeiba loisangba is not clearly explained in the vernacular manuscript. The Humai-roi department has to do with the Lois who make the hand fans (*humai* = fan). Khutheiba Loisang has to superintend the work of skilled artisans (*Khut* = hand, and *hei* = to be skilled). The Leikai Loisang deals with the housebuilder class. The Lāmmi Loisang is stated to be in charge of much the same work as the Leikai Loisang, but the chief officer of this department bears the military title *Senapati*.* The Sagontōngba or horse-riders are

* Probably lāmmi = lāl-mi = warriors. Hence the use of a military title.

mounted messengers. The Sanglinba provide substitutes for *lāl-lūp* duty. The Sang-cha-loi (or Lois who build houses) are entrusted with the same class of work as the Leikai Loisang above. The Tengkhul Loisang is the department in charge of the royal gardens. The Kōnsang (brass workers' department) draws its *personnel* from the following *sagei*: Tourongbam, Loukham, Angōnjambam, Kongābam, Keisham, Kōnsam, and looks after the manufacture of silver and brass vessels. The next three departments relate to the work of the special castes Ahaiba, Sanjam and Thāngjam. The Ningthou phisāba department is charged with the superintendence of the manufacture of the Royal clothes which have to be made with special precautions, lest through them any harm come to the Royal wearer. The Takhen pungaiba beats the gongs, and is in attendance on the Raja when he plays polo or witnesses a polo match. The Boldeb Seina are overseers of the supply of firewood. Meitan-sang provides fuel. The Khongjai Lambus deal with Kuki affairs. Tilli-loi-sang brings in the Lois for special work. The department of the Thouban-tong provides cooking pots, and therefore connects the central administration with the village governments in Chairel and Shuganu where pots are made by Lois. The Hisang deal with all matters relating to boats. The Penakhōngba accompany the Raja and Rāni on their travels, and play the *pena*, and also take part in the festival *Umang Lai haraoba*, or the feast of the Jungle Gods. The Maiba Sanglen, though low down on the list, is the College of the Maibas, and deals with all matters concerning the Pibaship of the *sageis*, both great and small, and also conducts the worship of the *Umang Lai*. The Ametpa seems to be connected with the preceding class, and is in charge of the Royal gongs. The Maibi Loisang corresponds to the Maiba Loisang, and is the College of the Maibis. The special duty of the Panji Loisang seems to be to forecast the future of the year, and, in particular, to predict whether any earthquake is likely to occur. The Lairik yengbam is the clerkly class with duties bringing it into contact with all the other Loisang departments. The duties of the Dhobi and Napit * class are obvious at once. The Mayang-sajik department supervises the supplies of fodder

* Dhobi = washerman, Napit = barber.—T. C. H.

and grass for the elephants and ponies. There were also minor departments entitled the Manang Usang, the Kunda Sang, and Mukna Kanba. The next group of departments is in charge of affairs relating to the Panggans of Muhammedan inhabitants, and consists of Panggan Sanglen, Panggan Inkhōl, Panggan Singa Loisang, Panggan phundrai Loisang, Panggan Kumar, Panggan Mall (apparently the Muhammedan acrobats and performers), Panggan Likli. The principal official here is the Kazi.* The Yaithibi looked after the sweepers who kept the Palace clean, and with this department we are introduced to the servile Naga communities such as the sweepers, and *mochis*. The Haojaopam dealt with cases of persons who had lost caste by reason of being degraded to Lois. The Duhon Loisang, Anik Loisang, and San-gōm Loisang were semi-private departments of the Raja, and provided water, materials for offerings to the Deities, and milk. Then in charge of the Keis were their own village officers at the villages Tingri Kei, Wākching Kei, Yairibok Ningthounai Kei, Tampāk mayum (in which there were fourteen minor subdivisions entitled Sanglen, Haomacha, Sanggai sanglen, Arongba, Akhonba, Loukhumta, Khudong, Sagon Sang, Pukei, Laikhong Siphai, Mapanthong, Brindabon Chandro pujari, Duhol and Bhandari). In the Manung Loisang were four departments Roul Loisang, Chakkon, Sebok Pukei, Bhandari. To the service of Gobinda (*Govindji*) were dedicated the Lai bhandari, Mantri sebok, and Kirtana. The Duhon Loisang scattered clean water over the people of the Deity. The Keis of Charang Pāt and Wangbon Ningthoukhong, and Thingnung, were also employed in the service of Govindji. The departments known as Palla-han Palla-yeima, Palla nahā, Sebok-palla and Yaripok Chāba, discharged duties in connection with the daily ceremonial of the *kirton* of the Royal Family. The Palla amanba seem to have been the choristers and musicians of Govindji, while the Bamjigi Palla, the Mahabali Thakur Palla, the Kallika Debi Palla and the Abdanta Prabhugi Palla, the Kammokha Debi (? Kamaikhya Debi) ministered unto their Deities.

In much the same thorough manner the Brahmins were appointed to offices, the titles of which are mostly of foreign

* Cf. McCulloch, *op. cit.*, p. 12.

derivation. They were equally liable to *lallup*, their duty consisting of ministrations to the Hindu Deities.

The Bijaya Garot, or Military Court, consisted of the Senapati, the Tuli Hal Major, the Tuli Yaima Major, the Tuli Nahā Major, Bhitna Major, Bishnu Soina Ahal Major, Bishnu Nahā Major, Top Major, Ayapuren Major, Pihila, Sajor, Subedar, Jamadar, Amandar Major, Kut, Agari Holdar, Awondar, Amandar, Garot Kothantor, Kothandor. The Tuli-Han regiment consisted of twelve companies known by the names of the villages from which they came. Tuli Yaima regiment consisted of eleven companies, Tuli Nahā of twelve companies, Bhitna Tuli of eight companies, Bishnu Saina Ahal of nine companies, Bishnu Nahā of the same number, and the Tōp Tuli (Regiment of Artillery) of twelve companies. There were other regiments, Kang Tuli (eight companies), Kangnao Tuli (seventeen companies), Oinām-nōng (seven companies), Nawa Tuli (twelve companies). I do not know the precise military duties of the Bamdiar who possessed a military organization, but were drawn from the four *pannas*. Possibly it was a Service Corps. In addition to duty in the Konung or Fort, there were outposts in charge of the military forces of the State, and it seems that in all there were thirty-six such posts. There also seem to be *lāllūp* officers attached to certain regiments, but whether they were merely put there for the purpose of providing the commissariat of the regiment with the necessary supplies or for any other purpose, is not clear. Each regiment of the First Class was commanded by a Major, whose second in command bore the title Pahila. There was one Havildar Major and two Kuts to each regiment. Each company was controlled by a Subadar, a Jemadar, an Agari Holdar, a Havildar and an Amandar. The total strength of officers in a regiment of twelve companies would thus be sixty-five, which seems large. There are no exact figures available of the strength of a company in normal conditions, but it may be surmised that no "actuarial calculations" would explain the inefficiency of the regiment as a fighting unit.

There are certain villages, such as the Loi villages, which are not worked by the ordinary *lāllūp* system, but possess their own officials. At Thāngā there are two classes of *lāllūp*, the one for the service of the Raja, and the second for the Rāni.

In each class there are fourteen grades. At Iting there are eleven grades. Chairen, Hairok, Kokching, (*Khul-len*), enjoy the dignity of a Ningthou as their chief officer, who at Kokching is known as the Budhiraj. The second official enjoys the military distinction of Senapati (Commander-in-Chief). The smaller villages, such as Tāngjing, Shuganu, Langathen, Kokching Yairi, Kokching Khunao, Andro, Kameng Kokching, Susa Kameng, Sekmai Awang, Kuru Khul, Kao taruk, Kameng, Chakpa Laimaram, are less endowed with officers, the chief of whom bears the title khullakpa. In the villages or hamlets occupied by Lois, especially the twelve salt villages, the chief village official is the hanjaba, but then these villages are under the care of the Thumjaorungba or overseers of salt, a *lāllūp* department of some importance. The list of offices at Moirang may be given in full, because while due to Meithei influence the list shows that the independence which Moirang has always claimed for its own affairs, has reflected on the village organization. The chief is the Moirang Ningthou or King, a title which at the present time is held by the grandfather of the Raja, although the right of the British Government to confer it was bitterly contested. Then in order of precedence we have the Khādarakpa, the Senapati, the Mantri, the Pukhramba, the Nongthonba, Ngangkharakpa, the Okchinglakpa, the Khoyal lakpa, the Khambi-rakpa, the Ngang-ngourakpa, the Ching-ngai-rakpa, the Higarakpa, the Yaosurakpa, the Thānggārakpa, the Kei-rung-pa (four in number), the Phang thou eight in number, and the Lairen lakpa and Lairen hidang. At Ningthoukhong, where resides the Piba or tribal head of the Kumul clan, we have in order of precedence the Ningthou, the Senapati, the Khullakpa, the Luplakpa, the Mantri, the Dewan, the Patchahanba, the Achrombi, the Keirungba, the Pakhanlakpa, the Nahārakpa, the Dulairoi Hanjaba and Hidang, the Boro and Choto Gayet, the Akhanba Hanjaba and Hidang, Hiruba, Hinaoba, and the Sellungba. The same officials in the same order existed at the village of Khangabōk. At Sekmai we have an officer named the Yupalpa or gauger, who is found in all the Loi villages in which *yu* or spirit is manufactured.

NOTE.—The word "Panna" is used to describe the Revenue Division in the Shan State, Keng Tūng. Cf. *Upper Burma Gazetteer*, part i.

MEITHEI WRESTLERS.

p. 72

INTERNAL STRUCTURE.

The Meitheis are divided into seven clans, Ningthaja, Kumul, Luang, Angōm, Moirang, Khābanānba and Chenglei. The vernacular name for these divisions is *salei.** Each of these *saleis* consists of a number of sub-groups called *yumnāks*, the number varying from one hundred and fifteen in the Ningthajā, or Royal clan, to seventeen in the Khābanānba. There is a tradition to the effect that formerly there were ten clans and that two, if not three, have been extinguished (*mut-khre*). In support of this tradition, reference may be made to the favourite ballad of Nūmit-kāppa or the man who shot the sun, where mention is made of the ten kings of the land. The head or *piba* of certain clans is still designated the *Ningthou*, or king of the clan, and it was suggested to me that the ten kings of the ballad were the *pibas* of the ten clans. The small clan, Khābanānba, is said to be a composite clan. The Kumuls and the Luangs are in some remote manner connected, with the result that they do not intermarry. It seems probable that in earlier days these clans occupied definite areas, as we know to have been the case with the Moirangs who stlll preserve a considerable degree of independence and autonomy and are mainly settled in the immediate vicinity of their eponymous village. Again, Colonel McCulloch refers to the fact that, "Tradition brings the Moirang tribe from the south, the direction of the Kookies, the Koomul from the east, the direction of the Murrings, and the Meithei and Looang from the north-west, the direction of the Koupooees." † It will be observed that this quotation seems to assume that the Meithei and the Ningthaja are identical, although, as a matter of fact, the name Meithei is given to the combination rather than to any single unit in it.

An ingenious theory in explanation of the extinction of the two clans which are believed to have disappeared, was once put to me by a Manipuri, who argued, that in earlier times the

vol. i. p. 329. It may be derived from the Manipuri root, *pān* = to rule.—T. C. H.

* *Salei* = tribe ; *sagei*, normally used in reference to a Naga clan, means "relationship ;" *yumnāk* = household.

† *Op. cit.*, p. 4.

clans occupied definite areas, and that the brunt of the Burmese invasions fell on them because they happened to occupy the area first attacked by the Burmese, who, as is well known from historical records, carried large numbers of Manipuris into permanent captivity. The point may be cleared up by a careful investigation into the reminiscences and traditions of the Manipuri settlers both in Burma and Cachar.

Another curious circumstance is that among all the hill-tribes, we find a similar organization of the unit into sub-divisions which are strictly exogamic, and among the hill-tribes these sub-divisions bear the Manipuri names, Ningthaja, Kumul and Luang. Only rarely do we find the name Angōm given to a Naga clan or *sagei*. The name Khāba occurs twice, but in both instances among the Tangkhuls. In one village, a Tangkhul village named Nungbi, we find Angānba and the names Atum and Kasu which are described by the Tangkhuls * as Manipuri names but are not now in use among the Manipuris. Apart from this, which may be pure coincidence, there is no material for holding that the names of the lost tribes were Atum and Kasu.

The Lois are divided into clans in much the same way and intermarry with other Loi villages if the industry of those villages be identical with that of their own. Thus the Lois of the salt making villages would intermarry, but it is not likely that they would go to Fayeng, a silk village, for wives, nor that Fayeng would give them their girls. Such Loi villages as are known to have originated as penal settlements for deserving Manipuris, claim a higher status in the world than other Lois and always grasp a chance of asserting their fidelity to Hinduism.

One of the earliest tokens of the progress of a Loi community towards Hinduism is the abandonment of delicacies in the way of food and drink. This sometimes involves them in serious loss when the industry of the community happens to be the distillation of country spirit.

* The Chronicles of Manipur make it abundantly clear that the Tangkhuls existed as an organized tribe in occupation of much the same area as at present, at a period coeval with the establishment of the Meithei hegemony in the valley, by the defeat of the Moirang tribesmen in A.D. 1431.—T. C. H.

MARRIAGE RULES.

The Meitheis are exogamous as regards the clans or *saleis* into which they are divided, but are endogamous as regards members of other tribes, though there are cases on record of marriages between Brahmins and Meithei girls. Such is the strict rule, but it may be inferred that it has not always been rigorously adhered to, since the Chronicles refer in more than one passage to the wrath of the Raja at the disregard of the proprieties and his orders that they "should not marry people of their own kins." There were special penalties on breaches of this rule in the shape of the loss of the privilege of giving water to the Raja, but their validity was derived, in the first instance, from the superstitious fear of divine wrath for the violation of an essential *tabu* (*nāmung-ba* in Meithei).

The general rule is amplified by further rules, which may be survivals from an order of things which has now passed away. Angōms were not allowed to marry with Khābanānbas, Moirangs, or Luangs. The Luangs were forbidden to take their wives from among the Kumuls, and the Moirangs were not permitted to marry the Khābanānbas, and one or two families of the Chenglei *salei* were also forbidden to them. The family of Moirang Laipham seems to have been prohibited to the Ningthajā clan, but the case is obscure, and, if genuine, constitutes the only prohibition affecting the Ningthajās. In one case only, that of the Kumuls and the Luangs, is an explanation afforded by tradition, which asserts that once upon a time a Kumul Wazir * saved the life of a Luang who had been sentenced to death. In the Kumul *lōl*, or account of the Kumul tribe, the following statement occurs, which may perhaps afford a further clue to the difficulty. "*Luang Ningthou Punsiba*, or the long lived, became the King of Kumul, and had two children, Nungthongai and Lungba. Lungba became the King of the Kumuls, while Nungba became Luang." It may be remembered that the modern rule in Manipur is that the succession to titles where the right of the strong hand fails to operate is by primogeniture,

* The use of the Muhammedan title Wazir is curiously paralleled by the title Shahi, used by the successors and sons of Garib Nawaz, and has been suggested to me as due to a temporary predominance of Muhammedan influence in Manipur.—T. C. H.

while the heir general is the younger son, as the elder son is provided for by gifts *inter vivos.*

There seems to be a rule requiring the Meithei Ningthou to be a close connection by marriage of the Angōm Ningthou, and by custom the formal coronation of the latter precedes by a few days that of the former. The relationship between the Meithei Ningthou and the Angōm Ningthou, the heads, one of the *Ningthaja,* or Royal clan, and the other of one of the most important clans, is generally that of son-in-law and father-in-law.

The Meitheis are polygamous,* and the Raja may have three principal wives, with as many as one hundred and eight subsidiary partners. Debindro Singh, in a short reign of three months, managed to amass ninety-six wives, but it is improbable that they were simultaneously members of the Royal household. The titles of the Raja's wives in order of precedence are, (1) *Mahārāni*; (2) *Apānbi* (which may mean either the preferred one or the one who rules); (3) *Laimakhubi.*

Further, there is a rule of general application that a man may not marry a woman of the clan from which his mother came. The prohibition goes no further than the one generation.

Colonel Johnstone † states that "they have a curious custom by which a man of low caste, marrying a high caste woman, can be adopted into her tribe (*salei,* or clan), the exact reverse of what prevails in India, where a woman of high caste marrying a low caste man is hopelessly degraded, and her children outcasts." The exact meaning of this statement is not quite clear to me, but if it means that marriages between Meithei women and Nagas or Lois are either common or capable of legitimation in the automatic manner implied, it is not in accordance with the facts I have observed. No doubt there are cases on record of the adoption of men of the subject communities by the Raja and of their subsequent marriage with Meithei women, but the important thing is that the adoption precedes the marriage. One of the Naga Lum Subadars was known to have been a

* The marriage of sisters to one husband is permitted, provided that the elder sister's marriage is prior to that of the younger.—H. A. Colquhoun.

† *Op. cit.,* p. 98.

Tangkhul Naga by birth, but he was taken prisoner when quite a child, and by his intelligence and good manners attracted the notice of the Raja, who not only made him a good Manipuri, but gave him office and the privilege of riding in a *doolie.* I made careful inquiries into the accuracy of the statement quoted above, and find that there is no system in Manipur which can be so described.

Widows may remarry, but not with their deceased husband's brothers. There is no ceremony for the remarriage of widows. In polygamous households the husband's attentions to the several wives are strictly regulated according to precedence, the eldest getting twice the nominal share of the wife next below her. In actual practice, I am given to understand that these rules are often broken. I have had to adjudicate upon complaints of conjugal discourtesy in polygamous households.

INHERITANCE.

There are some difficulties which must be cleared out of the way before the rules of inheritance, both of ordinary property and of offices and dignities, can be considered. In the first place it must be remembered that the security of property was never very adequately safe-guarded in Manipur, and that theories of recent date which assign the property in the land to the Raja, tend to destroy the few surviving relics of the earlier system.

The Chronicles of Manipur do not afford us much aid in ascertaining the rules of inheritance for private property, and at the present time the economics of the state are in flux under pressure of new ideas political and social. Land is regarded as held at the will of the ruling power of the State. As regards movable property the general practice seems to be to provide for the sons during the lifetime of the father, and to regard the youngest son as the heir general if at the time of the father's death he is still living in the ancestral home. If he had separated and was living apart from his father, the property should be equally divided among the sons. Marriage is of course the cause of the separation of the sons from the home, and is the occasion of finding provision for them as well as for the daughters. Mr. Colquhoun, I.C.S., states that in theory the rules of the Dayabhāga are followed, and notes that "the Manipuri Courts are not credited with much knowledge of that treatise." But the improvidence of the Manipuri is such as to render the rules of succession to movable property of little importance, because even those who are reputed to be rich, are very often found to be bankrupt on their decease. It is politically unwise to possess the reputation of wealth in a country where the conditions of life are as unsettled as they still are in many respects in Manipur, and those who held high offices, had to spend freely to maintain their position which might be at any moment taken from them and disposed of to a higher bidder.

Colonel McCulloch * says, "There is no law as to the descent of property. It is willed away according to the pleasure of the testator, but is generally given to those individuals of the family who are most in need of it without reference to seniority."

But the succession to dignities and offices, such as the kingship or the *pibaship* of the clans, is a matter concerning which there is a mass of material of extreme value and importance. Up to the reign of Churairomba the royal succession was fairly regular, though here and there the direct line was broken by some strong intruder. According to the general account the crown devolved by the ordinary method of primogeniture. There is, however, much mystery about the circumstances of the death of Churairomba and the succession of Gharib Nawaz (Pamheiba in Meithei style). Dr. Brown gives the following version of the facts as given to him: "In that year (1714), Pamheiba, who appears to have been a Naga boy brought up and adopted by the Raja Churai Romba, shot his adopted father, it is said accidentally, whilst hunting, and succeeded him" (McCulloch's account, p. 6). The following is the account of Pamheiba given by the authorities who deny that he was of Naga extraction:—"The father of Pamheiba was, they say, the Raja Churai Romba himself; the name of his mother was Noongtil Chaibee, one of the Raja's wives,

* *Op. cit.*, p. 20.

but not the head wife or Ranee. The custom at that time in Munnipore was to kill all male children by any of the wives except the Ranee. Noongtil Chaibee concealed the fact of the birth of Pamheiba, and anxious to save his life, persuaded her father to take charge of him. This he did, and carried off the child to a village named Lai Sangkong, to the extreme west of the valley. When Pamheiba was about four years old, the Ranee heard of his existence and sent secretly to kill him. The boy's grandfather escaped with him to the village of Tangal in the hills to the north occupied by the Quiron tribe of Nagas. Time went on, and the Ranee having no family there arose a difficulty about the succession. The Raja was unaware up to this time of the existence of his son Pamheiba, although he had a suspicion of the fact. He made a declaration before all his wives that, if any of them should have concealed a male child, they would be freely forgiven and the child made his heir. The mother of Pamheiba promised to make inquiries if the Raja would swear that no harm should befall the child, and on his doing so, she confessed to the existence of Pamheiba. The boy was sent for and acknowledged by the Raja and people to be the son of Churai Romba. The villagers who sheltered the boy were also rewarded. Churai Romba, according to the Munnipore account, was killed by a poisoned arrow in fighting a tribe to the south called Toosook, upon which Pamheiba, better known by his Hindoo name of Gurreeb Nawaz, ascended the *guddee*." *

The traditions which I have collected, both among the Manipuris and among the Nagas, modify the above account in some not unimportant particulars. In the first place they do not mention any custom by which the son of the Rāni alone was saved. The reason why the male children of Churai Romba were killed off was that there was a prophecy that he should die by the hand of his son. The child Pamheiba was concealed, and when the suspicions of Churai Romba were aroused, he ordered all the children from the village of Maikel, where young Pamheiba was in hiding, to be brought down to Imphāl and entertained. They were all bidden to watch the boat-races

* *Op cit.*, p. 59.

from a bridge the supports of which had been sawn asunder so that they broke and the children were drowned, but some one had warned Pamheiba's guardians and he escaped. To this episode they ascribe the origin of the custom which prohibits the spectators at the *Hi-yāng* (boat race, from *hi* = boat, *yāng* = swiftness) from standing on any bridge beneath which the rowers would have to pass.* Some years afterwards he returned to Manipur and by his charm of manner and readiness of speech drew upon himself the attention of the Raja, who made him his personal attendant. One day they were out hunting and the arrow from the bow of Pamheiba killed his father. Then the prophecy was recalled to mind, and at last the whole story came to light. Now to this day the Nagas of Maikel receive precedence over all other Nagas at the annual Naga sports as a reward for the protection which they afforded the king in his early days. Of course the divine ancestor Pākhangba is brought into the affair by the supposition that his accidental death at the hands of his son transmitted a sort of tendency to parricide to his descendants.†

The Chronicles do not afford any sort of warrant for either of these legends, and there is not the slightest hint that at any time was it customary for the succession to be restricted to the son of the eldest Rāni alone.

The long reign of Pamheiba, during which the fortunes of Manipur reached their zenith, ended by the black tragedy of the murder of the old King by his son Jit Shah or Shai. The eldest son Sham Shah or Shai was murdered at the same time, but the parricide did not long retain the throne, for he was driven out by Bharat Shai, who reigned for two years, when he was succeeded by Guru Sham. Colonel McCulloch says, and the statement is to some extent confirmed by the Chronicles, that "This Gouroo Sham was a cripple, and it is related that considering himself from his infirmity unfit to be sole ruler, he

* The custom really belongs to a group of customs which exhibit a belief in the peculiar sanctity of the head.—T. C. H.

† In the famous prophecy of "all the wonder that would be" that was made to Khāgenba, Pamheiba is given to the King, Churairōmba, by the Khullakpa of Thangāl—a Naga village in the north. Churairōmba is also said to be the last of the line of Pākhangba, and with Pamheiba begins the line of the descendants of Senamehi.—T. C. H.

associated with himself his brother Jaee Singh or Chingtung Komba, and that they ruled alternately. This arrangement lasted until Gouroo Sham's death, about 1764, when the sole authority fell to Chingtung Komba, who held it up to 1798." * Once again the close of the long reign of a fairly strong and capable king was followed by wild scenes of bloodshed, the numerous sons of Chingtung Kōmba, Rabino Chandra, Madu Chandra, Chourjit Singh, Marjit and Gambhir Singh all fighting for the throne. After the treaty of Yandabo, † Gambhir Singh, who had raised the Manipur Levy among the refugees in Sylhet, was recognized as King, and the independence of the State was formally guaranteed. On his death, in 1834, his son and heir, Chandra Kirti Singh, was a minor, and the Senapati, Nur Singh, a descendant of Churairōmba, became Regent. The Queen Mother is said to have been implicated in a plot to kill the Regent while he was worshipping at the temple of Govindji. The plot failed, and the Queen Mother fled to Cachar, taking the Minor Raja with her. Nur Singh was not allowed to remain quiet, and had to defend his throne against numerous attacks headed by members of the royal family, who, in their comfortable exile in Cachar or Sylhet, managed to collect adherents and arms. Nur Singh died in 1850, and was succeeded by his brother Debendro Singh, although he left sons who fled at once to Cachar. They returned with Chandra Kirti Singh, who drove Debendro Singh out with their aid. He was at once recognized by the people as the rightful King, and appointed the sons of Nur Singh to the offices of Senapati and Jubrāj. Chandra Kirta Singh had soon to contend with his friends and supporters, for Nur Singh's sons turned against him, and for some years the country was constantly harassed by attempts made by rival claimants to oust Chandra Kirti Singh, who succeeded in consolidating his hold on the throne. He had a large family of sons, all of whom held court appointments. Before his death, in 1886, the Government of India, on the request of Chandra Kirti Singh, acknowledged the Jubrāj Sur Chandra Singh as the heir and successor. Colonel Johnstone, who was Political Agent in Manipur at the time, has

* *Op. cit.*, p. 7.

† 1826. Mackenzie, *North-East Frontier of Bengal*, p. 150.

recorded the following account of what happened: "As soon as the Maharajah was again able to transact business, he begged me to write to the Government of India, and request that the Jubrāj should be acknowledged by them as his successor. I did so, at the same time strongly urging that the guarantee should be extended to the Jubrāj's children, so as to preclude the possibility of a disputed succession at his death. The Jubrāj earnestly supported this request; but the Maharājah preferred adhering to the old Manipuri custom which really seemed made to encourage strife. If, for instance, a man had ten sons, they all succeeded one after the other, passing over the children of the elder ones; but when the last one died, then his children succeeded as children of the last Rāja, to the exclusion of all the elder brothers' children. All the same, if these could make good their claim by force of arms, they were cheerfully accepted by the people who were ready to take any scion of royalty." * So far as the Chronicles of the State enable us to judge, there has never been a case of such regular succession, and the facts of all the cases point to one conclusion, that the only rule recognized is that the strongest member of the royal family held the throne as long as, and only just as long as, he could, and when a stronger man came, his day was done.

Sur Chandra Singh abdicated in September, 1890, and his brother, Kula Chandra Singh, who, till then, had been Jubrāj, became Regent. The brothers of the whole blood went to British India in company with Sur Chandra Singh, and their offices were taken by the brothers of the half blood who threw in their lot with Kula Chandra Singh. The circumstances of the abdication of the late Raja finally brought about British intervention, and on the unhappy events of March, 1891, the State passed into the hands of the Government of India, who, after full consideration of all the circumstances, decided to place a grandson of Nur Singh on the throne, and to administer the State during his minority.

Such is the history of the succession to the throne of Manipur, and from these facts it may be possible to disentangle some ideas as to the custom of the royal succession. The one fact that stands out most clearly is that the Raja must belong to

* *Op. cit.*, p. 195.

the Ningthaja or royal clan; but beyond that I can see no more than—

> "The good old rule, the simple plan,
> He takes that may, and keeps that can."

The explanation of the alternate succession of Guru Sham and Chingtung Kōmba is that the physical defects of the former made it impossible for him to take part in any of the sacerdotal ceremonies at which the presence of the Raja is regarded as necessary.

With regard to other offices such as the *pibaship* of one of the clans, the succession seems to be determined by primogeniture. This rule does not apply to the ceremonial offices of Kings of the clans which may be held by persons who are not the *pibas*. It is abundantly clear from the Chronicles that the Raja appointed whom he pleased to the Kingship of the Angōm clan, and it is to be remembered that the King of the Angōm clan is by custom the father-in-law of the Raja. It is not clear that he was always an Angōm. The British Government, therefore, in appointing the maternal grandfather of the present Raja to the Kingship of the Moirang clan, did not commit any unprecedented breach of custom.

It appears that the executive and judicial offices of the country were at one time hereditary; but Colonel McCulloch remarks that "in these days hereditary *fumtaus* do not suit the money-loving views of the authorities, and they are made arbitrarily for a consideration and as arbitrarily dismissed when another candidate offers a larger sum. The presidency of the Court (the Paja which dealt with cases connected with women) appears to be the right of the family called Paja Hulbum, which is descended from the royal family; that family, however, now only holds it when it suits the Raja's convenience." * I have had to deal with claims to succeed to village offices where the one party would strongly contend that the right was strictly hereditary, and the other would declare that the brother right prevailed in respect of the village offices and that therefore there ought to be a sort of general post at the death of any village office-holder. It may be pointed out that both contentions have some weight in them,

* *Op. cit.*, p. 19.

for among the Kuki communities with which Captain Butler, of the Naga Hills,* was acquainted, were some which practised this method of succession by gradual promotion. Among Naga tribes the village offices go by primogeniture. The utility of fraternal succession has been explained by Sir Henry Maine.†

Among the Lois the youngest son gets the house and land, but movable property is divided among the sons.

ADOPTION.

There is still in active progress a movement among the inferior tribes, such as the Lois and the Nagas, to seek admission to the ranks of the Meithei. The first step taken is to abandon the consumption of food and drink which are proscribed to good Hindus, and then, after a period of probation, to obtain the permission of the Raja to assume the sacred thread. Colonel McCulloch remarks that "The Raja, Brahmins, and members of the Royal family, give the thread indiscriminately, but to receive it from the Raja, and to become his disciple, seems to be the preferred method." ‡ Circumstances have changed, and the position of the Brahmin has become stronger, so that aspiration to the honour of Hinduism finds probably more difficulties than it did when those words were written. Much disgust was excited among the orthodox Hindus by the claims of the Loi villages to be allowed to style themselves Hindus when asked by the census officers to state their religion. Mr. Colquhoun thus describes the actual ceremony of admission: "Outsiders are freely admitted by the Meithei, provided that they can prove themselves to belong to one of the higher Hindu castes, *i.e.* those from whose hands Brahmins may take water, such as the Kahar, or gowalla. The lower castes are, in theory, not admissible. The rites of admission comprise ceremonial ablution, impression of the *tilak*, and investiture with the sacred thread, all accompanied by the recitation of Mantras, which may not be divulged. Presents are, of course, given to the presiding Guru. The candidate is then admitted as a member

* Butler, *Travels and Adventures in Assam*, p. 82.
† *Ancient Law*, p. 241 ; *Early Law and Custom*, p. 146.
‡ *Op. cit.*, p. 18.

of one of the seven *Yek* or *septs,* and assumes one of the *Yumnak,* or family names of that *Yek.* He is not at once accorded the full privileges of his position, *e.g.* men of the same *yumnak* will not ordinarily eat with him. Food cooked in his house by a Brahman would, however, be generally acceptable; similar principles given (? govern) the admission of children of foreigners by Meithei women."

TENURE OF LAND AND LAWS REGARDING LAND.

Dr. Brown states * that "The whole land system of the valley starts with the assumption that all the land belongs to the Raja, and is his to give away or retain as he pleases. Under the Raja is an official named the Phoonan Saloomba, whose duty it is to superintend all matters connected with land cultivation; he looks after the measurement, receives the rent in kind, and transacts all business matters connected with the land on behalf of the Raja. The land is subdivided into villages and their surroundings; the head man of each division or village looks after the cultivation, and is responsible for the realization of the tax payable by each cultivator; he holds no interest in the land, and is merely an agent of the Raja.

"Besides the land thus directly, as it were, cultivated for the Raja, grants of land are given to officials and favourites, sometimes for their own lives only, or for a specified time, sometimes for themselves and descendants. These hold their lands on payment of the usual tax in kind. Connections of the Raja, Brahmins, and Sepoys, pay no rent or tax on a fixed proportion of land regulated in each case, but on any increase on the land cultivated above that proportion rent is paid.

"The proportion of land cultivated under what may be called the direct system on account of the Raja is about a third of the whole; rather more than a third is in the possession of members of the ruling family, Brahmins and Sepoys: the remainder is in the hands of the head men, officials, etc., who hold it by favour from the Raja. Each individual liable for *lalloop,* or

* *Op. cit.,* pp. 11–13.

forced labour for the State, is entitled to cultivate for his support one *purree* of land, equivalent to about three English acres, subject to the payment of the regular tax in kind.

"The tax in kind realized from each cultivator, and which goes to the Raja, is liable to many modifications, although, in theory, the tax is a fixed one. The tax, as given by McCulloch, varies from 2 baskets to 13 from each *purree*. I am informed that the 2 baskets which nominally should be only taken from every one alike, is realized from favourites, and that the average from others may be set down at 12 baskets yearly; this is seldom exceeded, except in rare emergencies, as war, etc. This again will only apply to land cultivated for the Raja, or held by those subject to *lalloop*. In cases where lands are held by officials, etc., as middlemen, the burdens are more severe, running as high as 24 baskets per *purree*, which, I am informed, is the outside limit.

"The average yield per *purree*, or three acres, is about 150 baskets annually: each basket contains about 60 pounds."

On the subject of the cultivation of land, etc., Colonel McCulloch, in his report to Government, dated February 28, 1867, writes: "The Raja is the absolute proprietor of the soil, and can dispose of it as he likes. No one is prohibited from cultivating, but rather the contrary, for every male who comes on duty is entitled to cultivate one *purree* of land, paying a rent for the same. The State rent is nominally 2 baskets of rice in the husks, the basketful weighing 50 or 60 pounds; but usually 12 or 13 baskets are taken. Considering, however, that the worst *purree* of land yields 100 baskets and the best from 160 to 200, the 13 baskets is not a high rent; but so long as the rent taken by the State is given out as two, every basket over this is an exaction, and may be made a matter of grievance, as it is now. But this grievance can only be one as long as the *purree* of the cultivator is of the standard measure, which is very seldom the case—indeed, it has sometimes been found nearer two, and until a survey has been made, neither the Raja nor the people can be satisfied. Seeing the necessity for a survey the Raja has commenced one, but it is much disliked, and, I fear, though several persons connected with it have been punished for taking bribes, that they will still be taken, and that the measurement will not be honestly done, even if the people employed were qualified to do it, which I doubt.

"The land under cultivation yields sufficient for the wants of the people, but the action of the *Keiroi-thau* is against the extension of cultivation, and unless steadily looked to, would lead to its diminution. The latter result might be disastrous and though I cannot report any real improvement in the *Keiroi-thau,** I am glad to say that for some time past attention has been directed to it, and I hope, as the Raja is anxious to bring more land into cultivation, for which purpose water-courses are to be dug, he will see clearly the necessity of so reforming this *thau* as to make the people willing to take up the land which will be thus rendered fit for cultivation."

These quotations serve to make it clear that the theory of the vestment of absolute rights over the land in the Raja had firmly established itself in the minds of the officers who represented the Government of India in the State some thirty years ago, but the closer acquaintance with the people, which has been not the least important of the results of the occupation of the State by British officers, renders it no less clear that the people themselves are far from accepting this theory in the blunt and unqualified manner in which it is stated by the native authorities, most of whom were interested witnesses. The system is one of severalty, as is to be expected in a country where permanent settlement is possible, but the number and importance of the protests which have from time to time been made against the unrestricted alienation of land by Manipuris to Muhammedans and other persons of alien descent, the vigorous denunciation of the speculative tricksters, who took out leases for the waste lands near outlying villages and charged exorbitant rent for grazing or grass cutting, and the strength of the village system, afford evidence that the real nature of the tenure of non-arable land was communal and joint, while cultivated fields were held in severalty, a sure proof that we have to deal with a state of affairs halfway between absolute joint tenure and perfect severalty.

* *Keiroi-thau* = labour of Keis and Lois.

LAWS REGARDING OTHER PROPERTY.

Murder was generally punished with death, but in cases where extenuating circumstances were proved, mutilation was inflicted. Brahmins who committed murder, were banished from the country. In earlier times theft, especially cattle theft, still a common offence in the country, was punished with death, but banishment to a Loi village, a penalty which, if continued for any length of time carried with it degradation from caste, became regarded as more appropriate. More than once, cases of recidivism occurred which required rather special treatment, and perhaps on the principle that prevention is better than a doubtful cure, the authorities cut off the right hand of a thief on his second conviction, while one notorious housebreaker was permanently confined in a strong wooden box, a punishment which was recommended to us when the prince of jail breakers, Apaibi or Fly-away, was causing us some anxiety by his exploits. In modern times an improvement in the system of punishments was effected by the erection of a jail, which the native authorities did not manage on the theory that a jail should be a comfortable place for blackguards of the country to arrange plans of future campaigns against the peaceable people. The prisoners were freely employed on extramural labour without much serious interference with their health, which seems to have been regarded as of less importance than the protection of property and the prevention of crime by deterring the evil doers from a repetition of their misdeeds.

One of the most reprehensible features of the methods of the State was the partiality shown in judicial matters to the privileged classes such as the Brahmins and Rajkumars, but the blame which attaches to this must be held to be diminished by the tenderness they exhibited towards women, for whom the only punishments were banishment to a Loi village, which entailed at least temporary loss of caste, or the punishment known as *Khungoinaba*, which is thus described in the Chronicles: "She is made thoroughly naked, only a small bit of cloth tied round her waist, she is shaved off her hairs, and her bare head and face are painted with lime, ink and turmeric colours, broom-sticks are tied on her back with a drum, one man will pull her on the front by a piece of rope tied on her neck, and a large crowd will gather on her back beating the drum, at the same time her crime will be proclaimed to the public, and thus she will walk through the several streets and bazars." It is only fair to say that this method of punishment became obsolete by the beginning of the last century, and the passage quoted above bears the date 1696.

The methods of capital punishment varied considerably, and Colonel Johnstone states * that he was informed that it was the custom in Manipur to put a murderer to death in the manner in which he had committed the murder, and that by his representations he succeeded in persuading the authorities to adopt decapitation as the one method of carrying out the death sentence. Cases of high treason, when the offenders were members of the Royal family, were punished by death by drowning, the offenders being tied in a sack and thrown into a river at some place where another river meets it. The reason for this is obscure, but certainly connected with the belief in the special sanctity of such a spot.

Special mention must be made of the custom which required the presence of a high official at all executions to see that the sentence was duly carried out. If it happened that for good and sufficient reason no such officer was present, it was necessary for the fetters and manacles with which the prisoners were bound to be struck off by a blacksmith, before the execution, and taken to the Raja as a proof that the order had been given effect. The place of execution was either in front of the stone Dragons (the Nōngsha), which stood before the Kangla or Coronation Hall, or under a tree on the bank of the Nambol river. When decapitation was employed as the method of execution, the prisoner was placed on his back and his head cut off by a stroke of a *dao* across the throat. The executioner was a Naga of a special village.

The laws of the country regarding debt are simple. When a sum of money had been borrowed and not returned within a year, the sum due was double the sum borrowed, and either as a result of this rule, or even perhaps as the cause of it, we find

* *Op. cit.*, p. 139, where further information is given on the subject of the punishments inflicted on wrongdoers.

that the Manipuris have a bad reputation for neglect of their financial obligations. No doubt the security was often poor, and if the creditor had to wait a long time for his money when the rate of interest was high, he required the protection which this rule was intended to give him. As a fact, this rule is not uncommon among the people of the hills. But in Manipur, if it was not possible for an insolvent debtor to discharge his debts in full, he was allowed to make himself the slave, as it has been unfairly called, of his creditor. Now there were two kinds of slavery, the one originating, as I have stated, in simple debt, and the other where the slave becomes the absolute property of the master. Colonel McCulloch thus describes the two systems:* "Many become slaves voluntarily; some of them with the view of discharging a money debt which they cannot otherwise do, and some from sheer laziness. They live in the same house as their master, eat with him, and are altogether like members of the family. To abuse and ill-use slaves is the exception. These remarks refer more especially to Munniporees in a state of slavery. The hill people occasionally sell themselves; but more frequently they are sold by their relatives. There are two descriptions of slaves; the one, the absolute property of the buyer, called *meenai chanaba,*† the other *asălba*, or a slave for such time as the money paid to him, or advanced on him, may not be paid back. The latter is like giving work in lieu of the interest of the money paid, and should the person who becomes *asălba* get sick he is obliged to give a substitute or make good in coin the labour lost in the interval of sickness. Of course, to the *asălba* no considerable sum would be advanced unless he promised to work for at least one cultivating season. The hill people who are slaves are not perhaps so well treated as the Munniporees in a state of slavery, but there are many checks on ill use. If not satisfied with their condition they run to some other house where slaves are better treated. The master makes a point, if possible, of paying their price, usually, however, not in full, for the circumstance of a slave running to another's protection is considered a sign of his having been

* *Op. cit.*, pp. 24, 25.

† *Mi nai* = to belong to a man; *minai* = slave; *chā* = to eat; *na*, suffix of mutuality, *i.e.*, to belong to and be fed by a man.—T. C. H.

ill-treated, and as justifying an abatement. Slaves, too, often abscond to the hills, where they conceal themselves in the hill villages; but as they are apt there to be apprehended, they usually prefer passing into the British territory, where they are at once free. Thus, those who have slaves are under the necessity of treating them well, and slavery is much modified."

In another passage Colonel McCulloch says that "A man can put away his wife without any fault on her part, and if a person of influence he may do so without its being noticed. The rule, however, is that if a man puts away his wife without any fault on her part, she takes possession of all his property except a drinking vessel and the cloth round his loins. A man and wife may separate by mutual consent, and a wife may quit her husband on giving the value of a slave. Women are really the slaves of their husbands; they are sold in satisfaction of their debts, and I have heard of men pawning their wives for money to purchase some office, or even a pony." * I must say that I never came across any case in which the rule mentioned above was even cited, and inquiries made among Manipuris of good position only elicited a denial of its existence. The statutory penalty for adultery carrying with it divorce was fifty rupees, the price of an adult slave, and the statement that women are the "slaves" of their husbands, receives a curious confirmation from the fact that a woman is said to become the property of a man (*mi-nyonda nai-ba*) when she marries.

DECISION OF DISPUTES.

The Chief Court which administered the laws and customs of the country was the Chirāp, which was composed of twenty-four or twenty-five permanent members as follow: The Jubrāj, the Angōm Ningthou, the Wāngkhairakpa (*lakpa*, or manager of the north quarter; *wāng*, north; *khai*, division), Khurairakpa (manager of the *khurai*, possibly the skilled workers, *khutlaiba* meaning hand skilful), Mantri, the Jaisagun lakpa, Pukhrumba, Nongthonba, the Laiphamlakpa, the Ahalluplakpa, the Khābamlakpa, the Nahārup lakpa, the Luang Ningthou, the Moirang

* *Op. cit.*, p. 19.

Ningthou, Katnam, the Phungnai sang lakpa, the Laipham dewan, the Ahallup dewan, the Khābam dewan, the Nahārup dewan, the Laipham sanglenlakpa, the Ahallup sanglen lakpa, the Khābam sanglen lakpa, the Nahārup sanglen lakpa. There were, in addition, other officers of State entitled to or eligible for seats on the Chirāp. The grand total of Chirāp members was between sixty and eighty.* The Paja dealt with all cases in which women were concerned, such as divorce, disputed paternity, marriage rights, etc., and the president of this Court was known as the *Paja Hulba.*† The methods employed by the Paja in the decision of cases of disputed paternity were simple, and resemble those in vogue in Ancient Arabia.‡ The Tōp garde was the court which tried all cases in which sepoys of the military forces of the country were parties, and was a purely military court. The numerous *lalloop* officers exercised judicial functions, but the line which in the State organization divided the judicial from the executive functionaries, was so vague and uncertain that it cannot be said that there was any real separation of the two aspects of government, so that every village officer dealt, and was thought to be competent to deal, with all sorts of matters which Western methods relegate to a purely judicial body.

The first thing was to complain (*wā khatpa*, to present the story) to the proper authority, and at this, and at every subsequent stage in the proceedings, the offering of gifts was a necessary act. These gifts must not be regarded as bribes, for native opinion did not approve of the action of a judge who allowed himself to be influenced by these gifts. They really took the place of stamps and court fees, and were payments in kind as often as not. At the hearing and the decision of the case (*wā khaiba*, or the dividing of the stories) presents were made to the court by both parties. The employment of an oath seems to have been restricted to cases where Nagas or Kukis, foolish persons who attached some sanctity to an oath, were concerned, and the oaths then used are still recognized by them as binding. Water was poured over a gun and a

* See "Political Organization," above, p. 65.

† See McCulloch, *op. cit.*, p. 19.

‡ Robertson Smith, *Marriage and Kinship*, p. 169.

THE KOHIMA STONE.

***Erected by Raja Gambhir Singh*, 1833.**

p. 92

spear, and the Naga would then drink it, or he would take a tiger's tooth between his lips and swear to the veracity of his tale. The use of the ordeal is rare, but the Chronicles afford sufficient ground for believing that it was in earlier times much more frequent than in the period subsequent to the Hinduization of the Meitheis. We read how, in the course of a trial for high treason and conspiracy against the Raja Chourjit in 1804, one of the accused persons "pleaded himself not guilty, so he was examined before the public, when he put his hands on a burning fire saying that 'If I be guilty in any way, and if I have any connection with this conspiracy, my hands will be burnt, otherwise the fire will not injure even a hair of my hands.' To the surprise of every one present there they saw his hands were quite untouched by the fire, consequently the Maharajah was pleased to discharge him." The ordeal by water consisted in plunging the parties underneath the water, and in awarding the case to the party who remained below longest. In this form it is practised by the Nagas.

WAR.

The organization of Manipur, as has been stated in a preceding paragraph,* was at first directed solely for military purposes, and during the sixteenth, seventeenth and the early part of the eighteenth centuries was the instrument of the aggrandizement of the State, which at that period exerted considerable influence over the neighbouring territories, extending as far as the Shan States on the east and to Cachar on the west. Neither to the north nor the south did the sovereignty of the Meithei at any time reach beyond the limits which now contain the State. It therefore may rightly be held to have been an organized military power, although the numerous expeditions of which the Chronicles make mention, seem in many cases to have been little better that mere freebooting raids, in no respect different from those which, even in recent days, have been made by the Nagas and Kukis on the outlying villages in Cachar. The specialized organization which was effected by Gambhir Singh,† created a small but fairly homogeneous force, which against the

* P. 58. † P. 59.

loose and feebly combined array of the Naga tribes of the north was able to achieve some useful victories, and which, both in the dark days of the Mutiny, and at the anxious time of the siege of Kohima, rendered valuable help to the Paramount Power. Nevertheless, the inherent defects of the Meithei, his dislike of sustained discipline, his preference for diplomatic methods, his employment of irregular troops, such as the Kukis, and the lack of honesty in those who were responsible for the equipment and commissariat of the forces, deprived the troops of all military value which otherwise they might have possessed at the end of the period of independence in 1891. Yet the Meithei is far from being a coward, and in happier circumstances, with better leading, might be capable of military virtues.

HEAD-HUNTING.

The Chronicles afford sufficient warrant for the statement that, prior to the introduction of Hinduism, the Meithei were in the habit of bringing in the heads of defeated enemies as trophies of prowess. Doubtless this custom disappeared when the gentler customs which are associated with Hinduism became generally adopted in the State.

MISCELLANEOUS.

A Meithei, therefore, belonged to the *lăl-lŭp*, or militia, possibly to the *kei-rŭp*,* and always to a *Sing-lŭp*, or wood club, which anticipated the modern burial clubs in providing all that was necessary for his cremation.† There is reason to believe that occasionally the *Sing-lŭps* meddled in politics. These specialized associations stand in an interesting relation to the constituent elements of Naga villages, where the mechanism of social union is provided by the "genna" system.‡

* See page 46. † Cf. McCulloch, *op. cit.*, p. 25.

‡ *Journal Anthropological Institute*, vol. xxxvi., pp. 92–103.

SECTION IV.

RELIGION.

NATURE OF POPULAR BELIEFS.

WOULD that it were possible to imitate or transcend the easy brevity of Father Sangermano, who declares that the people of Cassay worship the basil and other plants after the manner of the ancient Egyptians.* Here we have the stately fabric of Hinduism with its elastic ease of accommodation, we have the fresh, healthy, indigenous system of animism, and as a result of the commingling of these forces at this point a medley of religious beliefs in which every phase of human imagination finds its place.

Hinduism is of comparatively recent origin, though the records of the Brahmin families in Manipur claim in some cases that the founder of the family settled in the valley at so remote a date as the middle of the fifteenth century. To the royal will of Pamheiba, the monarch in whose reign the fortunes of the State reached their zenith, Hinduism owes its present position as the official religion of the State. At first the decrees of the king received but little obedience, and the opposition to the change centred mainly round the numerous members of the royal family who were supported, not unnaturally, by the *maibas*, the priests of the older religion. Religious dissent was treated with the same ruthless severity as was meted out to political opponents, and wholesale banishments and execution drove the people into acceptance of the tenets of Hinduism. As a matter of fact the long reign of Chandra Kirti Singh witnessed the consolidation of Hinduism which had lost much of its hold on the people during the sad times of the Burmese occupation. Gambhir Singh once ordered

* *The Burmese Empire.* Sangermano, ed. Jardine, p. 110.

a Brahmin who had failed to take due and proper charge of a pet goose which had been entrusted to his care, to eat the bird which had died from neglect,* but in his son's time such an order was impossible.

The old order of things has not passed away by any means, and the *maiba*, the doctor and priest of the animistic system, still finds a livelihood despite the competition on the one hand of the Brahmin, and the Hospital Assistant on the other.

It is possible to discover at least four definite orders of spiritual beings who have crystallized out from the amorphous mass of animistic Deities. There are the *Lam Lai*, gods of the country-side who shade off into Nature Gods controlling the rain, the primal necessity of an agricultural community; the *Umang Lai* or Deities of the Forest Jungle; the *Imung Lai* the Household Deities, Lords of the lives, the births and the deaths of individuals, and there are *Tribal Ancestors*, the ritual of whose worship is a strange compound of magic and Nature-worship. Beyond these Divine Beings, who possess in some sort a majesty of orderly decent behaviour, there are spirits of the mountain passes, spirits of the lakes and rivers, vampires,† and all the horrid legion of witchcraft. *Quot homines, tot daemones*, with a surplusage of familiars who serve those fortunate few who are recognized as initiate into the mysteries.

It is not sound to regard these beliefs as "survivals" despite the official superstratum of Hinduism which exists in Manipur, solely in its exoteric form, without any of the subtle metaphysical doctrines which have been elaborated by the masters of esoteric Hinduism. The adherence of the people to the Vaishnavite doctrines which originated in Bengal, is maintained by the constant intercourse with the leaders of that community at Nadia. It is difficult to estimate the precise effect of Hinduism on the civilization of the people, for to the outward observer they seem to have adopted only the festivals, the outward ritual, the caste marks, and the exclusiveness of Hinduism, while all unmindful of its spirit and inward essentials. Colonel McCulloch remarked nearly fifty years ago that, "In fact their observances are only for

* Johnstone, *op. cit.*, p. 140.

† Hing-chā-bi (hing = living, chā = to eat, bi = honorific or respectful suffix), that which eats living persons.—T. C. H.

appearance' sake, not the promptings of the heart,"* and his criticism seems as true now as when it was written. It is, perhaps, too early to predict the influence of British rule upon the religious ideas of the people. The Penal Code is in some aspects a code of morality resting in native view on superior force rather than on divine authority or intrinsic virtue. The inevitable rise in morality which ensues from security of life and property, from increasing wealth, and from a greater range of needs, is slowly becoming evident in Manipur, and must sooner or later exert an influence on the religious life of the country. The *maibas* frequently adapt their methods to the altered circumstances in which they now find themselves, and realize that the combination of croton oil and a charm is more efficacious than the charm alone. It is too much to expect them to give up the charm all at once.†

In Manipur where Hinduism is a mark of respectability, it is never safe to rely on what men tell of their religion; the only test is to ascertain what they do, and by this test we are justified in holding them to be still animists.

It is curious to note the complete absence of any traces of Buddhism in Manipur, although it is reasonably certain that in historic times there has been a steady flow of intercourse with Buddhistic Burma. The Shans under Samlongpha who invaded Manipur in the beginning of the fifteenth century seem to have left no trace of their occupation of the State upon the religious belief of the people, for the records distinctly show that up to the formal introduction of Hinduism in the reign of Pamheiba the people buried their dead, ate meat, drank ardent spirits, and behaved just like the hill people of the present day. There is not a sign of contact with the lofty moral doctrines of Buddhism.

The Chronicles enable us to know the names, and in some cases also the functions, of a few of the popular Deities. Thus Panthoibi, to whose service Brahmins were appointed by Pamheiba (Gharib Nawaz), is said to be the wife of Khāba, probably the divine ancestor of the Khāba tribe, and to be the Deity of birth and death. She is certainly connected with the worship

* *Op. cit.*, p. 17.

† *Cf.* Sir A. Lyall, *Asiatic Studies*, vol. i. p. 113, Lord Avebury, *Origin of Civilization*, 6th ed. p. 24.

of the sun. The worship of Sena Mehi by a prince was regarded as a sure preliminary to an attempt by the worshipper on the throne, and was reserved for the Raja alone. The Deity Lairema is associated with oneiromancy, and is also the name given to private Deities. Of her magical nature there can be no doubt, for the Chronicles state that on the 17th *Langbon* (September), 1853, "There was a great fuss about Lirema Hooidompokpi. A sepoy reported to the Maharajah, that since Khuraijam established his God, Hooidompokpi, a considerable number of men died. The number of widowers and widows increased. The Maharajah ordered Losang Ningthou and Nongthonba to cause inquiry into this. It was turned out that there were two Liremas." Of the Deity named Noongshaba we know that he is associated with a stone, and is probably, as his name would show (*nōng* = stone, and *shāba* = maker, lit. maker of stones), the Deity of Creation of the rocks and stones. We do not know the reason why he, or Yumthai Lai, the Deity whom, on linguistic grounds, we may believe to be the establisher of houses, or the Deity Taibong Khōmbi, She who makes the earth to swell, should have been allowed to be served by Brahmins, while Pamheiba disestablished such Deities as Taibongkhaiba, He who divides the earth, or the clan Gods, or such Goddesses as Waihaiba. We know that Sena-mehi and Laima-ren are connected, and the name of the latter seems to mean "The Great Princess." * We may conjecture that the female Deity Laishing-choubi was the wife of Laiching, the Deity whose abode is on the hill of that name. Of others, such as Wāngpurel, Puthiba, Pukshore, Yumnam Lairema, Sarangthem Lamabi, Laisangthem Lamabi, we know little beyond the mere names. Some of them may be purely local, and their worship confined to the members of one family, or of one house, but even if *nomina* only, they are also *numina*, and rank above the vast crowd of *hing-chābis* or vampires (*hing* = alive, *chā* = to eat, that which eats live men), *lais hellois*, or demons, in which the people believe and, fear being the basis of their ritual, which they try to propitiate. Colonel McCulloch states that there

* *Laima* = princess, and *ren* or *len* = great, a word not now found in Meithei but common in Thado, and also found in *turen* = great water or river, from *tui* = water, and *khul-len* = big or parent village, from *khul* = village.—T. C. H.

were three hundred such deities, and that they "are still propitiated by appropriate sacrifices of things abhorrent to real Hindoos." *

Competent ethnologists † declare that the conception of divine beings as "Gods" connotes, firstly, the relationship of members of a family, subject to one head, who may be Lord of all, or attenuated as merely *primus inter pares;* secondly, their representation in human form; thirdly, the association of moral benefit with their worship; fourthly, their presentation as idealized human beings; and, fifthly, their occupation of a definite place in a definite cosmogonic system. Practically all these characteristics are lacking in Manipur. Indeed, it seems to be clear that deities like Panthoibi, Yumthai Lai, Laimaren, and Sena-mehi, are merely names of class spirits, for every householder is virtually the priest of these Deities, just as in ancient Rome every household had its Vesta. There are images of deities hewn from stone, but the more powerful Deities, if we except Govindji, the God of the Royal family, are represented by rough stones, which Manipuris regard not exactly as the image of the Deity, but as his abode.

THE WORSHIP OF ANCESTORS.

If the definition of ancestor-worship is strictly narrowed, we have in Manipur, among the Meithei only, the form of ancestor-worship which is practised by all Hindus, but if it be enlarged, as in the circumstances it ought to be, we find several curious phenomena to which attention should be given.

The worship of the clans which, seven in number, compose the Meithei nation or confederacy, clearly consists in the adoration and propitiation of the eponymous ancestors of the clan. The name of the tribal Deities is given as Luang pōkpa, or ancestor of the Luangs, Khuman pōkpa, ancestor of the Khumans, apparent exceptions to this being the tribal Deities of the Ningthaja and Angōm clans, which are called Nongpōk Ningthou, or the King of the East,‡ alias Pākhangba, whom we know from other sources to be the reputed ancestor of the clan

* *Op. cit.*, p. 17.
† Jevons, *Introduction to Plutarch's Romane Questions*, p. xxiii.
‡ Perhaps = the king whose Father is the Sun.—T. C. H.

in question (the Ningthaja), and Purairōmba. The aliases of the other tribal Deities are Poiraiton, for the Luangs; Khamdingou, for the Khābanānbas, Thāngaren, for the Khumans, and Ngāngningsing, for the Moirangs; and Nungaoyumthāngba, for the Chengleis.

The Hindu friends of the people have discovered for them a respectable genealogy by which they are descended from the Guru, the sage who is Lord of the Universe (*taibangpānbagi mapu*), but the accounts differ. In the version collected by me from the lips of a Manipuri, who had been a *sellungba*, or court officer, the Angōms spring from the brain of the sage, the Luangs from between his eyes, the Khābanānbas from his eye, the Moirangs from his nostril, the Chenglei from his nose, the Kumul from his liver, and the Ningthaja from his spleen. The account prepared for me by a very respectable Bengali clerk, states that the Ningthaja were born from his left eye, the Angōm from his right eye, the Chenglei from his right ear, the Khābanānba from his left ear, the Luang from his right nostril, the Kumul from his left nostril, and the Moirang from his teeth. It is a delicate matter to assign a preference to one version rather than the other, but the symmetry of the second version is apt to excite the suspicion that the orthodoxy of the reporter may have misled him.

In the case of the ancestor of the Ningthaja clan, Pākhangba, we have the curious superstition that he still sometimes appears to men, but in the form of a snake, which reminds one of the Zulu belief that their ancestors assume the shapes of harmless brown snakes. Another instance which may help to explain the Pākhangba worship is afforded by the classical instance of the Romans, who held that the "genius" of every man resided in a serpent. Cicero (*De Divinatione*, i. 18, 36), tells how the death of the serpent, which was the genius of the Father of the Gracchi, presaged, and was soon followed by, the death of Tiberius. Recent investigations prove that the genius was the "external soul" so familiar in the folk tales of primitive peoples. Here the snake is the external soul of the Raja, the *piba* of the Ningthaja clan, and the head of the Meitheis.* Speaking

* See also Miss Jane Harrison, *Prolegomena to Greek Religion*, pp. 327–332. Jevons, *op. cit.*, p. xlviii.

of the religion of the people, Colonel McCulloch* says that "The Raja's peculiar god is a species of snake called Pakung-ba, from which the Royal family claims descent. When it appears it is coaxed on to a cushion by the priestess in attendance, who then performs certain ceremonies to please it. This snake appears, they say, sometimes of great size, and when he does so it is indicative of his being displeased with something. But as long as he remains of diminutive form it is a sign that he is in good humour."

Whether connected immediately, or only remotely, with these associations of ancestor worship, I cannot say, but it is at least noteworthy that in the hymn which is addressed to the Raja by the man who is taking the sins of the country upon himself for the coming year, the Raja is addressed as "O Great God Pākhangba." This may, of course, be merely an honorific phrase in harmony with the extravagant language used to the Raja, who on all occasions is addressed as if he were indeed a Deity incarnate.

In contrasting the Meithei belief in Pākhangba with the Khasi faith in U Thlen, a clear account of which is given by Major Gurdon,† the author of the monograph on the Khasis and General Editor of this series, several points of interest issue to notice at once. Pākhangba is an ancestral spirit worshipped by women, while among the matriarchal Khasis, where women are priests, U Thlen is not regarded apparently as an ancestor. Both are associated with the fortune of the family, but while U Thlen may move from one family to another, Pākhangba is associated only with the Raja directly, but indirectly with the whole State. Both vary in size, and it is noteworthy that the occasions when they assume their largest and most monstrous form, practically signify much the same thing, viz. portents of evil and misfortune. I have no evidence of human sacrifices to Pākhangba.‡ In regard to the means adopted to get rid of the *thlen*, we may compare the transfer of sin by passing on the royal clothing with the sacrifice of property, money and ornaments which Khasis make when endeavouring to free themselves of the snake.

By the side of the road from Cachar not more than a mile

* *Op. cit.*, p. 17. † pp. 98–102. ‡ But see p. 108.

from Bishenpur, are two small black stones which are reputed to be *Laiphams*, or places in which abides a "Lai," a being whose exact equivalency is difficult of determination. At Hiyangthāng, about six miles distance from Imphāl, is a temple of considerable fame, for here abides the Hindu Goddess Durga, who is known to have avenged an insult to her shrine by causing the death of the sacrilegious. In this temple is a rough black stone which naturally I was not allowed to see close at hand, but which, so far as I could distinguish it, was entirely unwrought. This was the *laipham* of the dread Goddess. One of the last civil cases that came to my notice was a dispute about an ammonite of immense sanctity. In the course of the evidence it was proved that it had been looted from the Cachar Rajas at the beginning of the nineteenth century, and passed into the possession of Gambhir Singh, upon whose death it came into the hands of his widow, mother of Chandra Kirti Singh, who took it with her, when, after the attempted assassination of Nur Singh, she fled to Sylhet. The stone was quite small, and its curious markings showed to all but the densest eyes that it was a thing of high sanctity. It brought good fortune to its possessor, and in the disturbances of 1891 was seized by Angao Sena, brother of the Raja, who was sent to the Andamans, and who gave it to a Brahmin who sold it to a Bengali, when it was rediscovered and claimed by the heirs of Sur Chandra, who alleged that as it had always been kept in the *bāri* of the Royal Family, it was distinct from the regalia, and by the representatives of the present Raja, who asserted that it was impartible property attached to the office of Raja, while the Bengali claimed it for value had and received. I forget the finding of the learned Court on the case. In pre-Hindu times, as mentioned in the Chronicles, the worship of stones—perhaps as *laipham*—was regularly practised, and the luck of the State was symbolized by the great Nōngshā or animals of the Sun which, built of masonry to resemble stone, guarded the Kangla. In the Chronicles we read that stones were looted from defeated Naga villages and brought down to Imphāl. Now, at Maikel or Mekrimi, is a stone which, jealously guarded by the *khullakpa*, has great virtue in giving strength to warriors, and upon which no woman may look. I have heard it

NĀTCH-GHAR AND TEMPLE OF GOVINDJI.

(IMPHĀL—MANIPUR.)

p. 102

said in Manipur that it is worse by far to be reputed to be rich than to *be* rich, and the possession of so coveted an object as a war stone without doubt encouraged aggression and attack.

Lois worship Sena Mehi, and Laimaren the Imung Lai, and offer up pigs, dogs, ducks and fowls to them. The Sun God is worshipped by the people of Fayeng Loi in Sajibu (April), when they offer up a white fowl and a white pigeon. At Andro Loi, offerings are made to both Sun and Moon, the latter being worshipped every month on an auspicious day in the last quarter of the moon. They offer up each year a pig in honour of the Umang Lai or Deities, who control the prosperity of the crops, as Rain and weather Gods. Panam Ningthou and Purairōmba are their Umang Lai, while Khabru is the Umang Lai of Fayeng, and of Sengmai, where they told me he was the Lam Lai or God of the country side. They also worship the Clan God, whose names coincide with those of the Clan Gods of certain Meithei clans. Fayeng Lois assert that their ancestors were Meng-khong-ba and Hameng-mitpa.*

RELIGIOUS RITES AND CEREMONIES.

Colonel McCulloch states that "The Dussera, or as it is called in Munnipore *Kwaktalba*, is the principal festival introduced with Hinduism. At it the tributaries lay presents before the Raja and renew their engagements of submission. Honorary dresses, plumes of feathers, and other baubles which are highly prized, are distributed to persons who, during the past year, may have distinguished themselves, or to others who, at some former period, had done so, but whose merit had passed unrewarded." † *Kwāktālba* seems to mean the chasing of the crow (from *kwāk* = a crow, and *tānba* = to chase or pursue).

The Holi attracts a gay crowd of women to the capital who are seldom slow to take due advantage of the licence permitted to them, but from the coincidence of so many animistic or other festivals with those of Hinduism, a phenomenon which admits of an easy explanation, it is perhaps wiser to say that attention is paid to all and each of the various festivals which

* *Meng-khong-ba* = cat-voiced and *Hameng-mitpa* = goat-eyed.

† *Op. cit.*, p. 23.

are observed by the devout among Hindus of the Vaishnavite order.

The great and general religious festival of the *Laiharaoba*, or the rejoicing of the Gods (*Lai* = Deity, and *haraoba* = to be merry or to make merry), is thus described by Colonel McCulloch,* "Particular families have particular gods, and these at stated periods they worship, or literally 'make happy.' This worship consists in a number of married women and unmarried girls, led by priestesses, accompanied by a party of men and boys all in dresses of a former time, dancing and singing, and performing various evolutions in the holy presence. The women carry in their hands fruits, etc., part of which is presented to the deity, and part scrambled for by the girls. In some instances the god is represented by an image, but often there is no such representation, and a place is merely prepared in which he is supposed to be during the worship. The presence of the god, however, in either way, impresses the worshippers with no awe; on the contrary, it appears to be a cause of fun and jollity."

The next great festival to which attention is now to be drawn, is the *Chirouba*, a name which my informant, a Hindu of high caste from Bengal, stated to be connected with *charak puja*, a derivation with which it is impossible to agree. The festival is closely connected with the choice of a *chāhitaba* or name-giver for the coming year, and takes place at the end of the Manipuri month, Lamda, which corresponds with the middle of April. The Deity in whose particular honour the festival is held, is Senamehi, the administrator, as my friend and informant says, of the Universe. It is regarded as an auspicious day, and on it no work is done except that they clean their houses out very carefully. They wear new clothes and break all their old *chaphus* or earthenware cooking pots and eat alone without any guests. It is a day of powerful influence on the coming year, and on it takes place the selection of the *chāhitāba*, the man who gives his name to the year, who bears all the sins of the people for the year, and whose luck, good or ill, influences the luck of the whole country. The derivation of the word *chāhitāba* is obscure. *Kūm*, the word for a year in so many Tibeto-Burman

* *Op. cit.*, p. 17.

dialects, is not unknown in Meithei, but *chāhi* is peculiar to it. Some say that it is connected with the word *chāhi* or *chai* = a stick, and *tāba*, means to count, to count by sticks, the practice of the Manipuris being to calculate by means of a heap of sticks.* Others derive it from *chāhi* = a year, and *tāba* = to fall, because the fall of one year implies the commencement of a new year. According to another opinion, *chāhi* bears the meaning of a year, and *tāba* is connected with the root *tākpa* = to show or indicate, to point out—thus making the phrase to mean the person who indicates or names the year.

All reckonings of time are made by *chāhitābas* as well as by the Hindu system, and there are still men in the State who can repeat all the *chāhitābas* from the institution of the custom by Kiamba, in about 1485, who appointed Hiang Loi Namoi Chaoba to be the first *chāhitāba*.

The *maibas* nominate the man and compare his horoscope with those of the Raja and the State generally, and if they satisfactorily correspond, as is natural they should, the candidate together with the outgoing *chāhitāba* appears before the Raja and the assembled multitudes when, after worshipping his spiritual director, the Guru and his own God (probably his tribal deity), the retiring *chāhitāba* then addresses the incoming officer in the following terms: "My friend, I bore and took away all evil spirits and sins from the Raja and his people during the last year. Do thou likewise from to-morrow until the next Chirouba." Then the incoming *chāhitāba* thus addresses the Raja: "O son of heaven, Ruler of the Kings, great and ancient Lord, Incarnation of God, the great Lord Pākhangba, Master of the bright Sun, Lord of the Plain and Despot of the Hills, whose kingdom is from the hills on the east to the mountains on the west, the old year perishes, the new cometh. New is the sun of the new year, and bright as the new sun shalt thou be, and mild withal as the moon. May thy beauty and thy strength grow with the growth of the new year. From to-day will I bear on my head all thy sins, diseases, misfortunes, shame, mischief, all that is aimed in battle against thee, all that threatens thee, all that is bad and hurtful for thee and

* Omens are also taken by means of sticks thrown loosely on the ground.—T. C. H.

thy kingdom." The Raja then gives the new *chāhitāba* a number of gifts, including a basket of salt.* The *chāhitāba* is exempt from *lāllup*, and receives many privileges from the State. The *chāhitāba* offers brass plates accompanied by sacred offerings of fruit and flowers to the Raja, to the *maiba* and attendants of the Deity Pakhangba, to the *maiba loisang* or College of the *Maibas*, (exorcists' office as the term is translated by my Hindu friend) to the College of the Astrologers, to the Maharani, to the Overseer of the Royal stores, and last, not least, to the Hindu Deity Govindji, the Family God of the Royal family.

It is interesting to note that certain classes of persons are ineligible for this important office, such as Rajkumars, possibly because they are never out of the line of succession and therefore undesirable, Panggans or Manipuri Musalmans, Nagas who find consolation in an ampler dietary, and Thāngjams and Kōnsams, blacksmiths and brassworkers. I can give no reason for the ineligibility of the two last classes, except that it is possible that they occupy or once occupied so low a position in society that they were excluded.

The appointment of a *chāhitāba* rests on the desire to find a scapegoat to bear the sins of the community or of the individual Raja, the idea which is clearly the motive of the scapegoat ceremony which takes place at the foot of the holy hill Khabru on the grassy plain, to which the significant name Kaithenmānbi, the meeting place of the ghosts, has been given (*Kaithen* = market or gathering place, *mānbi*, from *mānba* = to resemble, to appear). Thither annually the Raja went in solemn procession to sacrifice a white goat, male without blemish, to the God Khabru whose abode it was, and to leave there fish and an offering of new cloths. But there come times when such ordinary devices as these fail of their purpose, and

* *Chi-rouba* may thus mean salt-taking. *Chi* is the word for salt in many of the cognate Tibeto-Burman dialects, and *rouba* = *laoba*, to take. There are many words which are obsolete or unused in Manipuri, or only used in a special sense, or in combinations, which are in common use in the other Tibeto-Burman dialects. The best examples are: *tui*, water, which in Meithei is found in *turen*, but is used by Nagas and Kukis; *lengba* = to go, to move, which, in common use in that sense in Kuki, is only used of the Raja in Meithei.—T. C. H.

it is necessary to have recourse to special sin-takers. Generally some criminal is found to take upon himself the guilt of the Raja and Rani who, clad in fine robes, ascend a staging erected in the bazar beneath which crouches the sin-taker.* The Raja and Rani then bathe in the screened tent on the stage, and the water they use in their ablutions, drops over the man below, to whom they give their robes and sins. Clad in new raiment, the Raja and his consort mix among their people until evening of that day, when they retire into a seclusion which may last for a week, and during which they are said to be *nāmungba*, sacred or *tabu*.

Sometimes the transference of sins has been satisfactorily accomplished by the simple device of presenting the Royal cloth to a "Sin-taker."

More than one ethnologist of note has pointed out that among communities which are animistic and which subsist by agriculture, rain-worship assumes peculiar importance, and to this statement the state of things in Manipur is no exception. There are Hindu ceremonies, performed by Brahmins, such as the milking of 108 milch cows before the temple of Govindji, or the presence of the images of Radha Krishna at the river bank, when the people cry aloud for rain and the priests mutter *mantras*. But the great characteristic of the rites of the pre-Hindu system is the management of these rites by the *maiba*, the *piba*, or in more important cases by the Raja, who is, in fact, regarded not only as a living Deity, but as the head of the old State religion and the secular head of the whole people, including the Ningthaja or Royal clan. The hill which rises to the east of Imphāl, and which is called Nongmaiching,† is the scene of a rain-compelling ceremony. On the upper slopes there is a stone which bears a fanciful resemblance to an umbrella, and the Raja used to climb thither in state to take water from a deep spring below and pour it over this stone, obviously a case of imitative magic. It was said that to erect an iron umbrella on the hill was an almost sure method of getting rain, when occasion needed. And there are many other

* *Cf.* The old Ahom custom, which was similar. It was called the *rikkhran*.

† See p. 8.

rites and ceremonies all of which are destined to provide the thirsty land with the rain, without which all are about to die, and at all of which the Raja should be present. Sometimes his great racing-boat was dragged through the mud and slime of the empty moat with the Raja and his semi-sacred father-in-law, the Angōm Ningthou, seated together in the stern.

The Kangla, the place where the most mysterious rites pertaining to the coronation of the Raja were performed, was the scene of a ceremony of which I have never been able to get a proper or intelligible account. Suffice to say that whatever happened there, it was sufficient to give rise to the story that human sacrifices had been made in the dire extremity of the country, for in older times, as I was told, the blood of some captive would have brought the rain. The sacrifice of ponies for this purpose may be due to the operation of what has been called the law of substitution. But the activity of the people does not confine itself to merely witnessing these official exhibitions. The men, headed on the worst occasions of prolonged drought by the Raja, strip themselves of all their clothes and stand in the broad ways of Imphāl cursing one another to the fullest extent of an expressive language. The women at night gather in a field outside the town, strip themselves and throw their *dhān* pounders into a neighbouring pool in the river and make their way home by byways. Of course there is the legend of a Peeping Tom, for whose outrage on the royal decency the country went rainless for a whole year. To some *maiba* the wicked act was revealed in a dream, and then justice was done and the country saved.

The Kumul Ningthou worships the Tribal Deity Okparen on behalf of the clan whenever rain is needed. He has to abstain from meat of any kind and from all sexual intercourse before this *puja*. To purify him water is poured over his head by a virgin from a new jar which is promptly broken. He does not worship Sena Mehi or Laimaren.

Dr. Brown * states that "in the event of Munniporie Hindoo losing his caste from any reasons, . . . the individual has to take up his abode in a Naga village, eating with the inhabitants.

* *Op. cit.*, p. 51.

. . . Its object seems to be to start the offender afresh from the lowest class." This is denied by many but has all the natural appearance of a purificatory rite. Does this throw any real light on the "affinities" of the Meitheis? *

SACRIFICES.

Each clan has its tribal Deity, and certain flowers, fruits, etc., are set aside for each Deity. Thus the Ningthaja clan offer the lotus, the lime, the mahāsīr fish, the *mōngba*—a small rat, I believe. Their special day is Monday (Ningthoukāba), and their special month is Ingā.

PRIESTHOOD.

Side by side with the Brahmin, there exist the priests and priestesses of the animistic faith who are called *maibas* and *maibis*, a word which also connotes, nowadays, the practice of the healing art because, as the language of the people clearly tells, a man is said to be ill (*a-nā-ba*) when he is possessed by a *nat*.† The heads of the clans are priests, and assume charge of the ritual of the tribal worship, while the Raja, the head of the Ningthaja clan and the head of the whole confederacy, is the high priest of the country.

The Chronicles of the State contain frequent and early mention of the *maibas*, while we have it on the authority of Colonel McCulloch that the *maibis* "owe their institution to a princess who flourished hundreds of years ago, but whether they have preserved all their original characteristics I cannot certainly affirm. At present any woman who pretends to have had a 'call' from the deity or demon, may become a priestess. That she has had such call is evidenced by incoherent language and tremblings, as if possessed by the demon. After passing her novitiate she becomes one of the body and practises with the rest on the credulity of the people. They put some rice or

* See p. 11.

† In Tibetan, *nat* or *nad* is "to be ill." The root *nat* is lengthened in Meithei by the suppression of the final consonant.—T. C. H.

some of the coin of the country into a basket, and turning it about with incantations, they pretend to divine from it. They dress in white." * Elsewhere he remarks that the priestess looks after Pākhangba the snake.†

The *maiba* is for the most part a medical practitioner with a good deal of empiric knowledge, which he supplements with brazen ingenuity, but he is also the rain doctor to whom men turn for help after the failure of all other methods. He is employed in all cases where purely magical ceremonies are performed, a sure sign of his true position.

The *pibas* or heads of the clans are now dignified officers holding in the case of the *pibas* of the Angom, Kumul and Luang clans, the title of Ningthou or king. They officiate at the annual ceremonies, which seem to be in honour of the eponymous tribal ancestor, or which are connected with the crops, and special precautions have to be taken against any impurity on their part. But pre-eminent above them all is the Meithei Ningthou, who is not only the head or *piba* of the Ningthaja clan, but the chief of his people as well. His appearances in a priestly capacity are infrequent, and limited to some great calamity, such as prolonged drought, when he will intercede with the powers that be, on behalf of his people. It is needless to say that the sacred person of the Raja is protected by many *tabus*. Some pertain to his royal office, while others are as distinctly intended to guard his priestly sanctity from pollution. He may in times of special distress avert the wrath of heaven by transferring his sins and those of the principal Rani to some wretched criminal, who thereby obtains a partial remission of his sentence and as a reward receives the discarded robes of the royal pair. In this connection it may be mentioned that the *chāhitāba*, the man who gives his name to the year, and who for the space of one year takes upon himself the sins of the whole people, enjoys for the term of his office a sanctity which is indistinguishable from that of the priest. Full details of the method and rites of appointing the *chāhitāba* are given above.‡

* *Op. cit.*, p. 21. † *Op. cit.*, p. 17. ‡ p. 105.

NATURE WORSHIP.

Indra, the Sky God, has his counterpart in the Meithei system, where the Deity Sorarel possesses all the attributes generally assigned to Indra, with whom he is now identified by the ingenious Hindus. The lofty hills which surround the valley are named after the Deities whose abode they are held to be. Khabru, on the north-west, looks down on the plain of Kaithenmānbi, the meeting-place of the spirits, and thither annually, in olden times, the Raja used to go in state to propitiate the Deity. When the thunder bursts on the summit of the mountain, men say the God fires his cannon; when they see in winter the snow fall on the topmost peak, the God is spreading his cloth. There are Thāngjing, Marjing, Laiching, and the sacred hill, Nọngmaiching, which seems to be derived from *Nong* = sun or rain, *mai* = face or in front of, and *ching* = hill, and to mean the hill that fronts the rain or sun. Does the Deity give the name to the hill, not the hill the name to the Deity?

From the ballad of Nūmit kāppa we know that they believed that once upon a time there were two Sun Gods riding on white horses, and now the moon is the faint pale image of the one that was wounded. Beneath the earth lives the earthquake Deity who shakes the earth, and to whom they pray *ngā chāk*, "Spare us our fish and rice," whenever he shakes the earth.

There are many rain *pujas*, but there does not seem to be any one rain Deity. In some cases the prayers of the worshippers are addressed to the tribal ancestor, and the *puja* performed entirely by the *piba* or head of the tribe. If we have not a thunder Deity, we have at least the legend of a Thunder Deity enshrined in the language of the people. In Meithei the word for lightning is *nōng-thāng-kūp-pa*, which is derived from *nōng* = rain, *thāng* = *dao*, *kūp* = to flash, and has therefore the meaning of the flash of the *dao* of the Rain God. Now among the Thādos we find the legend of the Rain Deity a mighty hunter coming home aweary from the chase and thirsty. Wroth was he when he found that his wife had no *zū* ready for him, and he brandished his *dao* at her, roaring hoarse threats of punishment for her neglect of her wifely duties, and then in his haste to quench his mighty thirst, he spilt the drink. It is curious to observe the *lacuna;* the Thādos have the tale but not the word,* while the Meitheis have the word but not the tale.

CEREMONIES ATTENDING BIRTH.

The Meitheis follow the ordinary rules of modern Vaishnavites in the matter of birth ceremonies, but have, in addition, a small *puja* in honour of the Imung Lai or the Household God, which is performed by the head of the household. This latter ceremony is, of course, non-Hindu.

NAMING.

Both Colonel McCulloch and Dr. Brown give explanations of the system of naming employed by the Meitheis, and concur in regarding the names as in many cases derived either from the profession or some personal peculiarity of the founder of the family. Colonel McCulloch † says that "Individuals are spoken of and known by their surnames; the *laiming*, or if I may use the expression, the Christian name, being seldom known to or used by any but the nearest relatives. All but the Royal family have surnames. The Christian name is written last. The introduction of surnames took place in the reign of Chalamba, about two hundred years ago, and of the *laiming* since the profession of Hindooism. The surnames are evidently derived from some peculiarity in the individuals who first bore them. The oldest family of Brahmins in the country is called Hungoibum. *Hungoi* means a frog, and that such a name should be given to a person who bathed so much more frequently than Munniporees had been accustomed to see, seems very natural. The same is the case with almost every family; all the surnames indicating either the profession or some peculiarity of its original holder."

Dr. Brown treats the matter in a different manner, and says

* *Wān aghin* is the Thādo for thunder, and means the noise of the sky, from *wān* = sky and *ghin* = noise; while *mē aying* is their expression for lightning, from *mē* = fire and *aying* = darkness.—T. C. H.

† *Op. cit.*, p. 22.

that "The names of the Munnipories are given on rather a complicated system, which may now be explained. In the first place, all the inhabitants have what is called a *yoom-nak,** or family name, corresponding with our surnames; some of these names are evidently derived from the ancestor's employment, as *Lairik-yem-bum,* corresponding with our English name, 'Clerk or Scrivener' †; *Phoorit-să-bum,* tailor; ‡ *Thăngjaba,*† smith, etc., etc. Next is the Hindoo name given by the astrologers, according to Hindoo custom, and, lastly, a nickname, or pet name, given to them when children, and by which they are known all their lives frequently. Sometimes the family name is alone used, occasionally the Hindoo, and very often the nickname; it is thus no easy matter some times to identify a Munniporie by name. I give a few examples of complete names, with their meanings when known.

Family name . .	Lairik-yem-bum (writer).
Hindoo name . .	Guneshur.
Pet name . . .	Baboo or Bapoo.
Family name . .	Phoorit-sa-bum (tailor).
Hindoo name . .	Moonee Ram.
Pet name or nickname .	Tuba Lokpa.
Family name . .	Sai-kom (no meaning).
Hindoo name . .	Kirtee Sing.
Nickname . . .	Chowba (large, fat).
Family name . .	Lai-hao-ta-bum (no meaning).§
Hindoo name . .	Gokul.
Nickname . . .	Cha-yem-ba (thin fellow).‖"

It thus appears that there is a name which is not permitted to be common property, that there is generally a nickname, or pet name, which is known to and used by the world at large, and that the family, or *yumnăk* name, is derived from either the occupation or some peculiarity of the original founder of the

* *Yum* = house, and *năk* is connected with the word *nai* = to belong to, *năk* also means near.—T. C. H.

† *Thăng* = dao, *chăn* = to manufacture, *lairik* = book, *yem,* from *yeng* = to look at. The man who looks at books.—T. C. H.

‡ *Phurit* = coat, and *să* = to make.—T. C. H.

§ Probably means giver of the flower known as the Lai-hao.—T. C. H.

‖ *Op. cit.,* p. 52.

family—that is to say, the *yumnāk* name is in origin descriptive in much the same way as the nickname or supplementary name now is.

Furthermore, it should be mentioned that it is customary for the Raja to assume a formal name on or after his accession by which he is described in all official documents. Thus, the Maharaja Chandra Kirti Singh was also known as Nowchingleng Nongdren Khomba after the year 1870, though he actually succeeded to the throne many years before that date. Thus the Raja, to whose reforming zeal the country owes the introduction of Hinduism, is variously known as Gharib Nawaz, Pamheiba, or Moianba. Doubtless the explanation of some, at least, of the Royal names is that they commemorate some incident or exploit which occurred during the reign, such as that of Khāgenba, whose name may possibly mean "Conqueror of the Chinese" (from *Khāgi* = Chinese, and *yānba* = to slaughter, or defeat).

TOGA VIRILIS.

The assumption of the sacred thread by a Meithei is regarded as proper when a lad has reached man's estate, but it is often delayed, and may be postponed without serious inconvenience. There is a curious custom which requires the eldest son of the Raja, when twelve years of age, to go into the jungles alone as a sign that he possesses the necessary strength and courage, and cut twelve bundles of fire-wood with a silver-hilted *dao*, which, tradition says, was presented to Khāgenba by the King of Pong, that mysterious kingdom whose exact geographical position has vexed the minds of so many inquirers,* who either forgot, or were never acquainted with, the peculiar laxity of the Meitheis in regard to the geography of unknown countries. The people of Pong were the Shans beyond their ken who visited them, and it is quite legitimate to conclude that the kingdom of Pong meant the powers who at the time were in supreme authority in the Shan States with which the Meitheis had dealings.

* *Gazetteer of Upper Burma*, vol. i. part i. pp. 188, 198, 255, 259, 270.

MARRIAGE.

The following excellent note by Mr. H. A. Colquhoun, I.C.S., gives all that can be desired in the way of an account of the marriage rites in vogue among the Meitheis:—"The usual marriage ceremony is that known as Prajapati or Brahma. After the parents have settled the preliminaries, the announcement of the forthcoming marriage or *Yathang thaba* takes place. This is followed by offerings of sweetmeats or *heijapot* on three separate occasions from the bridegroom to the bride's family. The actual ceremony is held at the bride's house; a large party assembles, and a *Kirtan* is held, the bride sitting in front of the bridegroom. Mantras are recited, and the ancestry of the pairs up to the great-grand-parents is repeated. The *sapta pradakhsin* follows: the bride walking ceremonially seven times around the groom and casting flowers upon him; garlands (*leipareng*) are placed on both, and the company prostrate themselves before them. They are then seated side by side, and their *innaphi*, or *chadars*, are fastened together. The *Hari Kirtan*, and the prostration are again repeated. The bride then enters the cooking-room followed by the groom. The pair sit on the same mat, and place *pan* (*panna khutap*), and subsequently sweetmeats (*kangsubi*) in each other's mouths. Offerings of *pan* are made to them by friends and relatives. The party then marches to the bridegroom's house, the bride being carried in a litter at the head of the party. A large and substantial wooden bed is a prominent feature of the procession.* On the sixth day following there is a feast at the house of the bride's family, and the ceremony is then complete.

"Other forms of marriage are also practised, the Sampati Rajbibaha, Rakshasa and Gandharva, the latter being, of course, constituted by simple cohabitation."

Colonel McCulloch states that "Although to become man and wife it is not necessary that the marriage ceremony should be performed, still it is usually performed, but as often after as before cohabitation." † It should be noted that the penalty on irregular marriages is the loss of the right to obtain offices about

* *Cf.* Robertson Smith, *Marriage and Kinship*, p. 200.

† *Op. cit.*, p. 19.

the Royal person and the inquiries which were necessitated by the census of 1901, caused some genuine alarm from the rumours sedulously spread that, as in the days of that stern old despot Chandra Kirti Singh, severe punishments awaited those who had taken advantage of the laxity of the British administration in these matters to contract connubial alliances without the usual sanction of the Brahmin. The fact is that most Manipuris regard cohabitation and public acknowledgment as sufficient, provided that due regard has been paid to the rules restricting marriage to members of the Meithei tribes and forbidding the intermarriage of persons of the same clan, *salei.*

Among the Lois gifts are exchanged and a feast prepared which culminates in the sacrifice to the Imung Lai, to the Lam Lai, and to the Umang Lai.

At Sengmai, where the manufacture of ardent spirits is the chief industry, presents of *zu* were offered to the girl's parents when the marriage was under discussion. If these gifts were peremptorily refused nothing further happened, but if the first invitation was accepted, the matter came into the range of practical politics and omens were taken to ascertain whether or not the marriage was favourably regarded by divine authority. Eventually the day was fixed, and the bride-price handed over, and the feast made ready.

DEATH, AND DISPOSAL OF THE DEAD.

All the rites and ceremonies consequent on the death of a Meithei are in the hands of the Brahmins, and there is therefore no feature to which attention should be specially drawn. Sepulture is only allowed in the case of children dying under the age of two years, and the burial takes place by preference on the bank of some river. I agree with Mr. Colquhoun in regarding the use of a box-like structure on the funeral pyres as a trace of the former method of sepulture for adults. It is well known that up to the advent of Hinduism, the dead were buried, and the Chronicles mention the enactment by Khãgenba of a rule that the dead were to be buried outside the enclosures of the houses. Gharib Nawaz ordered the Manipuris to exhume the bodies of their ancestors, which they formerly used to bury inside their compounds. At a later date in his reign, in the year 1724, Gharib Nawaz exhumed the bones of his ancestors and cremated them on the banks of the Engthe River, and from that time ordered his subjects to burn their dead. The system of cremation in vogue among the Meitheis is very thorough, as Mr. Colquhoun remarks, aud the frontal bone is preserved and thrown in the Ganges at a later date, as opportunity arises.

The corpse is never carried over the threshold of the main door, sometimes a hole is cut in a wall or the tiny side entrance used.*

FESTIVITIES, DOMESTIC AND TRIBAL.

Mention has been made of the various Hindu festivals such as the *Dussera*, and of the festival which is tribal in reality, known as the *Laiharaoba*. It is doubtful whether the *wāritābas* or parties given by wealthy folk, at which *iseisakpas*, or wandering minstrels, recite the stories of the wanderings of Chingthangkhomba, or of the unhappy loves of Khamba and Thoibi, or the adventures of Numit kāppa, are of a religious nature; but so closely are the threads of religion interwoven in the web of life of the people, that strange as it may seem to those who are accustomed to a religious system which provides for one day of the week only, it is probably just to mention these gatherings in this place. Recited in a dialect which is unintelligible to the listeners, despite the nasality of the tone in which they are recited, and despite the jangling accompaniment of the *pena*, these ballads possess something of real beauty. The audience knows not the exact import of the words they hear, but it knows the sad, the mirthful passages as they occur, and greets them with tears or with appropriate laughter. Meitheis or Moirangs, they listen with avidity to the trials of Khamba and Thoibi, the ballad which cannot fail to remind one of the stories of the Trials of Hercules, and which is held true by all, for to this day are not the clothes worn by these worthies still preserved in the temple at Moirang?

* See Jevons, *Introduction to Plutarch's Romane Questions*, pp. xxxviii, xxxix.

GENNA.

The detrition of the ancient customs which, begun by the introduction of Hinduism, has moved on with increasing rapidity since the country became the prey of the Burmese forces under Aloung Pra and his successors, prevents us from estimating the real extent to which the *genna* customs used to prevail among the Manipuris. If to-day they have not the thing itself, they have at least the memory of it in the word *nāmungba,* which covers precisely the same range of ideas as the word *genna.* There are even survivals of practices which among Nagas we call *genna,* and these I will now proceed to discuss.

It will be seen that among Naga tribes the head of the clan is divided from the common herd by *gennas* of food and speech. Thus it is *nāmungba* for any Manipuri to address the Raja except in a peculiar vocabulary.* We may compare this with the prohibition against the use of certain profane words by priests and kings.† Again they say that food cooked in a pot which has been used before, is *nāmungba* to the Raja. Indeed, of every prohibition which rests on vague indefinable sanctions, they use the term *nāmungba.* Each clan in Manipur regards some object as *nāmungba* to it, and believes that if by inadvertence some member of the clan touches one of these objects he will die a mysterious death, or suffer from some incurable, incomprehensible disease, pine away and die. The object which is *tabu* to the Ningthaja clan is a reed, that to the Moirangs the buffalo, in the case of the Kumuls it is a fish. Again, if a man falls from a tree, the elders of his clan may gather round that tree and solemnly declare it, even all others of its kind, to be *nāmungba* to their tribesmen. Yet another instance of the working of ideas which in other parts of the world have elaborated the system of *tabu,* the trees which crown the tumulus in Imphal, beneath which, according to common tradition, repose the bones of the Moirangs who fell in the last great battle with the Meitheis, are *nāmungba* to the men of Moirang to this day, and between them no Moirang may go, for,

* See J. G. Frazer: *Golden Bough,* vol. i. p. 144, 2nd Edition.
† Cf. Jevons, *Plutarch, Question* 44.

if one were so bold as to venture through, ruin would overwhelm his fellow clansmen.

It is remarkable that to this day the Moirangs whom I have described as still clinging to their independence and separateness, preserve something like a system of *genna*, participated in by the whole clan, and, like the Naga *gennas*, held periodically and connected with the times and seasons of cultivation.

Beyond these few cases it is now impossible to describe the *genna* system as it once existed; but I hope I have said enough to show that to this present day the fundamental ideas which underlie all *genna* rituals, are alive and active in Manipur.

To the curious in such matters the relationship of the three roots, *mang* = dream, *mung* [*nāmungba* = *nā* = *lā* = *lai* = Deity + *mung*], and *māng* = to be polluted or to be destroyed, may be commended for further investigation. We know that the legends of the country declare that the Gods appeared in dreams * and gave orders as to all sorts of affairs, thus legislating through the mouth of the dreamers. *Māng-ba* (to be polluted) has a religious significance, for it applies to cases of ceremonial pollution. If we admitted, and it is temptingly easy to do so, that *nāmungba* is derived from *Lā* = God and *mung* (? = *mang* or ? = *māng*), we should have an interesting instance of philology assisting our theory gratuitously. We have high authority for connecting the Meithei word *ising* with the Tibetan *chhu*, so that perhaps these humble guesses at philological truth are not of the order which neglects the consonants and is rude to the vowels. In fact, the connection between divine appearances in dreams, sacred prohibitions, *tabu* and pollution, is of the closest.

* *Cf.* Note on *Moirang Chronicle*, p. 131.

SECTION V.

TRADITIONS, SUPERSTITIONS AND FOLK TALES.

DR. BROWN has recorded some of the superstitions then current among the Meitheis in the following passage: * "The Munnipories are very superstitious. Demons of all kinds inhabit the small hills and other parts of the valley. They are also extremely superstitious with regard to days and dates for setting out on journeys in different directions, although on emergencies these ideas are put to one side. The following are unlucky days and dates for travelling in different directions—

Monday . . .	East.
Tuesday . . .	North and East.
Wednesday : .	North and East.
Thursday . . .	South and East.
Friday . . .	West.
Saturday . . .	North and East.
Sunday . . .	West and South.

The dates upon which it is unlucky to travel are as follows—

To the North . .	2nd, 10th.
,, South . .	3rd, 4th, 5th, 11th, 13th.
,, East . .	1st, 9th.
,, North-east .	8th, 15th, 30th.
,, North-west .	7th, 15th.
,, South-west .	4th, 12th."

It is clear from the Chronicles that Manipur is a land where strange things are in the way of happening. Now a God fires off a cannon, it may be that to-morrow two stars will rush together or that thunder will thrice be heard in a clear sky, an occurrence which from the times of Ovid we know portends the near approach of some great event. It is a land peculiarly liable to seismic disorders, and all the folk cry out aloud "*ngā chāk,*" "fish and rice," in order to save their food supplies from the demon who

* *Op. cit.*, p. 51.

is shaking the earth. Eclipses are due to the attack of the demon dog upon the sun or the moon, a story which is more fully explained by the Kabui version. At the death of Major Gordon in 1844, so the Chronicler records, a double-tailed star was seen in the sky, and in another passage the death of the eldest son of the Raja is connected by a sort of *post hoc ergo propter hoc* argument with an earthquake which occurred simultaneously. It is common to read of inanimate objects suddenly manifesting the power of locomotion. Stones raise themselves, guns fire themselves, drums beat themselves, the Royal cloth upon the loom shakes itself. Yet these things are the work of some Deity, for stones are well-known to be often chosen by Deities as places of abode, and if the divine inhabitant is displeased by being forcibly taken from some similar spot, he will show his wrath and produce a scarcity of food. The Royal cloth is destined for a being who is regarded as a God incarnate, and what he wears, or even what is destined for his wear before he has actually worn it, acquires something of his divine power. Rainbows have been known to form around the Royal head, and the very bow and arrows of the Rain God floated in the water of the moat close to the boat in which the Raja was sitting. This, of course, was an omen of exceptional felicity. But when rain fell like clay, when blood was found on the floors of the temples, when four suns were seen in the heaven, misfortune awaited the country. Sometimes we are enabled to assign to an omen a definite meaning, as when a swarm of butterflies is seen coming from the west to the east or when rooks fly from north to south, trouble in the shape of epidemic disease is at hand. The mysterious portent described in the phrase *sangaisel paire* or the flight of the *sangaisel*, betokens the death of some rich and important personage. It is not easy to ascertain exactly what is meant by the expression. One passage of the Chronicles says it is the flight of the spirit of a certain God, while in another it is said that a flame arises out of a holy stone, and I was informed that it was accompanied by a mysterious noise. We have in Colonel McCulloch's account the following reference to the superstitions of the Meitheis in regard to the erection of their houses:* "Connected with the making of their houses are many

* *Op. cit.*, p. 21.

superstitious practices. First, the house must be commenced on a lucky day, that day having been fixed by the astrologer; on it (it makes no difference whether the other materials are ready or not) the first post is erected. The post is bound towards the top with a band of cloth over which is tied a wreath of leaves and flowers. Milk, juice of the sugarcane and *ghee* are poured upon the lower extremity and into the hole in the ground in which it is to be fixed are put a little gold and silver. The number of bamboos forming the body of the frame for the thatch must not be equal on the north and south sides. If they were so, misfortune, they consider, would overtake the family. The other superstitions of the same kind are too numerous to mention. And it is not merely in reference to their houses that they are superstitious; they are so in every matter. Superstition constantly sends them to consult their *maibees* and *pundits*, who earn an easy livelihood by prescribing remedies to allay their fears." It will perhaps show the exact care and anxiety with which all house-building operations were carried on if a quotation is made from the Chronicles of a passage which describes the trouble which happened when something was done which ought not to have been done in the course of the erection of the *kangla* or Royal enclosure of the Coronation Hall. This is, of course, a peculiarly sacrosanct spot, not only from its association with the Raja, but as being the abode of the serpent as well. On the 15th of Mera, Sak 1771, *i.e.*, in October, 1849, Lairel Lakpa the astrologer declared that the place selected by the *pandit* for the site of the main post of the *kangla* was wrong because it would interfere with the place of the snake *annanta*. The *pandit* had his way and the hole was dug with the result that blood issued, and a bone and a stone were found there. Some days later the post was erected, but that night a white rainbow was seen over the post. The next day a snake entered into the hole where the post was and there was a frog on the back of the snake. Weeks later the king elephant went mad, and on the 5th of Hingoi (November) a fisherman at Wābagai caught in the trap a fish which he put in his bag. He was surprised to hear the fish say to him, "You want to eat me. I am the *lai* of the river." The fisherman replied that he had caught him in ignorance of his real rank. The fish then said,

"Go and tell the Maharaja to do worship on behalf of all the people," and jumped back into the water. A swarm of bees was seen at the gate of the Pāt, and Lairel Lakpa declared that all the "bad signs of the *kangla* had appeared," and then a trial was made of the value of the books of the Pandit and the astrologer Lairel Lakpa. The test was which book correctly gave the depth at which in the reign of Moyang Ngōmba Maharaja the stone of the tortoise or snake Pakhangba was found. The book of the Pandit proved trustworthy, and then the evil omens ceased to appear. Indeed, according to the Chronicles hardly an event of real importance ever occurred without some previous presage. Thus the shortness of the reign of Debendro Singh was foretold by the death of the king elephant and by the appearance in the *kangla* of a number of frogs which were seen there jumping about. The end of the dynasty of Gambhir Singh was foretold by a number of omens which are recorded in the Chronicles. "On the 13th of Kalen in the year 1813, the year of Ahongsangba Durlub Singh (1891, April). In the palace here a God's *dolai* with flag came down from the sky before the Bejoy Garōde at ten o'clock in the morning; it disappeared at the distance of 40 feet from the ground: the people witnessed the scene. The matter was reported to the Maharaja next day. The Maibas and the officers of the Tōp Garōde were summoned before the Maharaja, who asked Wikhoi Pandit what sort of *dolai* it was. Wāngkhai (or Wikhoi) Pandit replied that it was Pakhangba's *dolai*. Pākhangba's nine arms will come down in *koongkhookolen* (the *kangla* compound). The *dolai* was the first thing that had come down, and after this the country would enjoy happiness and peace, and the king would live long. Nongmaitemba Pandit seconded him and urged the Maharaja to worship Pākhangba. Touria Ashoiba Hidang replied that their prophecy might hold good, but it appeared to him that a calamity was coming.* Nahārup Lakpa upon this said that Touria was in terror and could not calculate properly. Men said in Maharaja's Sur Chandra's time that Maharaja Chandra Kirti Singh was ordained to reign for forty years, but

* Note the British troops had already reached the valley to avenge the murder of the Chief Commissioner and his companions, and this was known to all present.—T. C. H.

that he died before his time, having reigned only thirty-six years. Therefore the remaining four years were for Sur Chandra and Kula Chandra, and they expired this year. Upon this the Maibas fell to quarrelling and were dismissed by the Raja who called to his presence the Panjis, the astrologers, who declared that the appearance of Pākhangba's *dolai* was a sign of evil import to the Raja and his country. Then the Raja asked how these evils could be averted, and the Panjis said by offerings of tulsi leaves, of boiled rice with milk and sugar, and by feeding the Brahmins. But worse was to come, for on that night the moon was enveloped with red, green, and black mists, and on the following Sunday news came that the British troops had arrived from the north."

The country is full of legendary stories about the hills and river-pools. At Shuganu there is a deep pool which is the abode of an evil spirit which once seized the wife of the Raja who was travelling there in state, a story which is probably not without historical foundation, for in the Chronicles we find it told that Mongeanba's wife and daughter were drowned at Shuganu.

By the side of the road from Cachar about six miles from Imphāl, are two round hills known locally as Machi Manao (the two brothers). On the one are some trees, while the other is bare. The story goes that two brothers lived here, and one day quarrelled and fought. One pulled all the hair out of his brother's head but managed to keep a little of his own. The brothers are now the Lais of the hills. The hill Chingā Makhā in Imphāl itself is reputed to be the abode of a Lai who was once the inveterate enemy of the Royal family, and for this reason it is not possible for the Raja to set foot on the hill.*

Oneiromancy is among the accomplishments of the *maiba*, but his services are only called into requisition for the interpretation of dreams of very unfamiliar things. As among Nagas and Kukis every one knows fairly accurately the meaning of ordinary dreams.

It is, perhaps unnecessary to do more than to refer to the well-known legends of the origin of the Manipuri nation from the snake Pākhangba.

* Johnstone, *op. cit.*, p. 104.

THE NŌNGSHĀ.
(IMPHĀL—MANIPUR).

p. 124

The ceremony of ascending the throne (*phamban kāba*, or climbing the seat; *phamban*, from *phamba*, to sit, and *kāba*, to climb) was pregnant with varying incidents, all of which had their special significance. The Raja and Rāni, clothed in the garb of an earlier age,* passed from the house † (*sang kai pūnsiba*) within the walls to the *kangla* without, and as they went, careful note was taken of the stones on which the Raja trod. The Panji Loisang ‡ then read from them prognostications of the reign. Then in the recesses of the *kangla* was a chamber in which was a pipe leading, so I was told, to a chamber below, wherein dwelt the snake Pākhangba. The longer the Raja sat on this pipe and endured the discomfort of the unaccustomed pose and the torture of the fiery breath of his ancestor below, the longer and the more prosperous would be his reign.

The story of Numit kāppa is a folk tale, and its peculiar interest may afford an excuse for the literal translation which I now give.

NUMIT KAPPA (THE MAN WHO SHOT THE SUN).

"O my Mother, O Mother of the Sun who is the Father of the world, O Mother of all the Gods. She who was the Mother of the World gave birth one day to three sons. The first-born son was destroyed like withered paddy, and became like old dry paddy, and entered into the earth, and became even as the ant-heaps. Thereupon the Lairemma paddy and the great paddy were turned into Morasi and Iroya paddy. Her second-born son became rotten even as chicken's eggs, he became as the darkening rainbow. His eyes became like unto the eyes of a deer. Her third-born son was called Koidè Ngamba, the younger brother of the Sun. He was of a haughty temper and quick in spirit. He fell into a fishing weir and was killed. Thereupon his teeth became like the teeth of a wild beast, his rib-bones became the long *dao* of the Gods. The hairs of his head became like the flowers that men offer to Purairōmba and all the Gods. They became even as the flowers that men fasten

* See p. 6, *supra*. † See p. 8, *supra*. ‡ See p. 69, *supra*.

on the ends of their spears to catch *luangs* (small hill fish) in December, or like to the flowers that the King's wives and children present to the fields, such flowers as the Angōm Ningthou daily offers up, even as such became the white hairs of the God.

"Now the Sun and his brother Taohuirenga rose and set alternately. There was a man Khowai Nongjengba who had a slave, a lazy churl named Ekma Haodongla, who was wroth because the suns rose and set alternately. He said, 'I am a slave and twice have I to fetch wood, twice to bring in my master's paddy on my head. I cannot rear my children. I cannot see my wife.' So he said to his wife, 'My dear, go, get a bamboo from your father.' But her father would not give her a bamboo. 'Go to your uncle and beg a bamboo from the Thongkhongkhural, a bamboo that grows on the Khural King's Sōkpa Ching.' Thus he said, and sent her off. The Khural Lakpa gave him a bamboo from the hill. The slave of Khowai Nongjengba Piba in five days made a bow and arrows, and when he had dried them, he smeared the tips of the arrows with poison, and put the arrows in the quiver and rested. Then he said, 'Dear wife, Haonu Changkanu, my pretty one, go draw water and put the pot on your head. Then as his wife came from the water, he aimed and hit the pot on her head. One day he aimed and hit the hole in her ear. One day he aimed and hit a sparrow sitting on a heap of *dhān*. 'Wife, make food ready. A big boar has entered the field, a great python has come into the field. I will combat those strong things. I will kill that boar.' He slept by the side of the things he was going to take to the field, and for this reason the place is called *thongyala mamungshi*. The Great Sun set at Loijing. His elder brother Taohuireng arose in his splendour, and Ekma Haodongla the slave of Khowai Nongjengba Piba, a lazy churl, drew the string to his cheek and though he fired the arrow carefully at the sun, he hit the sun's horse on the leg, and it fell near the great Maring village. When the bright sun fell by the arrow of the slave of Khowai Nongjengba Piba, he was afraid and hid himself in the earth in a great cave by the big village near his father Pākhangba and his mother Senamehi. Then the Meithei land was dark by day and dark by night. The fields and the whole countryside looked to the Gods for pity because the day remained not. Weeds grew. Women that used to go to the fields went no more, women that used to toil in the fields went no more. The ten kings (Nongpōk, Chingkhai, Wāngpurel, Khāna Chaoba, Thāngjing, Sampurel, Loyarakpa, Kaobaru, Kaoburel, Marjing), these ten gods knew not how to look for the place where the sun was. A woman going to the field was holding converse with a woman going to sow, 'My friend, my companion, what is that fire in the earth shining there over by the great village?' said she inquiring. 'Yes, my dear, the Sun is hiding near his father Pākhangba and Senamehi.' 'It is the brightness of the Sun,' said the other as they talked. The ten Gods heard, and when they had returned to their own house, they called Thōngnāk, whose dreams were very true. 'Thōngnāk Lairemma, your dreams are very true, a dead person has entered into you. You do judgment on the dead. Call the Sun.' With these words they sent her. Thōngnāk Lairemma called the Sun. 'O Sun, by reason of thy disappearance, the land of the Meitheis is in darkness day and night. Bring thy warmth over this land and over its villages.' Thus said she, and the Sun made answer to her. 'Yea, Thōngnāk Lairemma, formerly my Mother, who is Mother of all the Gods and the Mother of the world, gave birth to five sons. One day my eldest brother shrivelled up like dry paddy and was destroyed. My second brother became rotten like the eggs of a fowl, my brother Koidè Gnamba fell into a fishing weir and was drowned. Now my elder brother Taohuirengba has fallen by the arrow of the slave of Khowai Nongjengba Piba, for his horse was pierced through the leg by the arrow which he shot, and so he hides in a dark cave.' Thus he spake, and would not come forth. Thōngnāk Lairemma returned to her abode. 'Ye ten Gods, hear. The Sun cannot remain alone in the world.' Then the ten Gods hired Panthoibi, the daughter of the King, the wife of Khāba. 'O daughter of the King, who art beloved of the King of the country, who causest to be born all the souls of men and dost cause them to die, who art the Mother of the Gods and the Mother of all the country, thy face is beautiful, do thou go, do thou call thy Father the Sun.' When they said this, the King's dear daughter who causes a flower to bloom merely by touching a big white leaf, assented to their request. 'Ye Ten Gods, if ye bid me to persuade the bright

Sun to come forth, make ready the roads, make men to go to and fro, build a *machan* five stories high, make the women all join in entreaties to him. In the baskets spread leaves carefully and set therein white rice, put eggs, fill the wine jars full of wine, wrap ginger in leaves and set it down, wrap cowries up in a black cloth and put them down near.' Then she took a white-cock and all the other things and went to the broad country to persuade the bright Sun.

"'O Sun, by reason of your hiding, in the land of the Meitheis there is darkness night and day; by your brightness warm all the country to Imphāl from here.' Thus she said and thus she persuaded him, for he assented, and when the white fowl lifted up its foot on the earth, the Sun also raised his foot from the earth five times and climbed to the top of the *machan*. Then the ten Gods looked and saw that the sunshine was pale. 'Let us make this right,' they said. Then Pākhangba's priest sat on the right, and the priest of Thāngjing, the God of Moirang, sat on the left. They took water from the river of Moirang, and an egg and yellow grass, and drew water from the top of Nongmaiching, and the priests, the children of the Gods, made the face of the Sun right, and his eyes and his face were bright and beautiful. Panthoibi holding the fowl soothed the Sun. Then the priest, who formerly guarded the seven branches of Nongmaiching, and who lived on that holy hill, whose name was Langmai Khoiri, who formerly worshipped the face of the sun, made prayers to the Sun. 'Thou hast come like the eyes of the hill. In the likeness of the eyes of the hill in thy brightness thou hast pitied us, the villages of Nongmaiching. Like the eyes of the Sun thou hast come. Like the eyes of the Sun by thy brightness the warmth of the sun has warmed all the ravines and jungle and all our villages on Nongmaiching.' Thus said he as he prayed. The great village also made prayers to the Sun, and its priests sang and prayed. The women also of the great village have crossed the river and have gone to the fields. The Tangkhuls have taken up their *daos*. Men see their shadow in the water. 'By thy brightness all the paths and all the trees and all the bamboos in our great village are warm with the warmth of the sun.' Thus said he and prayed. Then the brothers, the cunning priests, slaves of Thāngjing, prayed to

NŪMIT KĀPPA, MEITHEI CHARACTER.

Date not known.

the Sun God, 'O thou born on the stone, born on the white stone, who lightest the jungle, and the water, and who shinest up to the top of the loftiest bamboo, with thy brightness make warm the heat of the sun on the water of Moirang.' In the south the Khumal priest prayed. His father and his forefathers were very skilful, and his voice was very good, and his singing carried far. Than him there was none greater, his voice was like the cry of the crane, and in his singing there was no fault. Thus prayed he. 'O Sun, now that thou hast come, the trees, the bamboos, the grass, all are bright. O Sun by thy glorious brightness the leaves and the wood are as new, the heart is glad. By thy brightness make warm the heat of the sun upon the land of the Khumals.' Then the priest of the King of Manipur, who was skilled in the songs of the Manipuris, whose voice was like the running water, invoked by name his deceased mother, and singing sweetly the name of his dead father, having sung the names of men that were dead and making them to unite in the history, he makes birds and crows that are dead to be among the Gods. He knows the souls of men and their names, even though they are lost,* he knows them when they have become animals, though their names should be forgotten, he calls them in his song. Though hereafter the names of men be forgotten, he in his wisdom knows them, though they are wandering in the abyss among the demons, even though they have joined themselves unto swine, he knows them. Thus made he prayer. 'O Sun, Thou alone art beautiful, thou art the Father of all the unfortunate, thou art deathless, there is none like thee for truth and beauty. I cannot tell all thy names in my song, so many are they. Thou art the source of all good fortune, for in the scent of the earth is seen the warmth of the sun. O Bright Sun, thou art the source and the strength of all the world and of immortality.'"

Dr.Grierson gives the following folk tale in the Report of the *Linguistic Survey of India* †:—

"Once upon a time a man had two sons. After some time he died leaving behind him a buffalo cow, a pomegranate tree, and a curtain. When the two brothers proceeded to divide the

* *Māng* = to be lost, or ceremonially polluted.—T. C. H.
† Vol. iii. part iii., p. 41.

property, the younger brother, who was the more clever of the two, arranged the matter in the following way. He gave the front part of the buffalo, including the head, to his elder brother, and retained himself the other half, from the tail and forwards. And he gave his brother the lower part of the pomegranate tree, and took himself the top. With regard to the curtain, he used it at night, and left it to his brother during the day time. When the buffalo ate the crops of other people he made his brother give damages, because the outrage was done by the head, which belonged to the elder. But he claimed for himself the calves which were born and the milk. And he also reserved for himself the fruits of the pomegranate tree.

"In this way some time passed. The elder brother was advised by the neighbours, and one day he went to fell the pomegranate tree in order to get fuel. But the younger brother now proposed that they should divide the fruits between them, and thus prevented the felling of the tree. Now the elder brother declared that he would kill his part of the buffalo because it gave him such trouble in eating the crops of other people. The younger brother then stopped him, saying that they might also take each his share of the milk and of the young buffaloes. Then the elder brother took the curtain and kept it during the day in water. The other then proposed that they should use the curtain alternately. Both agreed, and after that time they lived without quarrelling."

THE HISTORY OF MOIRANG.

Moirang was created by the God, Thāngjing, who came down from heaven in the shape of a boar. Seven times did he incarnate himself and rule as King of Moirang. The first King of Moirang at the beginning of Kaliyug was Iwang Fang Fang Ponglenhanba, who was born of Moirang Leima Nangban Chanu Meirapanjenlei. He attacked Naga villages, brought Thānga under his rule, and fixed his boundaries to the north, where the Luang King bore sway. He brought in captives, and buried the heads of his fallen enemies in the Kangla or Royal enclosure. Then the God Thāngjing bethought himself that the King and his subjects were so prosperous that they were likely to forget their duties to him, and after taking counsel sent seven Gods, Yakhong Lai, to frighten the King and his people. At night there were mysterious sounds, but the soldiers at first could find no one. Then, when the sounds occurred a second time, they became aware of the Gods, the Yakhong Lai, and reported what they had seen to the King, who took counsel of his ministers. They besought him to call the famous *maibi* Santhong Mari Mai Langjeng Langmei Thouba. She was in the fields cultivating, but came running, whence (says the historian) all the dwellers of Moirang say *apaiba*, *i.e.*, "to fly," instead of *chenba*, "to run" which is the ordinary Meithei word.* The King begged the *maibi* "very respectfully" to raise the Khuyal Leikhong which the angry storm raised by the Gods had blown down, and by way of showing his respect said: "If you cannot raise the Khuyal Leikhong, I shall kill you." The *maibi* persuaded the seven Gods to tell her the *mantra*, and ordered her to convey a message to the King, who was bidden to send all the *maibas* and *maibis* of the country to sleep in the temple of Thāngjing wearing their sacred clothes. When she went to the Khuyal Leikhong she saw Pākhangba there. She raised the edifice by means of the *mantra* and then gave the message to the King, who bade the *maibas* and *maibis* go and sleep in the temple of Thāngjing in their sacred clothes. There in their dreams they were instructed to divide the people into sections, some for one duty and some for others. Then the village offices were created and their order of precedence fixed. The *maibas* chant the name of the God and the *maibis* ring the bell. Then, when they had told the King all the wonderful things communicated to them in their dreams, they were bidden to do as the God had said. Then the King died and was succeeded by his son Telhaiba, so called by reason of his skill with the bow. In his, and in the following reigns, there were raids against Nagas and various villages. Then we get into complications, for in the reign of King Laifacheng we are told, the Khumals were wroth with

* The logic may be deficient, but we may compare this statement with the fact that in the Royal Meithei vocabulary the word "to walk" "to go" is *lengba*, which in Thado means "to fly." The incident proves, firstly, a dialectical variation, and secondly, the imposition of a *tabu* on the use of the word *chenba* by the people of Moirang.—T. C. H.

Konthounamba Sāphaba and compassed his death. They took him into a wood and fastened him to a tree and left him, but by the aid of the Gods he broke the creeper and made his way to Moirang where he married and had a son. He left Moirang, and went to the land of the Meithei. The King kept the child, who by favour of the God Thāngjing grew so strong that the folk of Moirang begged the King to rid himself of the lad, for he would supplant the King. So they put the lad in chains for seven years, and all that time there fell no rain in Moirang. Then the God Thāngjing appeared to the lad and told him to ask the King to take off his chains. Then the King set the lad free, and the rain fell, but many had died of fever and cholera. The King implored the lad to pardon him for his cruelty and promised him, that when he was dead the kingdom should be his for seven years, even as many years as the years of his bondage. So it fell out, and for seven years the lad reigned as King where he had been in chains.

Raids against Luangs on the west against Naga villages, which the historian observes still pay tribute to Moirang, are all we have for a brief space covering some hundred years. The God Thāngjing kept his interest in the fortunes of the kingdom, and visited the King in his dreams and instructed him in many matters. The village grew and spread, so much so that in the reign of King Thānga Ipenthaba the small hill of Thānga was broken and the water let out. Then at the instance of two Khumal women the King slew the King of the Khumals whom he met by chance hunting. In a later reign, Moirang is invaded by the Khumals who assembled a force in boats. This force was defeated, and in return the Khumal villages were fired.

In the reign of King Chingkhu Telhaiba (skilful archer of the hill village), a Khumal, Aton Puremba, shot nine tigers with his bow and arrows and brought their skins to the King, who sought a gift worthy of the hunter's prowess. He would not give him clothes or such things. He had no daughter, so he gave him his wife, and by her the bold hunter had two children Khamnu and Khamba. Both their parents died, and by dint of begging from door to door, Khamnu got food for herself and her baby brother. Day by day the lad grew in strength and courage. So swift was he that none could race against him.

So strong was he that he and he alone dared to seize a mad bull that was raging in the land. Then Chingkhuba Akhuba, brother of King Chingkhuba Telhaiba and uncle of the Princess Thoibi, ordered his men to seize Khamba and have him trampled to death by the elephant. His sin was that Thoibi had made a coat which she gave to Khamba, for she loved him. The God Thāngjing warned Thoibi of the peril in which her lover was, and she arose and threatened to kill her father so that Khamba escaped. Then it befell a hunting party that a tiger killed a man in full sight of the King, but Khamba killed the tiger single-handed, and as a reward the King gave him the Princess Thoibi in marriage.* In 1431 the Meithei King slew the King of Moirang (at the battle of Moirang-khōng in Imphāl where there is a tumulus beneath which are buried the heads of the Moirang tribesmen that were slain in the fray). The later entries consist of names of persons who became Kings, and against one name is the remark "King Chandra Kirti Singh dismissed this King, and for twenty-seven years there was no King of Moirang." Last of all is the entry, "In 1813 Shak the Political Agent of Manipur appointed Romanando Singh as Moirang Ningthou."

One or two points occur. All the early Kings marry women of the Moirang clan, while even the change of the dynasty, when the son of the Khumal refugee became King, is not an exception, for the mother of Urakonthouba was a Moirang woman. Later on there are failures in the direct line, but a brother is recorded as successor. The incident of Khamba and Thoibi has no doubt been worked in by the chronicler, who seems to share the view held by Thāngjing that the people are forgetting their religious duties and need to be roused by some calamity.

More than ordinary interest attaches to the proof here afforded of the manner in which the divine ordinances regulating the structure of society and apportioning the duties of the citizens were promulgated as the result of dreams by the *maibas* and *maibis*—the soothsayers and wise women.

In conclusion it may be pointed out that there exists in Manipur a store of written records which, apart from historical

* See pp. 134, *seq.*

value, possess an ethnological importance as affording, unconsciously and unintentionally, remarkable evidence as to the level of culture from which as yet the bulk of the population has not emerged. There is yet a rich harvest to be gathered in, and, if the workers are few, their labour will be justified by its reward.

KHAMBA AND THOIBI.*

(The superior figures refer to the notes at the end of this tale.)

In the days of Chingkhu Telheiba, King of Moirang, Chingkhu Akhuba was Jubrāj, and his brother the King had no child. The daughter of the Jubrāj was Thoibi Laima. And in those days Yoithongnai was King of Khumal and he had three sons, Haoramba-hal, Haoramningoi and Haoram-thōl Louthiba. On a day it happened that Panji Thoiba,[1] the King's soothsayer, and his wife, Chaobi Nongnangma-chāk, went fishing in a lake at the foot of a hill whereupon there grew a Heibung tree. As the soothsayer rested in the shade of the tree, he saw thereon a necklace of beads which he plucked down and gave to his master, the Khumal King, who set it on the neck of his son Haoramba-hal. Then, as the King grew old, he set the necklace upon the neck of his second son, and then, last of all, upon the neck of his youngest son Haoramba-thōl.[2] In these days the Luang King Punsiba built him a new palace and summoned all the Kings to the great feast upon the day when he was minded to enter therein. So the sons of the Khumal King, Haoram-hal and Haoram-yeima were bidden, and put on their robes of State. And Haoram-hal entreated his mother to lend him the necklace, and she hearkened to his entreaty. Soon Haoram-thōl came home from his sport in the village and found not the necklace though he sought for it diligently. Then he was wrath and took his father's sword and sought his brothers so that he might kill them. Yet to none did he declare his purpose. So he met his brothers by the way and slew his brother Haoram-hal, for on his neck was the necklace, and Haoram-yeima fled to Moirang, where he took two women unto him as wives, and they bore

* See p. 56 and p. 133 above.

From a Picture by BHUDRO SINGH.

p. 134.

KHAMBA AND THOIBI

THE DANCE BEFORE THE KING.)

him each a son. Now Parenkoiba was the son of the elder wife, and Thāngloihaiba was the son of the younger wife. In his days Parenkoiba took unto him a wife, and she bore him a son whom they called Purenba, and in his days he took unto him a wife, and his wife bore him first a daughter whom they called Khamnu, and thereafter a son whom they called Khamba.

Now it chanced that upon a day King Chingkhu Telheiba of Moirang went a hunting in the jungles, and when the men fired the reeds,[3] five tigers rushed out, and the men who were with the King fled, all save Purenba who slew the tigers with his spear. So the King gave him his wife, for daughters had he none. And with her he gave rich dowry, even a store of goodly apparel, and he set the brave man in high office with titles of honour that all the folk might know his fame. Thereafter the King's soothsayer[4] chose the names for the children that his wife bore unto him, and the King assented to the names. Then it chanced that Purenba fell ill, for an evil spirit entered into him[5] so that he was vexed with a fever and died. Ere he died he sent for his friends, Nōngthōnba and Thōnglen, and commended his children to their care, and Nōngbal Chaoba betrothed his son Feiroijamba to Khamnu.[6] Then his wife, seeing that her husband was indeed dead, could not live when her lord and husband was taken by death from her. So she slew herself upon his pyre, and Thōnglen took charge of the two children, but they sorrowed and would not be comforted. So he let them go, and they went to their father's house, and were happy there. But there was none to help them, so Khamnu went among the village folk and husked paddy for them while the women gave the breast to Khamba.[7] Then one day it fell out that Khamnu went to Moirang to the bazar at the very hour when the Princess Thoibi was wont to do her marketing, and the Princess took note of the strange face, for she knew her not and asked her many questions and gave her gifts of food and jewellery; but Khamba was vexed, for there was nought for him. Khamnu met Thoibi again, who bade her come afishing with her on the Logtāk. When the King heard that the women who bore his daughter company were minded to sport on the lake, he gave orders that no man might go on the lake. So Khamnu told Khamba of this and left him at home the next day. As he slept, in his dream [8] the Goddess Panthoibi came to him in the guise of Khamnu, and bade him get the vegetables together. Khamba woke and wondered if he had indeed seen his sister or if it was a dream, but the God Thāngjing put it into his mind that he had indeed seen his sister. So he went down to the lake and got a boat there and rowed out, but in a wrong direction, so the God spread a veil of cloud over the hill. Anon a storm arose and blew the boat towards the place where Thoibi was fishing. On a sudden Thoibi turned and saw Khamba standing close to her. She asked Khamnu if she knew the stubborn man who dared disobey the orders of the King, but Khamnu denied all knowledge of him. Khamba stood there not knowing what to do, but when he heard his sister's voice, he went nearer, and Thoibi saw that he was goodly and well fashioned, as if daintily carved by some master hand. Khamba, too, wondered at the beauty of Thoibi, for it was the will of God that they twain should love. Yet again Khamnu denied knowledge of the man, for she feared for him that he would be punished for disobedience. Then Thoibi saw that Khamnu was wearing a piece of cloth which matched Khamba's *pagri*, and that Khamba wore the bracelet which she herself, but a day before, had given to Khamnu. Then Khamnu owned that he was her younger brother, and Thoibi was gracious to him and gave him of her sweetmeats, and then bade him go home lest the wrath of the King visit him, for he seemed goodly to her eyes. When Thoibi had returned to the Palace she bade Khamnu show her the place wherein she lived. So they went to Khamnu's house, and Thoibi saw that the gate was broken. But she sat on a red cloth near the post on the north side which men call *ūkōklel*. Khamba hid himself in the far corner where there was a mat, for the house was old and full of holes, yet Thoibi said nothing in blame, but only that the house was nice. She asked what the mat in the corner was hung for, and Khamnu told her that there was their God Khumalpōkpa [9] (the ancestor of the Khumals). Then Thoibi said, "May I pray to him, for I seek a mercy of him?" Then, so that Khamba might hear her words, she prayed aloud to the God to give her heart's desire to stay in the house and worship him daily. Then Khamba laughed aloud and both the women heard; then Thoibi said, "Your God has spoken to me." She sat down in the veranda and Khamba came out and sent his sister to the village to bring some fruit. When she was gone, Thoibi bade her maid Senu go to Khamba bearing gifts to him, and say, "My Lord, my Lady bids me give you these, for she desires to be your servant, and to think of none other. To you will she give herself." So he took the gifts and they two bound themselves by a mighty oath before the God Khumalpōkpa, and drank the water [10] in which the golden bracelet was dipped, and each vowed love to the other. Then Thoibi called Khamnu sister and bade Khamba go out among the folk and show himself to the King's officers. So Khamba went out and joined the young men who were learning to wrestle. An elder who stood by, saw the strength of Khamba and bade him wrestle, and he joined in wrestling, and at last the champion of the countryside invited him to wrestle, but Khamba was not thrown for all that the other knew many devices whereby he had often thrown great men. As it fell out, there passed by Nōngthōnba, the minister of the King, who stopped and asked the name of the young man whom the champion could not throw. With the great man [11] were the servants who followed him, his clients and those that sought to win his favour.

Then he sent for the great champion and asked of him the name of the young man with whom he strove, "for indeed I know him, yet cannot I mind me of his name." "I know not," said the other, "yet verily is he a strong man, like a rock so hard is he to move, like the might of a river that cannot be stayed." Then he asked of Khamba his name and the name of his sire, and Khamba answering said, "Men call me Khamba, but my sire's name I know not." "What manner of man is this," said the King's minister in wrath, "that knows not the name of his sire?" Then Khamba said, "My sire died when I was yet a babe, and my sister brought me to manhood. Peradventure she will know the name of my sire." Then the King's minister remembered the face of the lad, for it was even as the face of one who was his friend, and he was sorrowful, for he had spoken sharply to the lad in reproof. "True is it indeed that the elephant knows not his own brother, and kings forget their sons. Your father died ere his prime, even as a tree dies when men strip it of its bark." So he loved the lad, and in his delight went not to the

King's Durbar, but to his house, where he told the women folk of the lad he had met, and bade them take fine clothes and an offering of dainties, for he was minded that his first-born son should take Khamnu, the sister of Khamba, to wife even as he had promised to her father. So they went to Khamnu, who hid herself in the women's chamber, and they stood and wept outside, and lamented, so that Khamnu relented and spake with them, and took from their hands the apparel,[12] a dress for the morning and a dress for the time when women gather at the bazar, and a dress for the great days when the Gods make merry. Then ere Khamba set forth on the morrow, Khamnu gave him sage counsel. "If any, jealous, puts a stick in thy path, walk not over it, but round it, for they are minded to do thee harm who are evil. Jostle not in the crowd, for they envy thee." So the lad went with the King's minister to the market-place, where the Jubrāj sat, and the Minister, with a lowly obeisance, set Khamba before the Jubrāj, and told of his sire and of his strength. Then they set him before the King, who was gracious unto him and spoke of his father, and bade them enrol him among his servants, and bade them also set the great wrestler Kōngyamba among his servants, and when, according to the custom of the land, they had given largesse to the men of their village, the King bade them gather flowers for the service of the God Thāngjing on the morrow.

Then they set forth to their homes, and Khamba told Khamnu all that had befallen him, and how he purposed to gather flowers for the service of the God on the morrow, and the Jubrāj told his folk of the prowess and might of the son of his old friend, how the King had enrolled him, the son orphaned in his infancy, the child of a brave man, one who was wise in counsel, well versed in matters of state, and a leader of men in war, and made him his servant among them that bear office, for he was a man of high birth and a glory to his Panna. Then Thoibi said to her father, "In truth you should have honoured him yourself and built him an house, upon the north of your palace,[13] and you should have given him food daily." So she went forth and told her mother that the festival of the Gods was at hand. But she went to see Khamba, and he told her how the King had made him Khunthak Leiroi Hanjaba and had bidden him gather flowers from the hills. "Great trouble is in store for you if you essay to gather flowers on the hills. Rather will I collect them in the village and in the bazar"; and she cooked him food for the morrow and tied it in a bundle of leaves, fastening it with seven different kinds of silk. On the morrow Kōngyamba came for Khamba and chid him for being late, and, being the elder, bade Khamba carry his food. Khamba was wroth thereat, and flung it on the ground. So they went on to a place where the flowers grew, and Kōngyamba marked it with knots tied in the jungle[14] and claimed it as the place where his father was wont to gather flowers, and threatened Khamba with the wrath of the King. Then was Khamba wroth, and asked, "Where is the place where my father was wont to gather flowers?" Kongyamba pointed to the hills yet south of where they stood, and thither Khamba went, but he found no flowers. So he prayed to the God Thāngjiṅg, and the God had compassion on his servant's distress, and sent a whirlwind, upon whose wings was borne to the nostrils of Khamba a fragrance of many flowers. So Khamba went on and found a tree in a valley below whereon grew many flowers. He made obeisance to the God and did reverence to the tree ere he climbed it. So he gathered the flowers and threw them down, and by the grace of the God not a petal was broken. He sang on the way back the Khulang Isei, honouring the name of the Princess Thoibi, and Kōngyamba heard it and questioned him, but Khamba said, "I sing of *Toibi*."[14] Then they quarrelled again and fought, because Kōngyamba bade Khamba carry all the flowers and Khamba would not. Then they desisted and fell to eating, for it was late, and the odour of the savoury food which Thoibi had prepared for Khamba was very rich, and while Kōngyamba questioned Khamba about it, the crows came and ate the cakes which Kōngyamba had brought for his refreshment. So he was wroth, and when he had returned home, he was enraged with his younger wife, and would not let her wash his feet. But when Khamba had returned home, Thoibi said, "Here is my lord and master," and washed his feet and gave him fruit to eat. Meanwhile Kōngyamba sent his men forth to question whence Khamba had got such dainty food, and they went to the Palace to ask of the Ningon Lakpa[15] if there had been a feast, but they came back in sore haste, for Thoibi bade the porters drive them off. Then Kōngyamba was minded to vex Khamba, so he gathered the village folk at the gateway of Khamba's house,[16] and proclaimed to them all the King's orders, that on the morrow, the festival of the Gods, all should be clad in gay robes with jewels of gold and of silver. Then Khamnu came forth and asked him, "What sayest thou?" And he answered her roughly, "Hast thou no ears? Have I not proclaimed the will of the King all day long till my lungs are dry and my throat parched? Go to." So she wept for shame, and Khamba wept too, for the thought that he had no bright garments to wear on the morrow. But in the night, as they slept, they dreamed that they saw their father and mother standing by them, and that they told them to go to the house of Thōnglen, for there were stored their clothes of honour. So they arose, and even in the night went to the house of Thōnglen. The men seized them as thieves, and haled them before Thōnglen in the morning, but he knew them as the children of his old friend Purenba, and gave them rich clothes to wear and taught them the dance, and appointed men to follow Khamba and women to serve Khamnu. Also he sent men to build their house anew.[17] Then Senu and Thoibi came to the house bearing gifts of raiment and jewellery for Khamnu and Khamba, but they were perplexed, for they knew not the house, so well and truly had the men built it anew. And Thoibi was sore vexed when she saw Khamnu and Khamba in the verandah wearing rich clothes, for she feared that Khamba had married the daughter of some rich man. Then Feiroijamba, the son of Nōngthōlba, who was betrothed to Khamnu, joined them, and they went to the Pāt, where they met the Princess Thoibi riding in a rich *dooli*. Then Kōngyamba distributed the flowers among the great men, to the King first and then to the Queen, and then to the High officers of state. And Khamba, greatly fearing, asked counsel of the Maibi Hanbi, who first set flowers before the God Thāngjing. Then Khamba presented flowers to the great ones, first to the King, then to the Queen, and then to the High officers of state. Right pleased were they all with the flowers set before them by Khamba, and they gave him rare gifts, many times more than the customary presents which they had given to Kōngyamba.

Then the dancing began, and Kõngyamba and his wives danced. Then Khamba and Thoibi danced and sang before the God, and their party was great, and the people gathered together and shouted with joy as they danced, whirling together, till at last they knelt in salutation before the God. Then Kõngyamba was wroth and spake bitter words, and on the morrow the folk began to practise for the *lamchel* * and the wrestling, and the officers of the Pannas were bidden to choose their champions. So they chose Khamba, for he ran steadily in long strides with his chest low, even as those run who run far. They set him before Nongbal, who ran with his head high, swiftly indeed, but for a short distance. Then they ordained that this year the race be long. So of the two parties, both of the wrestlers and of those who run, Khamba was the chief, while Kõngyamba was chief of the other parties.[18] The Leikeirakpas were bidden to watch the start, and all the night Kõngyamba talked with his men how best they might hinder and overcome the party of Khamba for, said he, "Many are the races I have won, and heavy will be my disgrace if this year I am second to Khamba." And Khamnu feared for Khamba lest the friends of the other should do him harm, for they were many. On the morrow Nõngbal Kõngyamba set forth early with his party, and one said to another, "It is evil for the land if a poor man win the race.[19] It betokeneth scarcity more than the folk can bear. Let us say this among the people ere the race be run." So they hailed Khamba when he arrived, and said, "Hast not heard that thou art not numbered among those that run? Thy name is not set in the list." And the people that stood by assented thereto, and Kõngyamba said, "Of evil import is it that a poor man such as thou should run, for it betokeneth scarcity in the land more than the folk can bear." So Khamba believed and returned home very sorrowful at heart, and told his sister all that had been said to him. Then Khamnu bade him go to her father-in-law and tell him all. Then Khamba met Leikeirakpa Nõngthõlba, who was vexed with him and passed him in scorn, but Khamba ran before him and bowed himself to the ground before him and told him all. Then they went before the King, and the King bade Khamba run if there was yet time. So Khamba

* See p. 53 *supra*.

and his brother-in-law Feiroijamba sped to the starting-place, and they saw the runners kneeling and the bundle of grass was yet hoisted.[20] So they shouted, "We bear the King's order," but the people shouted so that the runners started, and Kōngyamba taunted Khamba, "Run with me," he said, but Khamba answered, "Not yet my friend." Then they entreated the Leikeirakpas, and Khamba went to the appointed place and there worshipped the Gods, and then he too shouted, and so swiftly he ran that he overtook Feiroijamba whose pony was startled and ran away.[21] Then the people of Kōngyamba were fain to stay him, but he dashed them aside. At last he caught up Kōngyamba, who ran slowly, for he was tired. Then fifteen horsemen, the men from the villages of Kōngyamba, tried to stay Khamba, and in his mind Thōnglen was aware of the evil things they did, and the tears came to his eyes and he started up and asked leave of the King to see what things they were doing to Khamba. Then Khādarakpa,[22] the friend of Kōngyamba, and Nōngthōlba set forth together, and Thoibi gave them *pān*, a gift for the swiftest in the race. Then turn by turn the twain ran, first one then the other, gaining but a little, and the women cried out to them. Then Khamnu cried out, "Run on, Khamba, for thy Father's honour," and Thōnglen shouted to him, "Here is the lion[23] thy Father touched, leap up and break his horn," and Khamba saluted the King and leapt up seven cubits high and brake the horn of the lion. Then Kōngyamba came up and in his turn greeted the King. Yet the King was more pleased with Khamba and gave him a gold embroidered coat, and the Queen gave him rich apparel, and the King's ministers heaped gifts upon him. So in the wrestling Khamba was the champion, and he surpassed all in putting the stone and tossing the caber.[24] Then he and his sister gave largesse of many cloths among the elders of the village.

Then Kōngyamba bethought him how best he might work evil upon Khamba. But the Gods taught him no hint of evil devices in his dreams, and he despaired greatly. Then he built himself a hut,[25] wherein he might consult a familiar spirit, but this availed him not. Then it fell out that one day he met women from Khumal fishing in the river of Moirang, and he questioned them. "Ye women of Khumal, why do ye fish

From a Picture by BHUDRO SINGH.

KHAMBA AND THOIBI

(THE CAPTURE OF THE WILD BULL.)

p. 143

in the river of Moirang?[26] Have ye not the waters of Ikōp and Waithou?" And they answered him and said, "There is a great bull that lurks among the reeds that border the waters of Waithou, and already he has killed a man. So we dare not fish there." Then Kōngyamba feigned that the God Thāngjing had given him the gift of divination, and he stood before the King arrayed as a Maibi,[27] and the King asked him "Wherefore art thou come?" and Kōngyamba said, "The God Thāngjing has spoken in mine ears, and I have his behest upon me. Verily saith the God, I am sated with offerings of flesh and fish, but this year my heart longs for the sweet savour of the flesh of the mighty bull that lurks in the reeds that border the waters of Ikōp and Waithou. My servant Khamba vows that he will kill it for mine honour and for the welfare of the land, for he is a brave man and set to do some great feat of strength." So they summoned Khamba and asked him of his vow, and he denied it saying, "I have not vowed this vow." Then Kōngyamba feigned that Khamba had bribed him with gifts to tell this thing in the presence of the King, and taunted him that all his caste were liars. Then they fell to a quarrel before the King. This was an evil thing to do;[28] none may quarrel or utter words of wrath in the presence of the King. Then the King reproved them, and Khamba did obeisance before the King and said, "If the God will, may I do this thing? I will go, catch the bull." Then was the King pleased with Khamba, and swore that he would give him Thoibi to wife, and Thōnglen set seven marks on the lintel post of the *kangla*,[29] as a token of the King's oath. Then Thāngarakpa, wearing a gay headdress of many rare feathers, went with 60 men on an embassy to the King of Khumal to bear tidings of the great sport that was to be. He bare his message to the Khumal King, who sat in Durbar and talked thereon with his ministers. But they assented not till they heard that one man alone was coming to kill the bull and that he was of the Khumal stock. So they built *machāns*, 700 for the Khumal folk, and 700 for the Moirang folk. So all was made ready for the morrow. Then Khamnu, who had treasured many things in her heart, was ill at ease for Khamba, and said, "This great bull was once the Lord of thy father's herd. Go to him, speak thy Father's name in his ear, and show him this rope of silk."[30] Then Khamba set forth to find the bull. At first he found him not among the reeds. Then he went to a low hill and saw the bull, and went towards him calling him to tease him. Then the bull ran at him, but Khamba bent aside a little and the people cried out, "Art afraid?" but Khamba answered them, "I fear not; I seek a good stance." Then he stood on firm ground and caught the bull by the horns, and they swayed together as they strove for the mastery. Then Khamba rested on the neck of the bull, who carried him into the jungle. And Khamba spake his Father's name softly into the ear of the bull, and showed him the silken rope. Then the bull remembered the name of his Master and knew the rope, and himself tied it round his own neck. Then Khamba brought the bull to the place where stood Khamnu and Thoibi. Then Kōngyamba joined him there and said, "Let me help pull the bull along," and caught the rope, but the bull would not move, and Kōngyamba said, "Look, I have rescued Khamba. I share the reward. Khamba had fallen into a ditch." Then Kōngyamba's friends shouted aloud, "Lo, he has rescued Khamba," and the Kings were sore troubled to know what was right, so they bade Kōngyamba fight the bull in an enclosure, but he was afraid and climbed for safety into a *machān.* Then Khamba fought the bull bravely; he caught it by the tail suddenly, and then on a sudden let it go so that it fell on its knees. Then he seized it by its neck. Then the Kings did honour to Khamba and gave him many gifts, rich jewellery and clothing, and the Khumal King said to the Moirang King, "My brother, childless am I, let this man be my man and live with me," but the Moirang King would not, and on the morrow Khamba killed the bull in honour of the God Thāngjing. Then it was ordained that at this festival there should be the archery as was customary in honour of the God Thāngjing,[31] and that Kōngyamba should pick up the arrows shot by the King and Khamba should gather those shot by the Jubrāj. It fell out that the Jubrāj asked Thoibi to give him his coat of gold embroidery, but she had given it to Khamba. On the morrow when the target was set, the Maibas[32] sang a charm over the arrows and the bow of the King, and the King tried the bow and then loosed the arrows from the string. Kōngyamba stood there girt ready and ran to fetch the arrows which he gave back to the King. Then Khamba girded up his loins, and when the bow and arrows of the Jubrāj had been charmed, the Jubrāj shot and so swiftly ran Khamba to pick them, that his cloth was loosed, and the Jubrāj saw and knew the gold embroidered coat below. Wroth, indeed, was he, and when Khamba bowed himself to give him the arrow, he would not take it and turned his face away from him. Then Kōngyamba took the arrow from the hand of Khamba and gave it to the Jubrāj, who was pleased with him and said, "My daughter Thoibi is thine to wive. In five days will I send thee the marriage gifts." Then Nōngthōlba asked the Jubrāj, "Wherefore art thou wroth with Khamba?" and the Jubrāj said, "I like him not; I will not see his face." Then said Nōngthōlba, "Is thy daughter a fruit or a flower thus to be given away as a trifle of no worth? On the day when Khamba slew the bull, the King, thy brother, promised her in wedlock to Khamba, in token whereof I set seven notches upon the lintel of the *kangla* for men to see and know." Then the Jubrāj said, "That I know not, but what I have said, I have said.[83] My daughter I give to Kōngyamba." Then the King was vexed, and the Jubrāj went to his house and bade his wives get ready the marriage gifts, "for in five days I will give my daughter Thoibi in marriage to Kōngyamba." Then, lest Khamnu and Khamba should give him gifts on the appointed day, he ordained that none should sell fruits but by his leave, and leave to buy gave he only unto Kōngyamba, and to none other. But Khamba set forth to the village where dwelt Kabui Salang Maiba.[84] When he stood at the gate, the Nagas who kept watch and ward there, seized him and took his load straps from him, and haled him to the *pākhanvāl*[85] where sat the Maiba. Then Khamba said, "Wherefore have thy men seized me and taken my load straps from me? I am come hither to see my Father's friend the Salang Maiba." Then the Maiba plied him with questions and knew that he was indeed the son of his old friend, and sent off men to gather fruit for him. Then he showed Khamba the spot whereon his Father had done great deeds of valour in battle against the Kabuis. The men brought in two weighty baskets of fruits, and the Maiba added thereto of his store gifts for Thoibi and Khamnu and Khamba. Then Khamba took the fruit home and Thoibi set it ready in eleven dishes,[36] and talked with the chief Rāni, who promised to stand ready with ten of the queens and ten maids to receive the gifts. On the morrow Kōngyamba brought his gifts, but Thoibi lay sick with a fever, for an evil spirit had chanced in her path. So the Jubrāj sent Kōngyamba away, saying, "I will send my daughter anon, for she lies sick of a fever." After a while Thoibi arose. Then the Jubrāj himself ailed and lay him down to rest a while. Then Thoibi's maid Senu swept clean the northern portion of the verandah,[37] the place that folk call *māngsōk,*[38] that is set apart for the women, and threw the dust on the southern part that is called *phamen,* which is set apart for the men. Then she smeared the northern part with fresh mud. Then came the Rānis and sat in their places, and Khamba's gifts were set before them and they partook of them and gave of them to the people. And it chanced, even as Thoibi had planned, that her Father, the Jubrāj, who meanwhile had risen and gone with the King to see the men shoot in honour of the God Thāngjing, returned home parched with thirst and craving the juice of some acid fruit. He asked of the queens, his wives, "Have ye any acid fruit?" and they said, "Lord, we have none," but Thoibi said, "Father, I have fruit in my basket," and she brake the fruit into a silver cup and gave the juice to her father to drink, who relished it and said, "What fruit are these?" Then said Thoibi, "Men call them *chā kao* and *mak kao,*"[39] and her father saw not the guile in her answer and again said, "These are strange names. Whence come they?" Then said Thoibi, "Father, dost thou not know the fruit? They are the fruit which Khamba, thy son-in-law, has set before thee on his marriage."[40] At this the Jubrāj waxed wroth and threw his silver *huqa* at his daughter. Then Thoibi fainted as if in a trance wrought upon her by the skyey influence of Laimaren and Panthoibi.[41] The Jubrāj was greatly terrified thereat, and the women wailed over her. So he said to his daughter, "Child, daughter, wife of Khamba, arise and go to thy husband's kin." Then Thoibi arose, and the Jubrāj was wroth again. Then he sent men to summon Kōngyamba, and to say to Khamba, "Come to thy Lord, the Jubrāj, for he is minded to give thee gifts."[42] Then Kōngyamba gathered men together and met

From a Picture by Bhudro Singh.

p. 147.

KHAMBA and THOIBI

The Torture by the Elephant.)

Khamba by the way, and said to him, "Art thou minded to give up Thoibi?" and Khamba answered him and said, "Jest not with me, for I will not give her up." Then they quarrelled and fought, and Khamba threw the man upon the ground and knelt upon his belly and pressed his throat, and was minded to kill him, but the men that stood by, the friends of Kōngyamba, dragged him off and beat him and tore his clothes, and bound him so that he could not move. Then the Jubrāj came up on his great elephant and bade the men beat him. Then they made him fast to the elephant with ropes, but the *mahout* who bound him, knew that Khamba was innocent, and so bound him that he yet had space to breathe. Then they goaded the elephant, but the God Thāngjing stayed it so that it moved not. At last Kōngyamba took a spear and pricked it so that it moved with the pain. But it harmed not Khamba. Then the dawn broke and the men said "Khamba is dead," and they loosed him from the elephant and moved him away. In the darkness of the night the Goddess Panthoibi came in a dream to Thoibi and said, "Dost thou not know that thy man is bound by thy father's orders to the elephant and they have nearly killed him." Then Thoibi arose and girt her petticoat close to her, taking with her a knife. She found Khamba still tied, and cut the cords that still bound him, and chafed his limbs so that the blood ran through them. Then Khamba came to and knew Thoibi, and bade her send for Khamnu, and one went and fetched her. When she came, she wept for sorrow at the plight of her brother. Then Feiroijamba came and gave help. Then Nōngthōlba was very wroth for all they had done to Khamba, and bade his son tell it all to the Chirāp. Then the slaves of Thōnglen told their lord that Khamba was dead, for the men had bound him to the feet of the elephant, and he was very wroth and went to the Chirāp with all his men armed and girt ready. Then Feiroijamba told the Chirāp thrice how cruelly men had tried to kill Khamba, but the Jubrāj heeded not the complaint. Yet again Feiroijamba told them, and Nōngthōlba in his wrath said, "Who is this that dared to touch my son-in-law." Then said the Jubrāj, "I bade them kill Khamba, and I believed him dead. Vexed am I that he still lives and, therefore, am I not minded to hearken to this complaint." Then said Nōngthōlba, "My Lord, hast thou the power of life and death ?" Then the Jubrāj answered and said, "Such power have I." Then said Nōngthōlba, "As I live and while I hold mine office, none shall dare to kill my son-in-law. Upon me is the task of guarding this realm. My counsel is ever before the King. Let us before my Lord the King." So they joined hands and went before their Lord the King, and the King was wroth with the Jubrāj, for Thoibi had told him all that they had sought to do to her husband. And the King forbade the Jubrāj to come in, for he said, "Peradventure he seeks to drive me out, and is leagued with mine enemies the Angōms.[43] When he has killed all my captains that are mighty in battle, then will he kill me also." Then Thōnglen came to the palace with all his men armed and girt ready, and vowed that he would kill all those who had sought to kill Khamba; but Nōngthōlba pacified him saying, "Shall a man wrestle with that great elephant and not get hurt ?" So Thōnglen laid his anger aside. The King sent his own leech to minister to the hurts of Khamba, and sent daily gifts of food and money. And in the Durbar he asked Nōngthōlba to give him counsel, and he punished all those who had laid violent hands on Khamba, and the Jubrāj he set in prison, and bade him stay there till Khamba was well again. So Thoibi tended her husband and he was well again. So the King set the Jubrāj free and hoped that he would bear no malice against Khamba. Yet the Jubrāj called his wives and summoned Thoibi, but she was tending Khamba. Then he said, "Better be childless than be the father of this evil girl. Sell her to Kubo and let me never see her more." And he would not relent for all that they entreated him. So he summoned Hanjaba, and bade him take the girl to Tamurakpa,[44] and sell her and bring back the price in silver and gold. Then Thoibi told Khamba, and said, "Dear husband, for thy sake I go to Kubo at my father's bidding. Forget me not, for I will come back." At daybreak she did obeisance to her father and mother, and wept so that the cry of her lamentations was like the thunder, and her mother wept also and all the maids. Then she went to Hanjaba, who had the secret orders of her father to Tamurakpa. He took away all her jewellery, and set out with her. On the way she met Khamba, and he wept with her for the happy days that were gone, and the grief of their separation.

Then Khamba gave her a staff to lean on by the way, but Thoibi planted it by the road and bade it blossom forth with leaves if she kept her love true and chaste for Khamba,[45] and she set a mark upon a stone by the roadside as a token. Then she reached Kubo, where Tamurakpa counted out her price in gold and silver into the hand of Hanjaba. But Tamurakpa had pity on her sorrow and bade her go in and be with his daughter Changning Kanbi. The evil women of Kubo whispered to Changning, and persuaded her to send Thoibi forth to catch fish and gather fuel.[46] While she was busied with her task, she dreamed that Khamba was with her, doing even as she herself, but when she woke, she knew that it was but a dream. Then the God Thāngjing took pity on her, and Tamurakpa bade the women weave each of them a cloth, for he heard them wrangling. Changning sought to reproach Thoibi, and said, "Wayward child thou art. Thou had'st the chance of marrying Kōngyamba a goodly man, a scion of a famed race, stout and comely, yet thy love turned to Khamba." And Tamurakpa heard, and his anger was kindled against his daughter, and he was fain to strike her, but Thoibi stayed him. So they wove together, and in the night Changning tore holes with a porcupine quill in the cloth which Thoibi had woven,[47] for she was jealous. When Thoibi arose, she saw all that had been done, but she sat to and so skilfully mended all the holes that Tamurakpa preferred the cloth she had woven, and threw aside the cloth which his daughter had woven. Then, while she worked at the loom, a wind brought ashes far drifting upon the loom, and Thoibi knew that they had come from Moirang. Then she wept as she thought of her husband and her home, and the God softened the heart of her father, and he sent men to bring her home again. But he warned Kōngyamba and bade him meet her by the way. So Thoibi did obeisance to the Kubo God, and thanked Tamurakpa courteously as she went back with the men her father had sent. And when she had come to the place where was the stone on which she had set a mark as a token, she worshipped it and put gold and silver on it; and when she came to the place wherein she had planted the staff which Khamba gave her, she saw that it had blossomed forth with leaves. Then Kōngyamba was near and bade his men see if

Thoibi was coming, and they shouted, "Lo, the Princess is at hand." Then Thoibi heard the shout and bade the slaves that Tamurakpa had sent with her as tribute to the King, "Go on and sit near if the man is Khamba, but far apart if he be Kōngyamba." She went on and feigned friendship with him, and sat on his red cloth,[48] but placed a stick between them.[49] Then she asked for fruit, and Kōngyamba brought her fruit, but she would not eat for she feigned that she ailed after her sojourn in Kubo. Then she asked Kōngyamba to let her ride on his pony while he rode in her *dooli*. And he was not loth. Then when she was near home, she galloped off on the pony to Khamba's house, and he took her and they all wept for very joy. Then Kōngyamba was sore vexed, for the girl had tricked him, and his friends availed him not, and he sought to win the King's ministers to hearken to him, but Thōnglen and Nōngthōlba sent men to guard Khamba and Thoibi, and on the morrow the matter was set before the King in his Durbar, and he bade them settle the matter by the ordeal of the spear, but as he spake an old woman came forth and said, "My Lord King, there is a tiger in the jungle hard-by that we fear," and the King said, "Let the tiger bear witness herein. Unto him that kills the tiger, will I give the Princess Thoibi." So they summoned the *hui rai*,[50] and fenced round jungle, and on the morrow the King and his ministers gathered there in *machans*. So many folk were gathered there that it seemed like a white cloth spread on the ground. Then they twain did obeisance before the King, who laid his behest upon them, and bade them slay the tiger, and he feared for them lest the tiger kill them. So they went and sought the lair of the beast, and in it they found the body of a girl but newly killed. Then they found the tiger, and sought to spear it, but it turned the spears away as they threw them. Then the tiger sprang upon them and bit Kōngyamba so that he died, but Khamba wounded the beast, and drove it off. Then he carried Kōngyamba to the *machan*, wherein sat his father. And Thōnglen taunted Khamba, "What! art afraid? Thy father slew five tigers and thou fearest one. Go to, I will come and kill the beast." Then Khamba entered the jungle once more and found the tiger crouching in a hollow half hidden by the jungle, but in full view of the *machan* of the King. As the tiger leapt upon Khamba, he speared it through the ravening jaws, so that it died as it fell. Then the King gave rich gifts to Khamba, and bestowed upon him wide lands and rights of fishery, robes of honour, and titles of high fame, and made him master of a salt-well, and ordained that men should call him Pūkhramba.

Thereafter Khamba and Thoibi were wedded in high state, and after them Khamnu was wedded to Feiroijamba.

Now it chanced one day that fear entered into Khamba's heart that Thoibi his wife was faithless to him. So he sought to try her and pushed a stick through the wall.[51] Then Thoibi was very vexed at this and cried, "Who dares to annoy me? I am a chaste wife," and thrust the spear through the wall and pierced Khamba. Then he called her and she knew his voice, and went out and carried him in, and was sore stricken with grief when she saw that he was wounded unto the death. As he lay, ere he died, she slew herself upon him, so the funeral flames ate their two bodies on one pyre. Gods were they, not as mortals,[52] and to them was denied the happiness of long life and children.[53]

NOTES.

1. The Panji Loisang, or College of Astrologers, is a great institution in Manipur, and its mysteries are not yet known in any degree.

2. The succession to the youngest son is by no means uncommon and is the centre of many legends among the hill people. Cf. p. 83.

3. The reeds which surround the low-lying marsh lands are often fired, and are inhabited by game of all sizes and quality. I have seen leopards driven out in this way.

4. Nowadays the horoscope is cast and the name selected in accordance with the precepts of Hindu lore.

5. The belief in possession by an evil spirit as the cause of illness is interesting, and explains the dual function of the *maiba* as the doctor and exorciser of evil spirits. Cf. p. 96 and p. 109.

6. Sati is a modern interpolation.

7. Women suckle children up to a considerable age in Manipur, and Khamba is said to have been "breast-fed" till almost adult.

8. The definite association of Panthoibi and Thāngjing with dreams is notable.

9. Khumalpōkpa = Progenitor of the Khumals. It will be remembered that Khamba is of Khumal origin.

10. An oath of this nature is very binding. We may compare it with the Kuki oath on the water poured over a gun barrel.

11. The technical names of the followers of a great man are: (*a*) *Loin* or *lois* who follow; (*b*) *Khāmin*, or voluntary followers who serve a great man; (*c*) *Haija*, persons who have some petition to make from *hai* to speak and *ja* or *cha* the suffix of humility; (*d*) *Chacha* are of a similar class to the last-mentioned.

12. Acceptance by Khamnu of these gifts is equivalent to betrothal with Feiroi-jamba.

13. Each side has a varying degree of importance, and the north is highly favoured.

14. Puns of this kind are much appreciated in Manipur. The aspirate is not very distinct.

15. The Ningon Lakpa is a Court official who had charge of the young ladies.

16. This is a common method of annoying a neighbour.

17. These were Lois, and the renovation of a house is no long matter.

18. Leikeirakpa, an official who looks after *leikei* or quarters of a village.

19. Superstitions of this kind are common in Manipur and Khamba readily believes it.

20. The bundle of grass is lowered as the signal to start.

21. The races are not fairly run, as hustling is permitted.

22. Khādarakpa is the title of a Court official at Moirang.

23. The *nōngshā* or lion here described is commonly held to be a Meithei emblem, but it is here associated with Royalty at Moirang.

24. The sports of Manipur are fully described above. See pp. 49 *seq*.

25. The hut was built of light lattice work, and the process of consulting a familiar spirit is technically and euphemistically known as *kharai changba*, literally to go into the latticed hut. The reason why a latticed hut is employed is to permit the spirit to enter and depart freely, which was denied to it in heavily-thatched houses or in *pucca* buildings. It is clear that Kōngyamba is recognized as having recourse to very shabby devices to defeat Khamba.

26. Each village has its recognized boundaries, and the jurisdictions of such tribal divisions as existed were also demarcated. It is worthy of note that the Moirang and the Khumal tribes each seems to have been associated with a definite locality.

27. Maibis are priestesses. See section above under "Priesthood," p. 109.

28. The use of words of evil import in the presence of the King was a dire offence. It is comparable with the old idea that fighting a duel in the precincts of the Court at St. James' was treason and punishable as such.

29. The Kangla is the Royal Hall of Coronation.

30. The curious may parallel this episode in that very modern novel, "The Car of Destiny."

31. The ceremony *ū kai kāppa* (*ū* = wood, *kai* = split, from *khai*, and *kāppa* = to shoot; it is just possible that *kai* = granary) has now been absorbed into the ritual of the Durga Puja, and takes place on the last day of the Puja. I am inclined to connect it with such a rite as that practised by the Kabuis, who place a straw image at the village gate and throw spears at it. The success or failure of the village lads affects the prosperity of the crops. The feature of the rite *ū kai kāppa* was that the

swiftest runners gathered the arrows as they were shot and brought them back.

32. The *maibas* are the ministers of the ancient animistic cults, and charm by their magic the implements used on all these occasions. The participation even to-day of a *maiba* in any religious ceremony is a sure proof that the ceremony is not Hindu in origin.

33. The exigencies of translation have revealed a curious anticipation of political oratory.

34. I do not know what were the exact relationships of the Salang Maiba, who seems to be a representative of Moirang in a Naga village.

35. The Pākhanvāl, or Bachelors' Hall, is an institution of very great importance in the Hill villages, and there is reason to believe that in early times it existed in Manipur. The question of the social importance of this institution will be discussed in a later volume.

36. The odd number is lucky. Compare the rain *puja* among the Tangkhuls, where the number of persons taking part is eleven also.

37. Each part of the house has its proper designation.

38. *Māngsōk*, the name of the part reserved for the women, is derived from *māng* = to pollute and *sōk* = to touch. *Phamen* = *pham*, to sit.

39. *cha kao* = *cha*, child and *kao*, to forget ; *mak kao* = *mak*, son-in-law and *kao*, to forget. We may compare *lūkhra pākhra*, widows and widowers, the name given to "speargrass" by the Manipuris.

40. The Jubrāj had partaken of Khamba's gifts, and would be held to have recognized him.

41. Laimaren and Panthoibi are deities of Pre-Hindu days. See section above on "Religion," pp. 97, 98.

42. This is formal recognition of the tie which had been created between the two. It is thus clear that there are two things essential for marriage according to the incidents of this story. The first is cohabitation, and the second is the exchange of gifts. In the scene in the house of Khamba when Thoibi worships the Khumal God in the corner, they are represented as cohabiting. Cf. note 12 above.

43. This curious association of the Angōms with treasonable practices is notably exemplified by instances in Manipur history, where the Angōm Ningthou was often the head and centre of disaffection and rebellion. The Angōm Ningthou is almost always closely associated by marriage with the Meithei Ningthou.

44. Tamurakpa is the *lakpa* appointed to reside at Tamu in the Kubo valley, and act as agent there.

45. The story of the staff that puts forth leaves in proof of the chastity of the woman who plants it is well known.

46. Thoibi is set to these menial tasks in order to humiliate her. The women of Kubo are not held in very great esteem by the Manipuris.

47. Compare Penelope's web.

48. Persons holding office are entitled to have a red cloth carried before them on which they sit. Cf. p. 13, *supra*.

49 When the man desires to keep separate from the woman whom he has married, he may place a sword or spear between them. This custom, which is described in *Romania*, Vol. 36, No. 141, pp. 36, *seq.*, 1907, is connected with the *tabu* prohibiting intercourse between warriors and their wives. This incident here is of importance, as the barrier is raised by the woman whose weapon is the stick, possibly the lineal descendant

of the digging-stick. By doing this Thoibi keeps Kõngyamba at a distance.

50. The *hui rai* are the trackers and scouts. *Hui* = dog and *rai* = to own. See section on hunting, p. 46, *supra*.

51. This is the usual signal to call a woman from her house. The mat wall is not damaged, and the lady within knows what is meant.

52. It is commonly believed that both Khamba and Thoibi were of giant size. This belief is not borne out by the clothes said to have belonged to them which are shown still at the shrine of Thãngjing near Moirang. I have seen them, and while they do not in general differ from the present costume, the patterns of the embroidery is not modern.

53. The translation which I possess omits several comic interludes in which Nongthõlba plays an important part. The interludes tend to increase in number, and the recitation of the ballad occupies two days at least. The pictures which illustrate it are by Bhudro Sing, a native Manipuri artist, who, if my recollection serves me aright, painted them while in jail undergoing a spell of imprisonment.

From a Picture by BHUDRO SINGH.

KHAMBA AND THOIBI
(THE TIGER HUNT.)

p. 154.

SECTION VI.

LANGUAGE.

We owe to the labours of Dr. Grierson and his colleague, Dr. Konow, the definite classification of the dialects spoken in the Manipur State. We are in this volume concerned with Meithei only, and of it, following strictly the conclusions of our authority, we may first say that it belongs to the Tibeto-Burman group of languages. In the next place it is assigned to the Kuki-Chin group, thus differentiating it from the Bodo, Naga and Kachin groups, while in regard to the other dialects (Northern Chin, Central Chin, Old Kuki, Southern Chin), which, for old association's sake, are assigned to the same group, it occupies a distinct and separate position.

This summary is a bald statement of the conclusions which are advanced in the relevant volumes of the *Report of the Linguistic Survey of India*, and it may be convenient to mention some of the facts to which Dr. Grierson invites attention. In the first place, Meithei has affinities with Burmese, especially in regard to the following points, the second personal pronoun and the adjectival prefix, while it agrees with Tibetan rather than with Burmese, as in the case of the suffix *pa* (Meithei) which exercises "almost all the functions of the corresponding Tibetan suffix."

There are many points of resemblance between Meithei and the languages of the Bodo group, and as they extend to structure as well as to vocabulary, the close relation between the two to which Mr. Davis drew attention in 1891,* must be held to be

* Census Report, pp. 163, *seq.*

satisfactorily proved. So also with regard to the Naga group; while of the relations of Meithei to the Kachin group, Dr. Grierson remarks that the two are closely connected, and that Meithei must be considered as the link between Kachin and the Kuki-Chin groups. Of its relationship to the numerous dialects composing the Kuki-Chin group, Dr. Grierson states that it must be held to be an independent member of the group with points of agreement, not only with the northern dialects but with the southern members as well, though differing from all in many essential points.

To make these conclusions more clear it will be useful to employ a scheme of comparison by which these facts will be exhibited. I propose firstly, to compare the structure of Meithei in the following points, (*a*) numerals, (*b*) negatives, (*c*) plurals, (*d*) relatives, (*e*) order of words, with the corresponding points in Tibetan and Burmese, then with the same points in Kachari (Bodo), in a typical Naga dialect such as Ao Naga, in Kachin in the next place, and lastly, with the same points in Thādo as representing the northern Chin sub-group, in Lushei as typical of the Central Chin sub-group, in Rangkhol as belonging to the Old Kuki sub-group, and in Khāmi as the representative of the Southern Chin sub-group. The same method of comparison will be employed in order to show similarities of vocabulary, although the comparison must be limited to a small number of elementary words. It would have been impossible to attempt this scheme without the comparative tables in the *Linguistic Survey Report*.*

To the kindness of Mr. J. E. Bridges, Reader of Burmese at the University of London, University College, I owe the notes on Burmese and the lists of Burmese words which appear below.

In the sketch of the grammar of Meithei which follows, no mention is made of irregularities and unusual forms, which are numerous enough and which will be dealt with at length in a separate volume.

* Vol. iii., part iii., pp. 10–14.

TABLE A 1.

Word.	Meithei.	Tibetan.	Burmese.
one	amā	chig	tit, ta
two	anī	nyi	hnit
three	ahūm	sum	thōn
four	marī	shi	lé
five	mangā	nga	ngā
six	tarūk	dhuk	chauk
seven	taret	dun	kun-hnit
eight	nipān	gya	shit
nine	māpan	gu	kō
ten	tārā	chu	tă-hse
eleven	tārāmathoi	chuchig	hsè-tit
twelve	tārānithoi	chunyi	hsè-hnit
thirteen	tārāhūmthoi	chusum	hsè-thōn
fourteen	tārāmari	chuzhi	hsè-lé
fifteen	tārāmangā	chunga	hsè-ngā
sixteen	tārātaruk	chudhug	hsè-chauk
seventeen	tārātaret	chudun	hsè-kun-nhit
eighteen	tārānipān	chogya	hsè-shit
nineteen	tārāmāpan	chugu	hsè-kō
twenty	kūl	nyi shu	hnă hsè
thirty	kūnthrā	sum chu	thōn zè
forty	nīphū	zhichu	le-zè
fifty	yāngkhai	nga chu	ngā-zè
sixty	hūmphū	dug chu	chauk·hsè
seventy	hūmphūtārā	dun chu	kun-hn ă-hsè
eighty	mariphū	gya chu	shit-hsè
ninety	mariphūtārā	gu chu	kō-ze
one hundred	chāmā	gya	tayā
two hundred	chāni	nyi gya	hnă-yā

TABLE A 2.

Word.	Meithei.	Bodo (Kachāri).	Ao Naga.	Kachin.
one	amā	māshī	kā	ai
two	anī	māginni	ānā	ni (lakhaung)†
three	ahūm	māgatām	āsam	masūm
four	mari	mābri	peza	mali
five	mangā	māboa	pungu	ma-ngā
six	tarūk	mādo	terok	khrū
seven	taret	māsinni	tenet	sinit
eight	nipān	mājai	tī	masat
nine	māpan	māsugū	tako	chakhu
ten	tārā	mājī	ter	si
eleven	tāramathoi		terika	shi langai
twelve	tāranithoi	zakhai tham*	teri ānā	shi lakhaung
thirteen	tārahūmthoi	zakhai tham se	teri āsam	shi masūm
fourteen	tāramari	zakhai tham ne	teri peza	shi mali
fifteen	tāramangā	zakhai tham tham	teri pungu	shi mangā
sixteen	tāratarūk	zakhai bre	metsa-māben terok	shi khiū
seventeen	tārataret	zakhai bre se	metsa-māben tenet	shi sinit
eighteen	tāranipān	zakhai bre ne	metsa-māben ti	shi masat
nineteen	taramapan	zakhai bre tham	metsa-māben tako	shi chakhu
twenty	kūl	zakhaiba	metsa	khūn (Eastern)
thirty	kūnthrā	zakhai sni ne	senar	hsūm shi (Eastern)
forty	niphū	zakhai zu	līr	nili shi (Eastern)
fifty	yāngkhai	madan	tenem	mangā si
sixty	hūmphū	—	rōkar	khrih si
seventy	hūmphūtārā	—	tenem ser metsa	sinit si
eighty	mariphū	—	lir ānāsa	masat si
ninety	mariphūtārā	—	telang takō	chakhu si
one hundred	chāmā	rajā-shi	meirang	la-chā
two hundred	chāni	--	—	ni-sa (Eastern)

* Plains Kachari. Cf. Grierson, *op. cit.*, p. 132.
† See Hertz Grammar, p. 12.

TABLE A 3.

Word.	Meithei.	Thādo.	Lushei.	Rangkhol.	Khāmi.
one	amā	khat	pa-khat	enkāt	hā
two	ani	ni	pa-hnih	enni	ni
three	ahūm	thūm	pa-thum	en tūm	katun
four	mari	li	pa-li	mīlī	mali
five	mangā	ngā	pa-nga	ringah	pangnga
six	tarūk	gūp	pa-ruk	garak	ta-u
seven	taret	sagi	pa-sari	sārī	sari
eight	nipān	get	pa-riat	garīt	kaya
nine	māpan	kō	pa kua	guōk	tako
ten	tārā	som	shom	shōm	hasuh
eleven	tāramathoi	som le khat	shom-leh-pa-khat	shōm le kāt	—
twelve	tāranithoi	som le ni	shom-leh-pa-hūih	shōm le enni	—
thirteen	tārahūmthoi	som le thūm	shom-leh-pa-thum	shōm le entum	—
fourteen	tāramari	som le li	shom-leh-pa-li	shōm le mīli	—
fifteen	tāramangā	som le ngā	shom-leh-pa-nga	shōm le ringah	—
sixteen	tāratarūk	som le gūp	shom-leh-pa-ruk	shōm le garūk	—
seventeen	tārataret	som le sagi	shom-leh-pa-sari	shōm-le sārī	—
eighteen	tāranipān	som le get	shom-leh-pa-riat	shōm le garīt	—
nineteen	tāramāpan	som le ko	shom-leh-pa-kua	shōm le guōk	—
twenty	kūl	som ni	shom-hnih	shōm ni	kusuh
thirty	kūnthrā	som thūm	shom-thūm	shōm tūm	ku-i-thun
forty	niphū	som li	shom-li	shōm mīlī	ku-i-mali
fifty	yāngkhai	som ngā	shom-ngā	shōm rin-gah	ku-i-pang-nga
sixty	hūmphū	som gūp	shom-ruk	shōm ga-rūk	—
seventy	hūmphūtārā	som sagi	shom-sari	shōm sārī	—
eighty	mariphū	som get	shom riat	shōm garīt	—
ninety	mariphūtārā	som kō	shom kua	shōm guōk	—
one hundred	chāmā	yā khat	za khat	rajā kāt	tarā
two hundred	chāni	yā ni	za ni	raja ni	—

TABLE B 1.

Noun.	Meithei.	Tibetan.	Burmese.
house	yum *or* im	khyim	ein
fire	mei	mē	mī
water	ising	chhū	ye
earth	lei	sā	myé (lè = rice field)
eye	mit	mik	myet
hand	khut	lakpa	let
head	kōk	go	gaung
pig	ōk	phakpa	wet
dog	hui	khyi	hkwé
bird (hen)	yel	jhā	hnget
egg	yērum	gong-nā	u
see	ū-ba	—	myin
eat	chā-ba	so	sā
drink	tak-pa	thung	thauk
speak	hai-ba	ser-shu	pyaw (hū = to declare)
ask	hang-ba (ni-ba)		me
good	a-pha-ba	yag-po	kaung
bad	pha-ta-ba	dūk po	hsō
north	awāng (lam)		myauk
south	makhā (lam)		taung
east	nongpōk (lam)		a-shé
west	nongchūp (lam)		a-nauk
woman	nupī	mi-mo	meim-ma
child	-cha	phugu	kălé
cloth	phī	gō	a-htè
tree	ū (sing = bush-wood)	shing dong	thitpin
leaf	(ū) ma-nā		ywet
sun	nong, nūmīt	nyi-ma	ne
moon	thā	dāwā	la
year	chahi		hnit

TABLE B 2.

Noun.	Meithei.	Bodo (Kachari).	Ao Naga.	Kachin.
house	yum *or* im	no	kī	ntā wa
fire	mei	wai	mī	wan
water	ising	dī	tzā	kha-nsin
earth	lei	ha	—	ka
eye	mit	mū	tenak	mit-myi
hand	khut	yao	ket	lata
head	kōk	kōrō	tokolāk	bōng
pig	ōk	—	—	wa
dog	hui	shīsha	āza	gui
bird (hen)	yel	dau-zu	oza	wū
egg	yērum	dau-dui	—	ti
see	ū-ba	—	—	mu-ai
eat	chā-ba	jī zā	chi	sha-ai
drink	tak-pa	lang	—	lu-ai
speak	hai-ba	—	—	sun-ai
ask	hang-ba (ni-ba)	(bi) (sangnu)	—	hsan-ai
good	a-pha-ba	hāmbī	tāzung	kaja
bad	pha-ta-ba	ā	ta-ma-zung	n'kaja
north	awāng (lam)	—	—	nda-de kha-khu *
south	makhā (lam)	—	—	nda de kha-nam de *
east	nongpōk (lam)	—	—	jan pru dē
west	nongchūp (lam)	—	—	jan shang dē
woman	nupi	māsaing jū	lār	nūm
child	-cha	ansā	tānur	-sha
cloth	phī	hi	—	pun ram
tree	ū	Bangfang	—	hpun
leaf	(ū) ma-na	—	—	lap
sun	nong, nūmit	shāin	āna	jan
moon	thā	dāi	ī	shata
year	chahi	lai-zau	—	shaning

* Cf. Hertz, *op. cit.*, p. 99.

TABLE B 3.

Noun.	Meithei.	Thādo.	Lushei.	Rangkhol.	Khami.
house	yum *or* im	in	in	in	in
fire	mei	mei	mei	mē	mai
water	ising	tui	tui	dui	tui
earth	lei	lei	lei	erneng	ka-lai-hong
eye	mit	mit	mit	mit	a-mi
hand	khut	khut	kut	kūt	aku
head	kōk	lū	lu	lu	alu
pig	ōk	vōk	vōk	vōk	wet
dog	hui	hui	ui	ui	ui
bird (hen)	yel	ā	vā	ār	kava
egg	yērum	ātui	vātui	ārdui	du
see	ū-ba	mū-ba	hmu	enroshe	—
eat	chā-ba	ne	ei	āfākrōshe	tsā
drink	tak-pa	don	in	—	nei
speak	hai-ba	ti	thu shoi	atiroshe	tapē
ask	hang-ba	dong	zawt	—	—
good	a-pha-ba	pha	tha	āsā	hui
bad	pha-ta-ba	pha-lo	tha-lo	shā-māk	s'hau
north	awāng (lam)	tui-nā (lam)	hmār-lam	—	—
south	makhā (lam)	tui-tā (lam)	chhim-lam	—	—
east	nongpōk (lam)	ni-shō (lam)	chhak-lam	mīsā āsh-ūok	—
west	nongchūp (lam)	ni-hlūm (lam)	thlang-lam	—	—
woman	nupi	nūmei	hmei chhia	dōnmāgtē (girl)	—
child	-cha	-cha	fa	naite nai-pang	—
cloth	phī	pōn	puan	pūn	
tree	ū	thing	thing	ting	akūn
leaf	(ū) ma-nā	thing-na	hnah	nā ting-nā	—
sun	nong, nūmit	ni	ni	misā	kani
moon	thā	hla	thlā	tā	la
year	chāhi *	kum	kum	kūm	—

* *Kum* occurs in Meithei as *hā-kūm* = last year. *Kūm-si* = this year. *Kum* is the vegetal year.

Meithei Numerals.—Of the simple numerals, those for eight and nine require special mention. *Nipān* and *māpan* seem to mean two "off" and one "off" respectively. Something not unlike this is found among the higher numerals in Ao Naga and Angami Naga.* The addition of what seems to be an otiose syllable *thoi* to the numerals, eleven, twelve, thirteen is notable. *Kūl* = twenty, is paralleled by the Eastern Kachin word *Khun*. *Kūnthrā* = *kūl tārā*. It is possible to equate the Meithei *tārā* = ten with the Ao Naga *ter*. In Meithei the higher numbers above forty are formed by multiplying in scores, the multiplier being prefixed to the word *phū* = score. Fifty (*yāngkhai*) may be resolved into *yāng* † = *chā* = one hundred, and *khai* = to divide, to half, cf. *makhai* = half. Sixty is three score. Seventy = three score plus ten. It will be noticed that the multiplier precedes and the addendum follows. In multiplying hundreds the multiplier follows the word (*chā*) for hundred.

Tibetan Numerals.—The Tibetan system of numerals follows a constant rule. The multiplier precedes while the addendum follows the theme, which is by decimals. Thus five hundred and ninety-two would be five hundreds, nine tens, two.‡

Burmese Numerals.—The Burmese system resembles the Tibetan, and is based on tens, not on scores, as in Meithei.

Kachari Numerals.§—Here we have a very curious system based on "fours." Thus we have *zakhai zu* = 40. *Zakhai* = four and *zu* = ten. For numbers intermediate between exact multiplication we have the rule that the multiplier immediately follows the "four," while the addendum come next. Thus *zakhai tham tham* = $4 \times 3 + 3 = 15$. This method carries us only up to 40, and is only used by the "Plains Kacharis."

Ao Naga Numerals.—Reference has been made to the meaning of the numerals 16, 17, 18, 19, in this language.‖ The forms for six, seven and ten, resemble those in Meithei. The higher numerals are formed on distinct lines. The forms for 30, 40, 50 and 60 are, so far as I can see, not "multiplied numerals."

* *Linguistic Survey Report*, vol. iii. part ii. p. 266.

† Cf. Burmese *yā*.

‡ Jaeschke, p. 15.

§ Endle, Kachari Grammar, pp. 12, 13. Grierson, *op. cit.*, Government Census Report, 1891, p. 159.

‖ See above.

The form for 70 is analysable into 50 + 20: that for 80 = twice 40. I cannot solve the mystery of *telang tako* = 90, for *telang* = 100, while *tako* = nine.*

Kachin Numerals.—Mention has been made of the similarity between the Meithei *kūl* = 20, and Kachin *khun* = 20. The higher numerals are formed by tens, the multiplier preceding the ten.†

Thādo Numerals.—The formation proceeds by tens throughout, the multiplier following the ten and the addendum being marked by the conjunction *le.*‡

Lushei Numerals.—The Lushei system resembles that of the Thādos as above described.§

Rangkhol Numerals.—It is interesting to observe that Rangkhol, which forms its higher numerals as Lushei and Thādo, has the syllable *rūk* in its word for six, like Meithei and Lushei, but not Thādo.||

Khāmi Numerals.—So far as my materials go, it seems that the higher numerals follow the use of Thādo, Lushei and Rangkhol in suffixing the multiplier.¶

It will be seen that up to one hundred the Meithei numerals show points of likeness to Tibetan numerals, where the multiplier precedes, and in the formation of "hundreds" follows the Kuki-Chin system where the multiplier follows the multiplicand. Resemblances of form as well as of formation are as widely and as strangely distributed.

PLURALS.

In Meithei the plural sign is often omitted. Where the fact of plurality is to be emphasized, the suffix *sing* is added to nouns denoting human beings, as *nupi sing* = the women. The same emphasis is obtained by using words as *yām,* which means many, as *mī-yām* = a crowd of men.

* Grierson, *op. cit.*, p. 273.

† See Hertz, Grammar, p. 13. Grierson, *loc. cit.*, p. 519.

‡ Hodson, Thādo Grammar, p. 17.

§ Lorrain and Savidge, Lushei Grammar, p. 8.

|| Soppitt, Grammar, p. 37.

¶ Grierson, *op. cit.*, vol. iii. part iii. pp. 351, 361.

In Tibetan the plural sign is often omitted, when, from circumstances, the fact of plurality is clear; but such words as "all," "many," and numerals, are used as plural affixes in addition to the usual affixes *nam* and *dag*.*

In Burmese the plural of nouns is formed by adding *myā* (which means many) or *do* to the singular. In colloquial *myā do* are both used together.

The plural suffix in Kachāri is *fur*,† which is used with nouns denoting inanimate as well as animate objects.

The plural affix in Ao is the suffix *tam*, which may be connected with the Thādo *tam* = many.‡

In Kachin the plural affix is suffixed to the noun and words of plurality such as *ni*, *bok*, *theng*, *yong*, which mean, heap, crowd, etc., are used.§

The plural affixes in Thādo are *hō* and *tē*, which are used with nouns of living objects, and *tampi* (*tam* = many, plus *pi* the magnitive suffix) and *ngē* with other nouns.‖

The plural suffixes in Lushei are *te*, *ho te-ho*, *ho-te*, *zong-zong*, and *zong-zong-te*.¶

There is only one plural suffix used in Rangkhol, *hai*.**

The plural suffixes in Khāmi are apparently *nai* and *na*, but words meaning "much" or "many" can be added to convey the idea of plurality.††

NEGATIVES.

In Meithei the negatives are the suffixes *da* or *ta*, *loi* (used only in the future tense of the verb), and *ganu* (used in the imperative). These suffixes follow the verbal root immediately, as root *pha* = good, *pha-ta-ba* = bad. The word *māi* is used in common speech as meaning "it is not." This word is derived from a lost root *mak*, a negative form in use among many other Tibeto-Burman tribes. It is formed on the known analogy of the word *lai*, which we know to be derived from *lak* = to come.

* Jaeschke, p. 11. † Endle, *op. cit.*, p. 9.
‡ Grierson, *loc. cit.*, p. 273.
§ Hertz, *op. cit.*, p. 5. Grierson, *loc. cit.*, p. 506.
‖ Hodson, *op. cit.*, p. 9. ¶ Lorrain and Savidge, *op. cit.*, p. 3.
** Soppitt, *op. cit.*, p. 34. †† Grierson, *loc. cit.*, p. 350.

The final consonant is elided as is common, this produces a lengthening of the vowel in the root, and the letter *i* represents the verbal sign of present time.

In Tibetan the prefix *ma* has a negative force, and is used with the verbal root. Negative adjectives are formed by the affixes *ma, mi, med,* and others, which are suffixed to the root thus modified.

In Burmese the negation is expressed by prefixing *mă* and omitting the temporal affix *thi* in the present and past tenses. In the future tense the negation is expressed by using *mă hok* (lit. " not true ") after the future affix *myi.*

In the imperative the negation is expressed by *mă* preceding the verb, and *hnin* (colloquial *nè*) following it.

In Kachāri * the suffix *a,* which is attached directly to the verbal *stem,* effects negation in all except the imperative tense, where the negative affix is *dā* and is prefixed to the verbal root.

In Ao Naga the usual negative is *ma* which precedes the verb, but in the imperative the form *ta* or *te* is used.†

In Kachin the usual negative is *n* suppressed, which is prefixed to the word or in compounds to the second part of the compound. With imperatives the prefixes *khum* and *phung* are used.‡

In Thādo the usual negatives are *hi* and *po* in the present tenses, *lo* and *hi* in the past, and *po* in the future. In the imperative *hi* is used. These affixes are found immediately after the stem (not the root) of the verb. In the future tenses the negative infixes follow the root and precede the tense suffix.§

In Lushei the negative suffix is *loh* which is affixed to the root, but in the imperative tense the suffix *shu* is used. There are also found in use the suffixes *nem* and *nang.*‖

In Rangkhol the negative suffixes *māk, nimāk* and *lō* are used.¶

* Endle, *op. cit.*, p. 24.
† Grierson, *loc. cit.*, p. 277.
‡ Hertz, *op. cit.*, p. 19. Grierson, *loc. cit.*, p. 509.
§ Hodson, *op. cit.*, pp. 18–24.
‖ Lorrain and Savidge, *op. cit.*, pp. 27, 28.
¶ Soppitt, *op. cit.*, p. 44.

The negative suffix in Khāmi is *o*, but the suffix *lo* is found. It is probably derived, as Dr. Grierson remarks, from the Burmese *lo* = to be wanting.*

RELATIVES.

The relative construction in Meithei is notable. It consists in the use of the verbal root with the suffix *pa* (or *ba*). Thus, "Ai-na ngarang yei-ba mī adu chenkhre;" lit. "By me yesterday strike man that run away has;" "The man I struck yesterday has run away." Or again, "Ai-gī pōt hū-ba mi adu phā-rak-pa ni-pa adu-da lūpā amāpi-gani;" lit. "Me of things steal man that arrest come man that to rupee one give will;" "I will give one rupee to the man who arrests the man who stole my things."

The relative construction in Tibetan is effected by a participial construction employing the suffixes *pō* (masculine) and *mō* (feminine), which are sometimes found attached to the simple root and sometimes to the participle in *pa*.†

There is no relative pronoun in Burmese, and its place is taken by the adjective connective *thaw* or *thi*. The order in Burmese of the sentence "The woman who cooked the rice is my mother," would be, "The rice cooked who the woman of me mother is."

There is no relative pronoun in Kachāri,‡ and a participial construction is employed.

The suffix *ba* in Ao and the suffix *er* are employed as relative participles, being added to the verbal root.§

The relative construction in Kachin is effected by the participle in *dai*. As in Ao, the interrogative pronoun is used as a relative.‖

The suffix *pa* is commonly used as a relative in Thādo; but I have found the verbal root with the (conventionally termed) antecedent noun immediately following it, having the force of a relative. It may be noted that the pronominal

* Grierson, *loc. cit.*, p. 354. † Jaeschke, p. 20, *sq.*
‡ Cf. Endle, *op. cit.*, p. 21. § Grierson, *loc. cit.*, p. 274.
‖ Hertz, *op. cit.*, p. 10. Grierson, *loc. cit.*, p. 508.

prefixes which are used with nouns and verbs, are not used with the verb in this relative construction.*

The relative construction in Lushei is expressed by relative participles or verbal nouns. Sometimes the demonstrative pronoun is used as a "kind of correlative." The plural suffix *te* can be suffixed to the verb in order to put the antecedent noun in the plural.†

The relative construction in Rangkhol as in Ao, is occasionally evolved from an interrogative pronoun, but more usually from a verbal participial.‡

The relative participle is used in Khāmi in much the same manner as in Meithei, though the evidence is not as clear as could be wished.§

INTERROGATIVE SENTENCES.

In Meithei we find a grammatical distinction between sentences involving as answer a simple affirmative or a simple negative, and those sentences which involve an extended answer. As regards form, we may say that where it is necessary to use interrogative words such as who, why, where, when, etc., the form of the verb differs from that used when the simple question is asked. Thus—

Nang Meithei lei-pāk-ta chat-pra, chat-ta-pra.
You Meithei country to going are, going not are.
Are you journeying to Manipur or not ?

Kari-gi damak Meithei leipāk-ta chat-page (*or* chat-pa-no).
What of cause Meithei country to going are.
Why are you going to Manipur ?

In the written works in Tibetan it seems that the suffix *am* is employed to mark an interrogative sentence, but it (or one of its variant forms) is omitted in the latter member of a double question, and when an interrogative pronoun or adverb occurs in the sentence.

In Burmese the interrogative affix *law* (colloquial *lă*) is used

* Hodson, *op. cit.*, p. 32. † Lorrain and Savidge, *op. cit.*, p. 13.
‡ Soppitt, *op. cit.*, p. 38. Grierson, *loc. cit.*, p. 185.
§ Grierson, *loc. cit.*, p. 352.

at the end of the sentence when the answer is simply "yes" or "no," and the affix *nī* (colloquial *lè*) in questions to which the answer is not simply "yes" or "no."

The distinction between simple and extended questions does not appear to be recognized in Kachāri.

There does not seem to be any distinction in Ao between simple and extended interrogations.

There is a formal distinction in Kachin between simple and alternative interrogative sentences. In the latter the particle *kun* is used, while in the former the interrogative particles *i ma,* and *kha,* which are suffixed to the verb, are employed.*

In Thado the use of alternative sentences in interrogation is very marked.†

Interrogative particles are freely used in Lushei, but there does not seem to be a clear demarcation between simple and extended interrogations.‡

The interrogative particle in common use in Khāmi seems to be *mo,* and the evidence for any distinction between simple and extended interrogations is not clear enough for any opinion to be offered.§

ORDER OF WORDS.

In simple sentences in Meithei the order is subject, indirect object, direct object, verb. The position of the subject and the verb is fixed, and between them are placed adverbs of time, manner, etc. We may note the order in the following typical sentences:—

Ai-na ma-ngon-da lūpā amā pigani.
Me by him to rupee one give will.
I will give him one rupee.

Ai-na mā-bu ngarang ū-re.
Me by him yesterday seeing was.
I saw him yesterday.

---

* Grierson, *loc. cit.*, p. 509. † Hodson, *op. cit.*, p. 34.
‡ Lorrain and Savidge, *op. cit.*, p. 15, and pp. 26, 27.
§ Grierson, *loc. cit.*, p. 353.

It may be noted that if it were desired to emphasize the fact that I saw the man *yesterday*, the order in ordinary speech might be "Ngarang ai-na mā-bu ū-re" = "Yesterday I saw him."

Jaeschke states the invariable rule in Tibetan to be, that in a simple sentence all words must precede the verb, while the order in which the subject, direct and indirect objects are placed is not so strictly defined. Adverbs and adverbial phrases of place and time are put at the head of the sentence.*

In Burmese *in a simple sentence* the subject or the object may come first, according as emphasis is placed on the one or the other, but the verb with its particles is *always* placed last.

The relative clause always precedes the noun or pronoun which is its antecedent in English.

In a complex sentence the principal clause is always placed last, and the subordinate clauses precede it; but the subject of the principal clause may be placed before the subordinate clauses.

In Kachāri † the verb is placed last. The subject may or may not come first, for the position of other words in a sentence seems to be determined largely by the emphasis placed on them.

As regards Ao, the verb usually comes last in the sentence, and the other words are placed as the necessity of the speaker's thought requires.‡

The order of words in Kachin is subject, direct object, indirect object, verb. Adverbs generally precede adjectives, and verbs and adjectives usually follow the noun they qualify.§

In Thādo the order is first the subject and last the verb. The indirect object, the direct object and adverbs come in between them in the order mentioned. Adjectives follow the noun.‖

The order in Lushei is usually subject, indirect object, direct object, verb. Adjectives follow the noun. In interrogative sentences the direct object is placed before the indirect object.

Here again, following Dr. Grierson in this as in practically the whole of this collection of notes, the order in Khāmi seems to be subject, direct object, indirect object, verb.¶

* Jaeschke, *op. cit.*, p. 42.

† Cf. Endle, *op. cit.*, p. 40.

‡ Grierson, *loc. cit.*, p. 277.

§ Grierson, *loc. cit.*, p. 509.

‖ Hodson, *op. cit.*, p. 33.

¶ Grierson, *loc. cit.*, p. 354.

SKETCH OF MANIPURI (MEITHEI) GRAMMAR.

The Article.—There is no definite article in the language. The demonstrative pronouns (*q. v.*) are used if any definite object is to be emphasized. The suffix *di* has an "intensive" action which seems to give it almost the function of a definite article. The functions of the indefinite article are performed by the simple numeral *amā* (one), but only when the fact of singularity is to be emphasized.

Number.—The ordinary plural suffix is *sing* (used only with personal nouns). The personal pronouns have the suffix *khoi*. *Sing* is only used when definite persons are referred to, as *lūkhrābi* = widows, while *lūkhrābi-sing* = the widows. The word *yām*, which means "many," is used as a plural suffix, both with such words as *mī* = man and with nouns of animals, as *mī-yām*, many men = a crowd, and *ōk-yām* = many pigs = a drove of pigs.

Gender.—In general there is only the "natural gender." But in cases where the gender is not evident, the words *nipa* = male and *nupi* = female, are used with nouns denoting human beings, while the genders of animals is shown by words as *amōm* = female and *a-lā-ba* = male. Thus from root *cha* = child, we get *ma-cha nipa* = his son and *ma-cha nupi* = his daughter. *Sagol a-lā-ba* = a horse and *sagol amōm* = a mare.

Cases.—There are six cases, instrumental or nominative, accusative, the case of the direct object, dative, or the case of the indirect object, which is also the locative case, showing the place or time at which the verbal action takes place, an ablative case indicating motion from, a genitive or possessory case, and a vocative case. In each instance the case is indicated by means of a suffix.

Instrumental or Nominative Case.—The suffix *na* corresponds to the Thado suffix *in* and the Lushei suffix *in*, and exercises similar functions to these suffixes.* It is possible that in Meithei this suffix is not used when the verb is of the order to which Aryan grammarians give the title "intransitive," but even this statement cannot be dogmatically asserted in face of

* See Thādo Grammar, pp. 9, 11, and 12 ; and Lorrain and Savidge, Lushei Grammar, p. 4. Cf. Jaeschke, *op. cit.*, p. 21.

passages in native texts. In common speech the suffix is often dropped, but it is most persistent in the past tenses of the verb.

Case of the Direct Object.—The suffix is *bu*. "*Nang-na ai-bu sok-le*," lit. "You by me as to touch was," "You touched me." But its use seems to be commonly reserved for personal pronouns and nouns denoting human beings. In other cases the order of the words seems to indicate the "object" with sufficient clearness, so that two linguistic tendencies are at work, the one indicating the functions of words by affixes, and the other by fixed arrangements of words.

Case of the Indirect Object.—The suffix is *da*, but the personal pronouns and the word *mi* (man) lengthen it and the ablative suffix by adding the syllable *ngon*. Thus *nupida* = to the woman, while *mi-ngon-da* = to a man. The suffix is also used to indicate the "locative" case.

The Ablative Case.—The suffix of the ablative case is *dagi*, which is also used with nouns of place to denote motion from.

The Genitive or Possessory Case.—The suffix *gi* denotes possession, and is affixed to the governed word which precedes the governing word. Often the suffix is omitted, and the relationship of possession indicated by the mere juxtaposition of the two words. Nouns of relationship and of the parts of the body, and the word *yum* (= a house) enjoy pronominal possessory prefixes (*i* for the first person, *na* for the second person, and *ma* for the third person).

The Vocative Case.—Sometimes the noun without any affix is used in the vocative case. The prefix *he* and the suffix *o*, which we may also regard as exclamatory affixes, indicate the vocative case.

Pronouns.—Pronouns are of three classes, *personal*, *demonstrative* and *interrogative*.

Personal Pronouns.—The personal pronoun of the first person is *ai* singular and *ai-khoi* plural, of the second person *nang* singular and *na-khoi* plural, and *ma* singular and *ma-khoi* plural of the third person.

The Demonstrative Pronouns.—The demonstrative pronouns are *masi* or *asi* = this, indicating proximity, and *adu* or *madu* = that, used of persons or things at a greater distance. In the locative case *asi* and *adu* are used as equivalent to "here" and "there."

Interrogative Pronouns.—The simple interrogative pronouns are *kanā* = who, and *kari* = what. The range of interrogative words derived from these two forms is large, as by the use of suffixes words may be constructed from them. We have *karigi* = why, which is derived from *kari* = what. The word is in reality an abbreviation of slovenly speech, as the suffix *damak*, which means "on account of," is omitted. Reference may be made to the verb* for the special changes which occur in the verb when these interrogative words are used. "Where" and "whence" have forms of their own which are notable. *Kadei-da* = where and *kadei-dagi* = whence. *Kadaungei* = when. *Kadōmda* and *Kadōmdagi* are honorific forms, and equivalent to *Kadeida* and *Kadeidagi*.

Adjectives.—Two things issue to notice about the adjectives in Meithei. The first is that all, or nearly all, assume the prefix *a* which we have seen above as the pronominal or possessory prefix of the third person, and assume also the so-called participial suffix, *pa* (*ba*). The second is that all are, or appear to be, capable of elementary modifications similar to those of the verb. The position of the adjective is but loosely determined. If, as is often the case, it precedes the noun, the case suffixes are attached to the noun, while if the adjective follows the noun, it receives the case suffixes. Occasionally feminine gender is denoted by the suffix *bi*.† Comparison is effected by either the use of adversative sentences as, "this man is short, that man is tall," which give the idea of comparison, or by the use of the adverb *hen-na*, which is derived from a root *hen* = to exceed, together with the suffix *dagi* (ablative case), which is suffixed to the noun compared. The superlative or absolute degree of comparison is effected in the same manner by employing, as the noun of comparison, some word meaning "all." Thus "this hill is high, all (others) are small," or (2) "this hill is higher than all others."

Adverbs.—Adverbs of manner are formed from the root of adjectives by the addition of the suffix *na*. This suffix is also added to the stems of participial forms belonging to the verb, which acquire thereby an adverbial sense. So, again, it is used

* See below, p. 178.

† "*Bi*" is also the magnitive or honorific suffix (see page 175).

as the suffix of instrumentality or agency with nouns with as wide a range of employment as the corresponding suffix *in* of Thādo or Lushei. Adverbs of place are formed from the demonstrative pronouns by the suffix *da* (suffix of the locative case) and the suffix *dagi* (suffix of the ablative case denoting motion from). These last are not true adverbs of place, as in each instance we often meet, in common speech, with the same construction, but with some word such as *mapham* = place, preceding the demonstrative pronoun which appears to be an adverb only by reason of the ellipse of the noun.

Simple adverbs of time are formed by the employment of the demonstrative pronouns in the locative case with the noun *ma-tam* = time, thus, *matam adu-da* = at that time. Some, again, are formed by the addition of the suffix *na* to the root of adjectives, while a temporal force belongs to some forms of the verbal participles with the suffix *da*.

Many adverbs of "time" are irregular in formation. The termination *mak*, which is associated with some of these irregular adverbial forms, appears in the adverb *mak-ta* = only, as the root of an adverb.

Numerals.—The table of numerals on page 157, shows clearly the method of notation in Meithei. With the exception of *a-hān-ba*, which means first, the ordinals are formed regularly from the cardinals by suffixing *sū-ba*, which probably means "completed." Thus *ani-sūba* = second.

Numeral adverbs are formed by the addition of the suffix *lak* to the cardinal, thus, *ahūm-lak* = thrice.

Verbs.—The verb in Manipuri ranges from very simple forms, as *tou-i*, to lengthy structures, such as *tou-ja-ru-ra-ga-daba-ni*, the synthesis of which can be determined without difficulty. It is not complicated by variations exhibitive of number, or person, or voice. The truth is that the Meithei verb seems to be what Aryan grammarians designate impersonal — an explanation given originally by Jaeschke of the verb in Tibetan.* The simple tenses, the present and the past, consist of the verbal root with, in the present, the suffix *i* or *li*, and in the past the suffix *le*. Thus—

tou-i = I am doing. *tou-re* = I did.

* Jaeschke, *op. cit.*, p. 21.

The imperfect tenses are derived from these forms by the introduction of an extra syllable *lam* or *ram*, thus—

tou-ram-li = I was doing, and
tou-ram-le = I had been doing.

These simple forms receive various additional significations by the interpolation between the verbal root and the tense suffix of infixes which are notable. The principal are—

khi = action at a distant place.
lu = action at a distant place.
la = action with purpose.
cha ‡ = action personally, also humility.
ri = present current action.
lu and *khra* = completed action.*
khat = gradual action.
gal and *ram* = repeated action.
tōk or *han* † = causality.
na = reciprocal action.
ning † = desiderative.
pi ‡ = honorific force.
man = excessive or intensive action.

The future tenses are formed by the syllable *ga*, which is placed between the verbal root and the tense sign (present only). An intensive form denoting immediate action is produced by the addition of the syllable *gē* to the verbal root. A sense of necessity is imparted by the addition of the suffix *daba* as—

chat-ka-ni = I shall go.
chat-ke = I shall go at once.
chat-ka-daba-ni = I shall have to go.

Future tenses with the modifications shown above as due to infixes, are also found, as *chat-khi-ge*, *chat-cha-ge*, *chat-lu-ge*. A future perfect tense is formed thus, *chat-la-ge* = I shall have gone. In ordinary use it means, "I am going now."

We also find a form, *ga-doure*, as *tou-ga-doure* = I am about to do. This seems to be in reality the future stem with *toure*, the past tense of *tou* = to do, added.

* These forms are used only with the past tense, and of the two the latter is more emphatic.

† These infixes are used independently as verbs—a fact which helps to the belief that the other infixes may originally have been capable of similar use.

‡ *Cha* and *pi* are the diminutive and magnitive suffixes used with nouns. Cf. Thādo Grammar, p. 8. They are by transference used with "verbs" to express humility and importance, and are often contrasted in antithetical sentences.

The negative forms are produced by the infix *ta* in the present and past tenses, and their derivatives, and by the infix *loi* in the future tenses, and their derivatives. Thus—

chat-te = I am not going.
chat-lam-da-ri, abbreviated to
chat-lam-dri = I was not going.
chat-loi = I will not go.

The imperative form (positive) is produced by the suffix *lu* (*ru*) added to the verbal root—

chat-lu = go ; *tou-ru* = do.

The negative imperative form is produced by the suffix *kanu*, or *ganu*, added to the verbal root—

chat-kanu = do not go ; *tou-ganu* = do not do.

The positive hortative form is produced by the suffix *si*, added to the verbal root—

chat-si = let us go.

The negative hortative form is produced by the introduction of the negative infix *ganu* (*kanu*) between the verbal root and the hortative suffix *si*—

tou-ganu-si = let us not do ; *chat-kanu-si* = let us not go.

Participials—There is an abundance of participial forms, the constant element in nearly all of which is the suffix *na*, which we know to be the suffix, firstly, of the agent case, and, secondly, of the adverbs derived immediately from adjectives. We have also negative participials in which the negative infix is *ta* (*da*), with present or past forms, and *loi* (*roi*) with future forms. Thus—

hai-na and *hai-du-na* = saying.
chat-ta-na and *chat-ta-du-na* = not going.

The future forms, present and past, are undifferentiated, the one form (in reality a past form) being *la-ga*, as *chat-la-ga*, which really means, "when I shall have gone." It must be remembered that the difference between present and past time is not very strongly marked in the simple forms of the verb. Connected, at least in form, with the future tense is the "gerundial" participle—which is formed by the addition of the syllable *daba*, to the future tense form in *ga* (or *loi* in the negative) as—

tou-ga-daba = shall have to do.
tou-roi-daba = shall not have to do.

The temporal participial has the locative case suffix *da*, and is formed by the suffix *lingai* (*ringai*) thus—

tou-ringai-da = at the time of doing.
chat-lingai-da = at the time of going.

The negative temporal participials are two, and each possesses a distinctive meaning; they are—

(1) *tou-da-ringei-da* = at the time of not doing.
(2) *tou-ram-dei-da* = at the time of not doing.

The first has gradually acquired the sense of "some time before doing," while to the second is now attached the meaning of "just before doing."

Purpose is shown, firstly, by a typical construction in the future with the participle *haiduna* = saying, as *ma-na ai bu hāt ke haiduna chat-khie* = he set out to kill me; and secondly by participial constructions as (*a*) *gadaba-gi* and (*b*) *na-naba*, thus—

ai-bu hāt-ka-dabagi chatkhre, and *ai-bu hāt-na-naba chat-khre* = he set out to kill me.

It may be noted that the participial form *gadaba-gi* is incomplete, as from the use of the genitive suffix *gi*, it is clear that some word, such as *damak* = for the sake of, has been elided.

The participial *bani-na* means "by reason of," as—

tou-bani-na = by reason of doing.

The conditional participial is *ba-di*, thus—

ai na-chat-pa-di = if I go.

The suffix *di*, it will be remembered, has an intensive force, and may thus here mean, "I go, indeed, then," etc.

The suffix *sung*, which is denasalized in ordinary speech, has a concessive force. The potentiatives, *hei-ba* = to be intellectually able, and *ngam-ba* = to be physically able, follow the verbal stem in *ba*, which we may conventionally regard as the infinitive form of the verb, and receive the usual suffixes of tense, as—

Meithei lairik-pā-ba hei = I can (I know how to) read a Manipuri document.
ai-chat-pa ngam-la-roi = I shall not be able to go.

The verb *yā-ba* (to be permitted, it is agreed) has also the same construction.

nangna-chat-pa-yāi = you may go.

Yā-na-ba in the reciprocal form means "to be mutually agreed"—

makhoi-na yānei = they have come to an understanding.

The inceptive *hao-ba* requires the governed verb in the infinitive, but it is also used idiomatically when affixed directly to the verbal root, thus—

lei-hao-re = I remained behind, and
Khong hao-dre = I knew nothing at all, I had not begun to know.

The affix of the infinitive, (to use the conventional though, in this connection, misleading terms of Aryan Grammar), is *ba*. We get *tou-ba* = to do, and *tou-da-ba* (negative) = to abstain from doing. Combined with *yā-ba*, we get sentences such as this—

Khajona-pi-da-ba yāi.
Lit. Rent not to pay is permitted.
You are exempted from rent.

The interrogative form of the verb varies, if the question asked be capable of a simple affirmative or negative, or if it requires an extended answer. Or, to put it in a more formal way, if an interrogative word is used, the form of the verb in the sentence differs from that in an interrogative sentence where no interrogative word is used. All sentences where no interrogative word is used should strictly be in pairs, thus *nang chat-ka-dra, nang-chat-loi-dra* = will you go, will you not go, are you going or not. In the present tense the suffix is *bra*, thus—

nang ū-bra, nang-ū-da-bra = do you see him or not.

With interrogative words, as—why, when, where, whence, whither, etc., the suffix is *bage* (*page*), as—

nang kadei-dagi lăkpage = where do you come from.

Honorific forms.—The Meithei is a ceremonious person, and, in his intercourse with persons acquainted with the niceties of etiquette, observes certain rules which will be only briefly summarized here. In addressing the Raja* and members of the Royal Family, a special vocabulary is used; in speaking to men of equal and superior rank, the speaker addresses the person spoken to (if a man) as *i-pu* = my grandfather, and if a woman as *i-be*, while *i-be-ma* = my dear, is familiar. If the speaker is addressing an officer of state, he speaks of himself as *na-nai* = your slave, and introduces into the verb the honorific † suffix *pi* or *bi*, and the suffix *ja* or *cha* which conveys a sense of humility. Thus—

Na-nai-na khat-ja-ning-i. Na-naigi wă tă-bi-u.
Your slave desires to make a complaint in person.
Be pleased to hear the complaint of your slave.

All verbs are regular except the verb "to be." The verb *lei-ba* = *worden* rather than *sein* in the present tense, for which the word *ni* is used. In the past tenses *lei-ba* is used as equivalent to *sein*, while *oi-ba* in all its tenses is identical in meaning with *worden*.

The relative construction is a function of the verb, and is formed by the suffix *pa* to the verbal stem, and almost produces the effect of an adjective, as *ngarang* = yesterday, *chen-khi-ba* = having run away, *ni pa* = man, *adu* = that, *hal-lak-le* = has returned.

Ngarang chen-khi-ba ni pa adu hal-lak-le.
The man who ran away yesterday has returned.

The order of words is usually subject, indirect object, direct object, verb. Adverbs usually precede the verb immediately, but their position in the sentence may be altered if additional emphasis is to be laid on the verb.

All speech is reported direct, thus avoiding the bewildering maze of pronouns which disfigures oblique narration. The use of adversative sentences, both in interrogation and comparison,

* See M'Culloch, *op. cit.*, p. 22. † See note above, p. 175.

is notable. It is common to have the verbal root repeated, as if some greater emphasis were gained thereby, as—

ikai-kai-re = I am ashamed ; *iloi-loi-re* = it is quite finished.

Meithei vocables are for the most part composed of monosyllabic roots. There are some di- and poly-syllabic roots.

A specimen of Meithei literature is given below in Appendices II. and III. The Chronicles (Ningthou-rōl) have also been translated, and, apart from their value as historical records which has yet to be determined, are documents of singular ethnological interest. Excerpts from the history—such as those which record the "*wars*" with Burma or with Tippera, or those which narrate the steadfastness of Ching Thang Kōmba—are very popular. Translations of passages from the Indian Epics have been made, and the influence of Hindu ideas upon the growth of the literature of the country is considerable.

An Alphabet of the Meithei Character is given by Dr. Grierson on page 22, Volume III., Part III. of the Report of the Linguistic Survey of India. Its origin is said to date to the rise of Bengali influence in 1700 A.D., but local tradition declares that the Chinese immigrants in the reign of Khăgenba first taught the art of writing. I understand that the Meithei word *che* = paper is of foreign origin—not Indian.

LIST OF AUTHORITIES CONSULTED IN SPECIAL REGARD TO THE CHAPTER ON THE LANGUAGE AND GRAMMAR OF THE MEITHEIS.

(1) Grierson, Dr. G. A., C.I.E., PH.D.

Report of the Linguistic Survey of India, vol. iii. parts ii. and iii.

(2) Primrose, A. J.

Manipuri Grammar.

(3) Damant, G. H.

Notes on Manipuri Grammar.
Journal Asiatic Society of Bengal, vol. xliv. p. 173, *seq.*

(4) Jaeschke, H. A.

Short practical Grammar of the Tibetan language. Kyelang, 1865.

(5) Endle, Rev. S.

Outline Grammar of the Kachari language. Shillong, 1884.

(6) Hertz, H. F., C.I.E.

Practical Handbook of the Kachin or Chingpow language. Rangoon, 1902.

(7) Hodson, T. C.

Thādo Grammar. Shillong, 1906.

(8) Lorrain and Savidge.

A Grammar and Dictionary of the Lushai language. Shillong, 1898.

(9) Soppitt, C. A.

Grammar of the Rangkhol Lushei Kuki language. Shillong, 1887.

(10) Assam Census Report, 1891.

Notes by A. E. Gait and A. W. Davis. Shillong, 1892.

(11) M'Culloch, Major W.

Account of the Valley of Munnipore. Selections from the Records of the Government of India, No. xxviii. Calcutta, 1859.

APPENDIX I.

THE ORIGINS OF THE SEVEN SALEIS OR SAGAIS (KINSMEN OR A COLLATERAL RELATION).*

Exogamous Groups.

THE originator of the Seven Saleis: (1) Ningthouja, (2) Angom, (3) Chengloi, (4) Ngangba, (5) Looang, (6) Khoomon, and (7) Moirang, is Gooroo (the most excellent Spirit).

The Seven Saleis were brought forth from the different limbs of the Gooroo, *i.e.*—

(1) Ningthouja was born from the left eye.
(2) Angom from the right eye.
(3) Chengloi from the right ear.
(4) Ngāngba † from the left ear.
(5) Looang from the right nostril.
(6) Khoomon from the left nostril.
(7) Moirang from the teeth.

The pedigrees (or genealogical tables) of the seven brothers or saleis are as follows:—

List of the Yumnaks of No. 1. Salei Ningthouja. Shandilla Gotra.

1. Enkhom
2. Kaithel lakpom
3. Khoirom
4. Nahakpom
5. Thongabom
6. Shanglen-moum
7. Mairenbom
8. Fairenbom
9. Eroom-Hairom
10. Khongnam
11. Nowkon Shangbom
12. Ta-yumjom
13. Nowrem
14. Ipoo-Shangbom
15. Le-u-Shoongbom
16. Khoomon-lambom
17. Khoisnam
18. Shingam
19. Namoijom
20. Mayang-lambom
21. Nowroibom
22. Kanga-Shenbom
23. Chong-ning-Henbom
24. Nga-ri-yanbom

---

* Lists prepared in connection with the census, 1901.—T.C.H.

† Or Khăbanānba.

25. Loitam
26. Kham-langba-Shangbom
27. Erom
28. Laishongbom
29. Thingnam
30. A-khom
31. Khoondrakpom
32. Kangabom
33. Howkhom
34. Shanoujom
35. Lai-Kangbom
36. Wa-reppom
37. Lourangbom
38. Eangnoo-Eaibom
39. Shairem
40. A-khongbom
41. Sho-yam
42. Mutum
43. Hairang-Khongjom
44. Haisnam
45. Hooi-rongbom
46. Kongbajom
47. Sapom
48. Ahanthem
49. Laichonbom
50. Kaisam
51. Erengbom
52. Satokpom
53. Choribom
54. Loitombom
55. Atom
56. Paonam
57. Eroongbom
58. Lookram
59. Laimram
60. Nongthonbom
61. Famdom
62. Hemnam
63. Cherom
64. Khoidongbom
65. Namoi-rakpom
66. Huidram
67. Yumnam
68. Laimapokpom
69. Khoomon-Cha-rappom
70. Langpok-Lakpom
71. Ningthoujom
72. Na-kanbom
73. Shingam
74. Shoram
75. Enshenbom
76. Thoudam
77. Hodam
78. Sagonsem
79. Senasam
80. Namoirakpom (Moirang Ning-thoumoum)
81. Paobom
82. Fouroongbom
83. Sangai-Senbom
84. Khoonjahanbom
85. Sanabom
86. Waikhom
87. Khang-Jrakpom
88. Eng-pokpom
89. Feejam
90. Thang-gan-Shabom
91. Ahaibom
92. Wangkhei Falambom
93. Fe-lem
94. Lourembom
95. Laitonjom
96. Moichem
97. Houdeijom
98. Khoinoojom
99. Nowtam
100. Lantham
101. Kontha Howbom
102. Shorenshonbom
103. Khoondom
104. Shingkhangbom
105. Shaikhom
106. Khoori-eanbom
107. Shouka-rakpom
108. Chanjanbom
109. Nongmai-kappom
110. Tensoobom
111. Wangkheirakpom
112. Khooai Rakpom
113. Wangkhei moum
114. Sharoongbom
115. Kanghoojom

List of the Yumnaks of No. 2. Salei Angom. Goushik Gotra.

1. Longjom
2. Lairen Lakpom
3. Wang Khem
4. Kashuwam
5. Akoijam
6. Ningonbom
7. Laitonjom
8. Hooirem
9. Eumlembom
10. Longmaithem

11. Longmaithem(Telongba Shangbom)
12. Hidam
13. Sheram
14. Naroombom
15. Pong Shoombom
16. Achoowam
17. Hai-Haibom
18. Ngarenbom
19. Ongnam
20. Hongnem-Shoongbom.
21. Kongbom (Khoira *i.e.* eldest)
22. Chakprom
23. Mang Sha Tam
24. Aengbom
25. Wanglembom
26. Chingangbom
27. Terem
28. Loitanthem
29. Shairom
30. Khangembom
31. Kaikonbom
32. Nongthonbom
33. Nakpok-Hanchabom
34. Khoimom Tabom
35. Thangjom
36. Moirang Laishangbom
37. Ekhoi Shangbom
38. Achoibom
39. Poshangbom
40. Nganglenbom
41. Angom Yumkhaibom
42. Nganoo Kappom
43. Khana Choubom
44. Kho-Younthen
45. Moong khom
46. Shangombom
47. Pooton jom
48. Shangdon jom
49. Kiam
50. Mandingbom

List of the Yumnaks of No. 3. Salei Chengloi. Bharadaj Gotra.

1. Thangjom
2. Tongbrom (Khoira *i.e.* eldest)
3. Aekpom
4. Shoorai shom
5. Loishangthem
6. Chongtham
7. Kha-Gokpom
8. Now Shekpom
9. Yumgoodom
10. Shorangthem
11. Wairokpom
12. Chanam
13. Elangbom
14. Chinga khom
15. Maiba Thiam
16. Shamnom
17. Tourangbom
18. Thoom Gan bom
19. Ngathem
20. Loushigam
21. Hooi wam
22. Loitam
23. Moinam
24. Sharak Khaibom
25. Kharaijom
26. Konsom
27. Langon Jam
28. Moiang Lambom
29. Maibram
30. Khoisnam
31. Hai-wam
32. Pot Sangbom
33. Konthoujom
34. Howrokcham
35. Thangjom you pambom
36. Wakambom
37. Konjengbom
38. Loktambom
39. Yanggoijom
40. Hemoibom
41. Amam

List of the Yumnaks of No. 4. Salei Ngangba. Noimisha Gotra.

1. Maihoubom (Khoira *i.e.* eldest)
2. Tekchom
3. Thongam
4. Ahaibom Thongam
5. Hentakpom
6. Howbajom
7. Thinbom
8. Langonjom

9. Sanjeeram
10. Kaborambom
11. Khaidem
12. Khoomoo Jom
13. Feejam
14. Wangbajom
15. Khoondangbom
16. Nongjenbom
17. Khooroijom

List of the Yumnaks of No. 5. Salei Looang. Kasshop Gotra.

1. Ashangbom (Khoira *i.e.* eldest)
2. Arambom
3. Tinbijom
4. Lairongjom
5. Toibijom
6. Aboojom
7. Mayengbom
8. Oorit Khinbom
9. Aroobom
10. Nongthonbom
11. Poongraijom
12. Ngangom
13. Looang Shangbom
14. Wanglenbom
15. Haitham
16. Fam-mi-hanbom
17. Thamang Jan
18. Wakongthem
19. Khoonjao Moum
20. Kambang Moum
21. Thangjam Shoran
22. Khoomook Cham
23. Fairoi Jom
24. Thiam
25. Shembangjom
26. Waikhom
27. Maiboong Lakpom
28. Shoubam
29. Maisnam
30. Maitram
31. Yumlembom
32. Thounoujom
33. Athokpom
34. Hijam
35. Salam
36. Nong pokpom
37. E-a-Ngambom
38. Chingan bom
39. Howrongbom
40. Laishom
41. Thangjom
42. Thoudoijom
43. Nahakpom
44. Loukhom
45. Nowroibom
46. Wahengbom
47. Laikangbom
48. Nanbom
49. Lairenjom
50. Loija-e-ang-bom
51. Ngoubom
52. Chingjabom
53. Ningchitpom
54. Khoknam
55. Shambam Tooram
56. Khoibom

List of the Yumnaks of No. 6. Salei Khoomon.* Madhookoilla Gotra.

1. Tentha Maibom (Khoira *i.e.* eldest)
2. Thoidingjom
3. Eanglem
4. Thingoojom
5. Pookrem
6. Fairenbom
7. Chandam
8. Pankhaijom
9. Mongjom
10. Langdem
11. Ngangbom
12. Akangjom
13. Oenam
14. Maimâm
15. Khamnam
16. Ahong Shangbom
17. Chaboongbom
18. Thongram
19. Ahongbom
20. Hekroojom
21. Senam
22. Thongbom
23. Eang-noo eaibom
24. Hanglem
25. Karam

* Or Khumal. I have not interfered with the writer's spelling.—T. C. H.

26. Laikhooram
27. Thoudem
28. Konom
29. Shougaijom
30. Ashem Nga kha khoi moum
31. Wa-reppom
32. Taipongjom
33. She-atpom
34. Houbijom
35. Kabo-rambom
36. Thangjom
37. Pookrambom
38. Maitan-keishongbom
39. Likmabam
40. Maibom
41. Thingom
42. Moiang Lambom
43. Chingkhooam
44. Maifuuam
45. Amakcham
46. Charoibom
47. Khoolem
48. Akooam
49. Khoirishoongbom
50. Lamabam
51. Tourem
52. Yaithingbom
53. Lang-Gam
54. Shamook cham
55. Thingbaijom
56. Khoirom
57. Na-maran
58. Howbom
59. Mairengbom
60. Hentakpom
61. Neprom
62. Im-goo-doom
63. Laisram
64. Amom
65. Tonjam
66. Pooyam
67. Shangkhom
68. Moijem
69. Langhaibom
70. Fanjom
71. Paloojom
72. Lantham
73. Eam-bem
74. Tourem
75. Nga-Sheppom
76. Shantham
77. Toumom
78. Pang Ngambom
79. Tokpom
80. Shan-Shen-bom
81. Kadam
82. Enshenbom
83. Chingtham
84. Sha-ka-pom
85. Howronbom
86. Lantham
87. Thangjam eou sham
88. Thangjam
89. Khoomonthem
90. Wankom
91. Ahaibom Tonbom
92. Eanglaibom
93. Polembom
94. Terem
95. Tonthrom
96. Howaibom
97. Thangang shabom
98. Khoothaibom
99. Langkhombom
100. Shoram
101. Ha-wai-bom
102. Shendam
103. Akham

List of the Yumnaks of No. 7. Salei Moirang. Atreya Gotra.

1. Chongtham
2. Melem
3. Wa-enbom
4. Pookrambom(Khoira *i.e.* eldest)
5. Mairang Narengbom
6. Narengbom
7. Kabo-rambom
8. Thangjam Shangkhom
9. Moirang Nongthombom
10. Poothem
11. Konjengbom
12. Chakpa-fiam
13. Ley-u-jom
14. Namboojom
15. Wangbijom
16. Kaba-jom
17. Ngangnom
18. Noongleppom
19. Thangajom
20. Ningthou-khongjom
21. Kong-kham
22. Moirang-Kaithel-lakpom
23. Okrom
24. Eaikhom

25. Kumabom
26. Hanglen Chakpatabam
27. Moirang them
28. Thongjom
29. Akhoo-eaibom
30. Namoojom
31. Wanglembom
32. Fairenjom
33. Moirang yumkhaibom
34. Khoo-Youm-them
35. Moongkhom
36. Khoieangbom
37. Howrongbom
38. Laikhoojom
39. Eao-renbom
40. Konjengbom
41. Akooram
42. Lisham
43. Moiang Lombam (Moirang Anouba is included into Moirang Salai)
44. Thock chom
45. Polem
46. Shoibom Pookrambom
47. Shoibom
48. Maifooam
49. Laifrakpom
50. Lairenmoum
51. Nga-Ngom
52. Khoinaijom
53. Laimajom
54. Wangkhem
55. Hitom
56. Shingkhangbom
57. Ha-wai-bom
58. Kaithel-Lakpom
59. Ngangkhom
60. Ahaibom
61. Ngasep-pom
62. Moirang Moum
63. Laima-khoojam
64. Khooai-rakpom
65. Ashem
66. Khondram

APPENDIX II.

NUMIT KĀPPA.

THE version in archaic Meithei followed by a translation into modern Meithei with (as far as possible) a word for word rendering in English.*

1. Haya he he liklai o oima-yai taodalba mapal
2. He imā he taipangbānbagi mapā oiriba nūmit
3. O Mother, O world of Father that is sun

1. korounongbu kholbi malem leibu lambina korou
2. mamā lai pumnamakkisu mamā oiribi taipangbānbagi
3. mother Gods all of also Mother that is world of

1. numitmada mapari ama satle haidabara. Mapari
2. mamā oiribina nōngmagi nūmitta macha nipa amā
3. mother that is sun of day on child male one

1. hanna satpa amadi thangyigum chi satna loi-mom-
2. pōke. Tao. Macha nipa hānna pōkpa amādi phao
3. bore. Hear. Child male firstborn one paddy

1. gum hamgangnare malem loida kumana loison khoimit
2. akangbagūm māngkhre, phao ahamba phaohamgūmle
3. dry like destroyed (was) paddy husked paddyhusks became like.

1. manaba oikhia. Thangyi ahangba loimom achaobigi
2. leipāk manūngda changduna leishao mapi mānba ōnkhire.
3. earth inside entering white-ant nest like became.

1. hoina motunginna thangyi morashi loimom madangbu
2. Phao lairemma phao achaoba adugi matūnginduna
3. Phao lairemma phao achaoba these behind following

* The lines marked 1 are archaic Meithei. Those marked 2 are modern Meithei.

1. salonakhi. Mapari konna satpa amadi kairoi arum
2. phao morasi phao iroya ōnkhire. Macha nipa kōnna
3. phao morasi phao iroya turned to. Child male afterwards

1. tugu mababu pumkangnare korou chumithang wangbal
2 pōkpa amādi yelgi marūm gūmna pūmkhre, chumthāng
3. born one fowl (its) seed like swelled, rainbow

1. numidang oina salonakhi. Aroi sangai lalabicha
2. amamba ōnkhre. Sangai sangai adugi mamit gūmna
3. dark turned to. Deer deer them of eyes like

1. yaoroi motunginna sangai ahingmitbu salonakhi.
2. sangai mamit ōnkhre. Tao. Macha nipa amā pōkpadi
3. deer eyes turned to. Hear. Child male one bearing

1. Haidabara. Mapari ama satpadi numit manao Kaidangba kaoa.
2. nūmit manao Kaidengamba kaoe.
3. sun brother Kaidengamba called (was).

1. Numit manao Kaidengamba mama hukamala hamalaba
2. Numit manao Kaidengamba mana phingmanba thakmanba
3. sun brother Kaidengamba he proud very swift very

1. yang mala paimalabagidamak thingnang lepalu
2. ithak thak manbana moianggi lepna * changba yāba
3. swift swift very (meaning very indistinct) allowed

1. kaojao sorarudа changna nong haimale. Yarel khong
2. sorarūda changsinduna sīre. Mayā aduna sāgi mayā
3. weir into entering died. His teeth beast of teeth

1. phoi tolana likao maya manaba oikhia, nakalao
2. mānba leikōn oikhre, nākanggi saru aduna laigi
3. like cowries became, side of bones it by God of

1. moiphangtuna thangsang nain manababu salonakhi.
2. thāng asāngba ōikhre.
3. sword long became.

1. Tangjam masamtouana chingnung chinga chanukhunda
2. Makōktagi masam-na chingda haoba Pureirombadasu
3. His head from hair hill on growing Pureiromba to also

* Text obscure.

1. loi Kaba loikham loi lambu khamaba purumarai nong
2. katpa lei luang phānaba tākhakta hāppa laisam mānba
3. offer flower Luang catch to spear on fasten God hair like

1. bala lou khamba phabi khokalang tolong loi oibu
2. Wakching thāda ningthoumatu machana louda katpa
3. Wakching month in King his wife his children by fields to present

1. wakching loima mangsa hombi khaloi loukoi loi
2. lei Angōm Ningthouna lamthōng khudingda katpa lei
3. flowers Angom King by field gate daily offer flowers

1. angouba ningthou tora thonglen laikham loi laisam
2. laisam angaoba oikhi.
3. God hair white became.

1. tolong angaobabu oikhia.

1. Oima yai taodalaba sena khomba dal atolabaga masabi
2. Nūmitka numitki mayāmma Taohuirengba nūmit anīna
3. Day day of his elder brother Taohuirengba day two by

1. Taohuireng ahalabaga numit ani chayonna thabi leng
2. sinna sinna nūmit anīna amūk thak amūk tana thōk-labagi
3. exchanging suns two again rising, again setting

1. leng sinana palobagi Khoainongjengbam paija Ekma
2. Khoainongjengba mīgi manai Ekma-hao-dangla atal-ba-na
3. Khoainingjenba man of slave Ekma-hao-dangla laziness by

1. haodangla namupongba raj atalabana wa oirokoi
2. saoe, nūmit asina nūmit anī sinna sinna amūk thak
3. wroth is Sun this by suns two by exchange again rises

1. Oi mayai taodalabana numit ani chayonana thabi ani
2. amūk tāre. Ai di minai oibanina ūyūng sing put
3. again sets I indeed man slave being because wood root firewood bundles

1. asibu lengsinanoia. Ai di tayum minai oibanina
2. kōkthōng anīrak halle, phaokōk thōngsu anīrak
3. head load twice caused, paddy head load also twice

1. langbol uyung singjalpot anirak hal waia tara lou
2. halba ngamdre. Ichanipa Haodongkhu ichanupi
3. cause cannot. My child male Haodongkhu my child girl

1. chanpotsu anirak onde ngamde, ipari Haodangkhu
2. Haodonghanba yōkpa ngamdre, nupi itu Haonuchang-
3. Haodonghanba rear cannot, woman my wife Haonuchang-

1. imom Haodanghalbu noak phade moumanu taloi oirambi
2. -khanubu tinnaba ngamdre haiduna saokhie.
3. khanu converse with cannot, saying, wroth became.

1. Haonuchangkhanubu lang kao pha de, haina we oikhie

1. Khoai nongjembom piba Ekma Haodangla namupangbaroj
2. Khoainongiemba piba Ekma haodongla minai atalbana
3. Khoainongjemba chief Ekmahaodongla slave lazy being by.

1. kadambana momanu taloi marumbibu phao kaokhie
2. nupi matubu kaoduna hai, itu nupi pema Haonuchang khanu
3. woman his wife calling said, my wife woman dear Haonungchang khanu

1. oibunai momanupema Haonuchangkhanu

1. safbio napam wabu wa ni ruo napam seloi longmai
2. phajabi napamdagi wā nīru o, napamo-Nongmaiching
3. beautiful your father from bamboo beg, father Nongmaiching

1. wa longmai khuchum miyum wa niruo, haina thaosikhi babu
2. dagi aphaba wā nīru o haiduna chathankhibabu wā pirakte
3. from good bamboo beg, saying sending though bamboo gave not

1. wa pirakhate mopum thongkhong laralawabu wai niruo
2. mamāga pōkminaba mamāda thōngkhōng kurāldagi wā
3. maternal uncle gate ditch Kurāl from bamboo

1. haina thousikhibu thongkhong karala wa karala
2. nīru o haiduna chathankhibabu Kurāl Ningthou shōk
3. beg, saying sending though Kurāl Ningthou

1. Ningthou sokpamba maching lel Kurāl lakpa thoumala
2. pagi chingda haoba, Kurāl lakpa māgi chingda haoba
3. belonging to hill on growing, Kūral lakpa his hill on growing

1. taoba maching sangda pamba wabu wa nibabu wa pirakke.
2. wā nībabu wā pirake.
3. bamboo asking bamboo gave.

1. Khowainongjembom pibana korou numit manganibu
2. Khowainongjembom pibana nūmit mangāni lirung tel
3. Khowainongjembom chief by days five bow arrows

1. likhai tel khaikhi. liphao tel phorabaga
2. sai. Lirung tel adu phaodōklaga
3. makes. Bow, arrows that sharpened having

1.
2. tel tōngda hāpsinduna ngaiduna leirē
3. arrows quiver in placing standing was

1. hugatoi paloga thongna ngaimakhie. Oibunai momanu
2. tel machinda hū teire. . . . Itu nupi
3. arrow head on poison smeared. My wife woman

1. pema Haonuchangkhanu sa pa bi o nangbu laij
2. pema Haonuchangkhanu phajabi nang ising sōktuna
3. dear Haonuchangkhanu beautiful you water drawing

1. ipal langma pulolang loroi thongloko hania
2. pūl adu nakōkta hāplako haiduna
3. pot that your head on place saying

1. thousikhie. Momanu kaloi marumbina lonai
2. chathankhi. Nupi matu aduna isingdagi
3. sent. Woman his wife that by water from

1. hinson karakabada pulalang loroi thongbabu
2 changjaoda pūl makōkta hāplakpa adubu
3. getting pot her head on placing her

1. pāchare kaorao numitmadi momnu taloi
2. pāndambada pālle. Nōngma nūmit amana
3. shooting hit. Day day one on

1. mamunbigi chomlang kaobi manasibu
2. nupi matu adugi chōmlang manāda siba
3. woman his wife that of hole her ear in pierced

1. patambasing paehure. Korao numit madi sentang
2. aduba pāndambada pālle. Nōngma nūmit amana sentang
3. it shooting hit. Day day one on sparrow

1. khrapālbalu tongpatumbasung paehurubagi. Khawai
2. phaorāda tōngba adu pāndambabu pālle. Khawai
3. dhan floor on riding it shooting hit. Khawai

1. Nongchengbom naija yeakma Haodongba Khābā
2. Nongchengba manai Ekma Haodonglana itu nupi
3. Nongchengba slave Ekma Haodongla by, my wife woman

1. phaldongna yoipunai momuu taloi arimbio tārā
2. itu nang chāk chaiom yōmmo yusu yukhōmda hāllo
3. my wife you food edibles collect wine also wine gourd in pour

1. Chāomo wanglei khombalo. Oklel tāba lonehangba
2. ōk achaoba louda changle, lairel achaobasu
3. pig large field in entered python big also

1. loutababu leia. Thinglou soknaruge, oklel
2. louda changduna leire. Akamba sing adu sōknaruge
3. field in entering was. Strong cunning that I will encounter

1. hānamge hania khomlang thengkoo—nikna
2. ōk adu hātluge haiduna yu-khōm pugadaba pōt ka
3. pig that I will kill saying wine gourd to carry things

1. yāta khie, adu nongibu thengya lomnungshi kaoe
2. loinana hipkhre. Adugi damak Thongyalamanungshi kaoe
3. together slept. That of cause Thongyalamanungshi called is

1. Thengyalamanungshida tangja lom phangle.
2. Thongyalamanungshida ngairure.
3. Thongyalamanungshi at he woke.

1. Lil lana thetrol lābāda yorinayai taodalba sena
2. Lōttuna leirabada nūmit ti lam achaoba Loijing
3. hiding remaining on sun region vast Loijing

1. Khommadal di lomlci roiehing sārāda tareng tareng
2. manunda tārang tārang tākhre
3. shade in falling falling fell (set).

1. leitha khie.

1. Moshabi Taohuireng ahalbadi numit mashong
2. Mayāmma Taohuirengna nūmit mangālna
3. Elder brother Taohuiring sun glory on

1. Choona ahel karaklabada khowai-nong-chengbom piba
2. thōklaklapada Khowai Nongjengba piba
3. Setting on Khowai Nongjengba chief

1. Ekma Haodongla namu pongpalacha aking
2. Ekma Haodongla migi manai akalbana liri adu
3. Ekma Haodongla man of slave strong by bowstring that

1. tolpama liri thamoiting lākā telmoi lāknā
2. thamoi yaona chingduna telna nūmitpu tamna
3. chest up to pulling arrow by sun at full

1. yorinayai Taodalbabu tomnā kāpkhibabu taodalba
2. kāpkhibabu nūmit ki sagol sātōng adudā telna
3. shooting sun of horse beast riding that to arrow by

1. lang koi makhumelta tel pallabagi damak
2. pālluraduna
3. hitting (or being hit)

1. Maring khun birakta loture—Angālba Sena
2. Maring khun birakta tākhre. Angālba nūmitsu
3. Maring villages among fell. Bright sun also

1. Khommadalsung Khowai Nongjengbam Piba
2. Khowai Nongjengba pibagi telna tārabada kīraduna
3. Khowai Nongjengba chief of arrow by falling on being afraid

1. waira matelchabu song kirabagi damak laimmral
2. leipāk maral tarūkta leikhā mangādā lam
3. country away from (?) six days cavern five day country

1. torukta lei haoral mangada Lemlel khulbi lomda
2. achaoba khunbirakta mapā Pākhangba Senamehi
3. large villages among his father Pākhangba Senamehi

1. mapal lariel taororinai tubi mayanungda shul
2. Senamehi Pākhangbagi manākta lōt-tabada
3. Senamehi Pākhangba of his vicinity in hiding

1. thuplabagi poiroi miltri machil wangma thamle.
2. Meithei leipākta nūngthilsu mamle, ahing
3. Meithei country in daytime also dark was, night also

1. lompu tupu laikomthal nekta shoiona narol
2. mamle lousu lamsu ngākōina ure. Nūngthil
3. dark was fields also folk also terrified looked. Daylight

1. singloulabagi haikhu loukumbira loukumda
2. naidarabada nāpisingbi haoraduna loukūmbina
3. not being by grass jungle growing cultivators

1. haichek loutadara haki.
2. loukūmdare, loutābina louda tārabagi.
3. did not cultivate cultivators field in falling.

1. Ningthou Pongba taramana yoimayai taodalbagi tang ja
2. Ningthou Pongba tāramana lai tāramana nūmit ki
3. Kings ten Gods ten sun of

1. makhong khulbu thi khongdarabada khomia mata heiku
2. leiphambu thība khongdarabada mata lou kūmbi
3. being place search knowing not then cultivator

1. lou kumbana haichek loutabi aminana hania ngamme
2. lou tāba anīna ngāngnaramme. Itā loinarakhibi
3. cultivator two by conversing were. Dear companion

1. Khonion ita ngairoinaio lomlel khulbi lomda lomu
2. lam achaoba khunbirakta leipākta ngālliba
3. distance great villages among earth in shining

1. niltush leinil hao ngaltum ngalba asibu karimemo
2. asibu karamba meino haiduna hāngbabu hoi ita
3. that what kind fire is saying asking yes dear

1. haina pao hangbabu hoida khoinao itao, taodalba
2. nūmitna mapā Pākhangba Senamehigi ma-nāk-ta
3. Sun by his father Pākhangba Senamehi of vicinity in

1. Lena khomdalbu mapal lairel taoroinagi
2. lōtlie, nūmit-ki mangāl arābane—haiduna
3. hid is sun of brightness far is saying

1. tubi mayanungda salthupba numit mangal
2. wā ngāngnarambabu lai tāramana
3. word conversing Gods ten

1. tarabane haina paomelna ngambabu
2. tāraduna mayūm mayūmda hōmlaklaga
3. hearing their house house to gathering having come

1. Ningthou Pongba taramana natarabagi malrol
2. Thōngngāk Lairemma mamang yāmna
3. Thōngngāk Lairemma her dreams very

1. aldé lamlabada chakpa lomlang meipi
2. chūmbibu kaokhi. Thōngngāk Lairemma
3. true are called. Thōngngāk Lairemma

1. mangpat chadang yapibu pao kaokhie.
2. namang yāmna chūmmi asibana nangonda
3. your dreams very true are dead by you to

1. Chakha Lomlang meipi khomlel mangchang
2. changlaklibani asibabu bichar toubi
3. entering come is dead as to trial who doest

1. thaobi khamnung chatwai tambi amal
2. nang nūmit-pu kao-thaklo haiduna
3. you sun call saying

1. Kham butla lapinang lao o yoimayai
2. chathankhi. Thōngngāk Lairemma nūmit pu
3. sent Thōngngāk Lairemma sun to

1. Taodalbabu pao kaoro'o haina thousikhie
2. kaothōklie— nūmit nangna thorak-tareduna
3. called sun you by happening not

1. Chakpa lomlang maipina Taodalbabu pao
2. Meithei leipāk asi nūngthilsu mamle ahingsu
3. Manipur country this daytime also dark is night also

1. themelue, yoimayai Taodalba Sena Khomdal
2. mamle, lam achaoba khunbigi leipāk mathak
3. .dark in distance great villages of country it upon

1. nongbu nangna sal thupbagi poiroi chiltuchil
2. asida nūngsā sāraru asūmna haijababu
3. this in sun heat make hot thus speaking

1. wangngam thamle lomlel khulbi lomgi malem
2. nūmitna khūmlake hoi Thōngngāk Lairemma
3. Sun by answered Yes Thōngngāk Lairemma

1. manamsida nong salaru asum pao thembabu
2. mamangeida imā lai pumnamak-ki-su mamā
3. formerly my mother gods all of also their mother

1. angalba Sena khomdalsu pao khulake, hoida
2. oiribi taipangbān-bagi mamā oiribina macha
3. being universe of its mother being by her children

1. lehakpa lomlang maipi o lāhal palem ima korao
2. nipa mangābu pōklamme nōngmagi nūmitta
3. males five bore day of sun on

1. nongbu khalbi malem hiburmbina mapari
2. iyāmma hānna pōkpa amadi phao akangba
3. my eldest brother first born one indeed paddy dry

1. mangamabu hothae korao numitmadi ishabi
2. gūmna māngkhre, phao ahamba gūm phaoham
3. like perished, paddy dry like paddy husks

1. hama satpa amadi thang ekum chitsatna
2. oikhre iyāmma kōnna pōkpa amadi
3. became my elder brother next born one indeed

1. loimomkum hamkongnare, ishabi konna satpa
2. yelgi marūm gūmna pūmkhare iyāmma
3. fowl of its seed like swelled my elder brother

1. amasung kaie lei yelrum gumbabu pomkongnare
2. Kaidengambasu moianggi lepna changba
3. Kaidengamba also

1. ishabi kaide gumba sung thongnang chatlu
2. yāba sorarruda sire. Iyāmma Taohuirengsu
3. weir in died. My elder brother Taohuireng also

1. kaochao soraruda nonghanule. Ishabi Taohuireng
2. Khowai Nongjengba pibagi telna tāraduna
3. Khowai Nongjengba chief of arrow by having fallen

1. ahalbasung khowai nongchengbom Piba waira
2. nūmit ki sagol sātōngda telna pāllabagi
3. Sun of horse animal riding on arrow by hitting of

1. matelchana numit langkoi makhunetta
2. atinga dagi amamba leikhāda lōtlie
3. fear from dark earth cave in hiding is

1. tel pallabagi koraomakhalma wāngpal
2.
3.

1. mololta salthuplie
2.
3.

1. Taipang nongshapalda numit itom lep ngamlaroie
2. Taipangbānbada nūmit itomtana thōkpa ngamlaroi
3. Universe on sun (I) duly light shall not be able

1. hania wakallabada chakha lanlang maibisung
2. haiduna yāramdarabada Thōngngāk Lairemma su
3. saying not consenting on Thōngngāk Lairemma also

1. maral onde rakle. Ningthou Pugba taramao
2. mayūmda hallakle. Lai tārana nūmitti
3. her house to returned. Gods then sun indeed

1. yomiayai Taodalbana taipong palda numit itom
2. taipangbānbada nūmit matōmatana thōkpa
3. universe in Sun duly light

1. lepugam laroi hania paoa ngamde haidibara
2. ngamlaroi haiduna yāramdre tao. Lai
3. shall not be able saying agreed not. hear Gods

1. Ningthou pongba tara mana tompha wangmalal
2. tāramana ningthougi macha nupi
3. Ten King of his child girl

1. khabi lengmao khombitu thaonebkhie. Tompha
2. Panthoibi-bu thaoneki
3. Panthoibi summoned

1. wangmalal khabi lengma Khombibu lūbi
2. Ningthou macha nupi kābada onglūbi
3. King his child girl coming on Mistress

1. ngaye chanu toula nongtonglengpi kuyal
2. ningthoucha chanu leipāk ningthou gi
3. King child child woman country King of

1. phaitangloupi korao nongnea halbi malem
2. mabemma mi pumnamakki thouaibu
3. his dear men all doings

1. leibu halbi angalba helloi changbio
2. amūk pōkhanba amūk sihanba lai
3. again betime cause again die cause Gods

1. mapal lairel taurimaiba pimama piro'o
2. aikhoigi imāsu oiribi leipāk pumnamakki
3. us of our mother also being earth all of

1. wahalabada tompha khonguing pibu yoibu
2. mamā oiribi masaksu yāmna phajabi
3. its mother being her appearance also very beautiful

1. una chambi pamel intha raobi tompha.
2. nangmak chatpio napā nūmitpu
3. you yourself go please your Father sun

1. wangngam louner pao yarabagi Ningthou pongba
2. kaothak-piru hairabada ningthoucha chanu
3. call please saying on King child child woman

1. taramana angalba Sena khommadalbu pao
2. ū manā achaoba anouba amābu hekpairabada
3. wood its leaf big new one even seizing on

1. themo heirabadi malem leipi khong wai shemi
2. lei hekma oihambi ningthougi macha nupina
3. flower even to be causing king of his child woman by

1. paki parom tābada pálák manga sabio. Moaki
2. wā adu yāre. Lai tāramana o angālba nūmitpu
3. word that agreed. Gods ten by O bright sun

1. nuran tabina pao themo, phairoi mang
2. thembu hairabadi lambi semlamu
3. persuade say if roads prepare

1. ngariak ngai khongdalba manoruk
2. nipanasu chatnabasu semu. Sagai mathal
3. men by also go in order also prepare. Machan stage

1. manemg khomo irukta chamba loraloth
2. mangā sāromo. Nupibasu them-halamusu
3. five build. Women also persuade also

1. ngaithing yoio ching ngonpa hamna yel rum
2. lūkmaida thūm mukta lā ningthīna thāraga
3. basket in basket in leaves beautifully having spread

1. koing khilna khabi khoinka halshing singlaka
2. ching angaoba hāppu. Yerūmsu hāppu yūsu
3. rice white put egg also put wine also

1. yepo saret mālaire kailei angoubabu nakta
2. yūkhōm thamna hāllaga hāppu singsu lāna
3. gourd full up pouring put ginger also leaf in

1. yepha mangpat chatangpuna lomlel khulbi
2. yōmlaga hāppu, selsu kakup thūmsu kakup
3. wrapping put sel also covered salt also covered

1. lomda malem leibikhal waikumna mapal
2. hāppu phī amūbana kupsindo yel
3. put cloth black in wrap up (cover) fowl

1. leirel taoroinaibu penemlue. Angalba
2. angaoba pūduna Athelpāt yaona lam
3. white bringing Athel lake up to distance

1. mahūi taoparoibu pao themlue Taodalba
2. achaoba khunbirakta pumnamakka loinaduna
3. great villages among all accompanying

1. Sena Khommadal nangna sal thuplabagi
2. mapā nūmitpu themlue angālba nūmitpu
3. her father sun persuaded bright sun

1. poiroi chiltum chil wangngam thamle
2. themlue nūmit nangna lōtluna leirabagi
3. persuaded Sun you by hiding being of

1. lomlel khulbirom malem levialphaona kanglei
2. Meiteida nūngthilsu mamle, ahingsu mamle
3. Meitei (land) in day also dark is, night also dark is

1. pumna ngalna nongshallaru haina paothembabu
2. lam achaoba khunbirakki leipāk maralshi
3. country large villages among of land even from

1. hoi yarabagi macheng kairoi angaobana
2. phaona Kōnung pumnamaksu ngālna nūngshā
3. up to Palace all brightness by sun warmth

1. malem leibi khoug wai amaga nakhong
2. sāroro haiduna thembabu hoi haiduna yārabagi
3. make warm saying persuading yes saying agreeing of

1. khenabaga yoimoyai taodalbasung malem
2. yel angaobana leipākta makhōng-amūk thāng-
3. fowl white by earth on its foot again lifting

1. leibi khongwai mangaga pathum taruk tal
2. lakpada nūmitsu leipāktagi khōngthāng
3. on sun also earth from footraising

1. palak manga gana angalba sena khanmadalua
2. mangārak thānglaktuna. Sagai mathal mangāmada
3. five times raising machan its stories fivefold

1. ning ming khel karaklababu ningthupongha
2. nūmitna tārang tārang thaklakpabu lai tāramana
3. sun by by degrees lighting Gods ten by

1. taramana mityeng sal kheibabu numit mamai woke
2. yengbada nūmitki mamai makle nūmit
3. looking on sun of his face dim was sun

1. thabi mamai taie yoimayai taodalba numit
2. mamai makladuna nūmitki chōp sābisi
3. his face dim being sun of virtue let us make

1. masansabu sabiahe haina nongda lairel
2. haiduna Pākhangbagi maiba Konderak
3. saying Pakhangba of maiba Konderak

1. Pakhangbagi mama ifa koldel makthangmai
2. Thangmai Leikang Leikalbana yetlōmda
3. Thangmai Leikang Leikal by right side on

1. leikang leikalbana sarel yettompham keke
2. phamle Moiranggi Lai Thāngjinggi maiba
3. sat Moirang of God Thāngjing of maiba

1. mana ifa thingkal mari phaobiyacha
2. Khuyal Urakalbana oirōmda phamduna
3. Khuyal Urakalba by left side on sitting

1. langchinglang maiba khuyal urakalbana
2. Moirang-gi tūreldagi isingga yel marūm
3. Moirang of river from water with fowl its seed

1. somu oiromphan purem Chingyai koirel
2. amaga nāpi napu matōl Nongmaiching dagi
3. one with grass orange its top Nongmaiching from

1. iga kaileipa mayelrumga yempong phaipangbabu
2. isingsōktuna maibana nouhing kaoba nāpi
3. water drawing maibas by nouhing called grass

1. phai tolyampa thinkhai thingna tao o namai
2. singbi yaona Laigi nipasing aduna nūmitpu
3. grass up to God of boys those by sun

1. nana tāngba nouhing nahakpa sheda nadábá
2. chōp sābirabada angālba nūmitti mamit
3. virtue making on bright Sun indeed his eyes

1. yaona laiba thou Ipi yashengna numit
2. mamai iseng sengle. Nūmit gi mamai
3. his face cleanness clean were. Sun of his face

1. machupsalu salriabada angalba Sena
2. phajere. Nūmitpu Panthoibina yel
3. beautiful was. Sun as to Panthoibi by fowl

1. Khommadaldi numit lunaga thabi hennaga
2. angaobabu paiduna themlui, mamangeida
3. white taking persuades formerly

1. numit mamai lure thabi mamai pālle
2. Nōngmaiching chingsu taret longba laigi
3. Nōngmaiching hill also seven (branches) God of

1. Taodalba Sena khommadal atolba tombuwang
2. chingda leiba langmai khoiri kaoba lam adugi
3. hill on being langmai khoiri called district that of

1. ngam lonna macheng kailei angaobabu nangba
2. ahal nōngmaibu lātpa maibana nūmitpu laishi
3. old sun face worshipping priest by sun as to Divinity

1. yepua paothumphababu lahal mayumshel
2. laithōllabadi chinggi mamit māuna thōklake
3. God praying if hill of its eye like happened

1. loi asāba mapal taretchinggi lairu phaheha
2. chinggi mamit mānba aikhoibu chānbire
3. hill of its eye resembling us as to pitied

1. sang chinggi Khongyaphabicha langmai
2. nōnggi mamit mānna thōklake nōnggi
3. Sun of his eye likeness in happened sun of

1. khoiri haiba chingba kaosing ngamba
2. mamit mānba nanggi na-ngāl-na Nōngmai
3. his eye resembling you of your brightness by Nōngmai

1. langmaithel bung lāt pana yoimayaibu
2. ching-gi khun aikhoigi lōk sādu ching
3. hill of villages us of ravines and jungles hills

1. tenthabadi chinggi mamit manana thoklakle
2. pumnamak ngālna nūngsā sāre haiduna
3. all brightness by warm warmed saying

1. Chingmit malgi yoirelba nongi mamit
2. laishi lai thōlli. Heirem Khoalchaina
3. Divinity God prayed. Heirem Khoalchai-by

1. manana thok lakle nongmitmalgi yoingalba
2. nūmitpu laishi laithōlbadi Heirem khoan-
3. Sun as to Divinity God prayed Heirem khoan

1. selloi ayumnakpu thaobi lokmaithel sadu
2. chan-gi maibana matōmta isai saktuna
3. chan-of priest by alone sing singing

1. chinglai ngalna nongsalao hani tengthanei
2. laishi laithōlbadi Heirem Khoanchan-gi
3. Divinity God praying if Heirem Khoanchan of

1. Mayum Heirem Chaopapung Khoalchang
2. nupina tūrel lānna lou kūm laokre
3. women by river crossing (by) cultivation cultivated

1. sangba yaida Yoimayai Taodalbabu teng
2. Tangkhul-su thāng paire, isingdasu
3. Tangkhuls also dao took up, water in also

1. thabadi Heirem aseiba khoalchal tengthaba
2. nami ūre, Heirem khul chan aikhoigi
3. shadow seen was, Heirem village chan us of

1. lengnao haokhomba haotang pungtoiba
2. khullak leirak sādu ching pumnamak
3. village up to paths jungle, hills all

1. kangku naocha thingkal manasu
2. ūmang wāmang ngālna nūngsā sāre
3. wood jungle bamboo jungle brightness by suns warmth warmed

1. phaklang lol chaningda matom wari wakna
2. haiduna Laishi lai thōlle Heirōmdasu
3. saying Divinity God prayed Heirom at also

1. tengthabadi mayum Heirem kei manung
2. matōmta laishi lai thōnjai Shanthōng-pangba
3. alone Divinity God pray Shanthōng-pangba

1. leima khulchal thong kal telhaiba chanu
2. Moirang leipākki ahal lūchingba khul
3. Moirang country of chieftain village

1. turel namphao machan khabi loukum
2. aduda pōkpa Thāngjinggi manai
3. that at born Thangjing of his slave

1. loukashi Tangkul mara thangkul khut
2. isaisakpa machi manao pōkbadagi atōlba
3. song-maker elder and younger brother born from younger

1. naija chakmitsel apaba o ayum Heirem
2. maiba ningthougi mikal Thagonbana
3. priest king of direction Thagonba by

1. chaobapungbu thaobi lekmaihel sadu
2. nūmitpu laishi laithōnbadi nūnggi mathakta
3. Sun as to Divinity praying stone of its top on

1. Chinglai ngalua pamel ukhanglouna
2. pōkpa nūng achaobagi mathakta
3. born stone big of its top on

1. nongsharo haina tengthānue. Heirom ashaibana
2. pōklaba tōnnā khoirelba ising mathakta
3. born younger by winding water its top on

1. tengthabasung matom tengthānue Haoroi nong
2. ming thalba wānglaba wāgi matōn
3. name full lofty bamboo of its top

1. chup khánā pangba ramda kē ke chambapung
2. yaona thorakpa Moiranggi isingda
3. up to lighting Moirang-of water in

1. moirang sángba yaida tengthaba khuyal
2. ngālna nūngsā sāroro haiduna asūmna
3. brightness by sun warm make warm saying thus by

1. chúmaba cheima mukiba muyam
2. laishi laithōlle Moirangda laishi
3. Divinity God prayed Moirang at divinity

1. safaba hao wangpong manao lihal
2. laitōnsu matōmta laishi lai thōlle
3. God prayers also alone Divinity God prayed

1. khoirisu maroi kachenglom thengai
2. makhā pangba Khumal leipākta nūmitpu
3. south (being) Khumal country in sun as to

1. thongai atolba ke ke pung yang chumaba
2. laishi laithōlbadi Khumalgi maiba laishi
3. Divinity God praying Khumal of priest Divinity

1. mingba cheimaba cheima asheiba kaning
2. laithōlba mapā mapu achaobana pōkpa mapā
3. worshipping his Father his ancestors big by born his Father

1. mikaowāngna yoimayai Taodaldabu
2. mapu yāmna heisingbagi macha magi
3. his ancestors very cunning of their son his

1. tuigthabadi nungmu thakta naopangba
2. ma-khan-jilsu yāmna pha-ba mana
3. his voice also very good him by

1. nungmu Raja angaoba munggao thaktā
2. sak-pu sōl-bada lam yāmna ninba
3. Song as to invoking distance very steep

1. nao naoba nungngao Raja asheiba
2. mābu hen-ba leitaba ainu-gi makhal
3. him as to exceeding not being crane of his voice

1. pana lam thang thaona khoiralba
2. gūmba māna sākpu salbada chit-thaba
3. like him by song as to invoking fault

1. laija ipāk thakta me hoalara langlel
2. leitaba maibana laishi lai thōl-la-badi
3. not being priest by Divinity God praying

1. kongyang watal thokta ming takpa
2. nūmit nangna thōkpa-da ū wā
3. Sun you by lighting (happening) wood, bamboos

1. maibu mayum ke ke chanba pungbu
2. nāpi singbi angāl ngālle. Nūmit
3. grasses brightness bright were. Sun

1. laija irai ngalna nongshalao hania
2. nang-gi amengba na-ngāl-na manā
3. you of clear your brightness by its leaves

1. asum tengthanai heayum ke ke chaoba
2. ma-sing i-nao-naore pukning
3. its wood newness new are stomach-wish

1. pungda tengthabasung motom tengthanei
2. nūngaire Khumal leipāk-ta ngālna
3. pleased was Khumal country in brightness by

1. haoroi khaneipangba ramda mongyai
2. nūngsā sāroro haiduna laishi
3. day warm warm make saying, Divinity

1. paobapung atol shangba yaida
2. lai thōllabadi Meithei ningthougi
3. God praying Manipuri King of

1. yoimayai taodalbabu tangthabadi
2. maiba isai sakpa mamā Likshisuna
3. priest song maker his mother Likshisu by

1. nongyai ashaiba khumal tengthaba
2. pōkpa Meithei isai heiba makhalsu
3. born Manipuri songs knowing his voice also

1. mapal shoalon ngahongba chami paima
2. pha-ba ising chenba gumba mamā
3. good water luming like his mother

1. lel koigi thoibalang khomsu chikham
2. si-khribabu maming panduna sakpa
3. deceased as to her name taking singing

1. uirishu Chenwak thoubal thonkaba
2. mapā si-khrabagi mamingbu pha-ja-na
3. his father deceased of his name as to well

1. lomloi waklom kaba watha wāk
2. isai sakpa mi si-khrabagi mamingbu
3. song singing man deceased of their names as to

1. yenkhom moinuwak hiitrugun
2. saklaga pūrōnda tin-han-ba
3. having sung the chronicles in making to join

1. langwak imu khongkonwak tolba
2. ūchek koak oiduna panglei
3. birds crows being

1. Thang chingsu nonghao mapu khumal,
2. leirababu lai marakta tin-halli
3. being as to Gods among makes to join

1. adusung khadomde naodabal ashaibana
2. thowai ming mānglabu shā oikhriba
3. names having perished animals having been

1. tengthabadi yoimayai Taodalba yellangpangi
2. tākpa oinaduna lamlakta chenduna
3. showing being country among in running

1. paiyaoba chaokhongpangi narekpa
2. khonglaba ma-mingsu mānglababu
3. having known their names also having been lost though

1. yonshing tolki taraba lairel yoishom
2. māna saklaga kake migi maming
3. him by having sung man of his name

1. ping khe shompeng leihaoba yoikhom
2. ma tha māngkhrababu mana khongsi
3. his work (?) having been lost though him by knowing

1. thokkhom thokna lonba yoibaleng
2. lamlakta leiriba ōk-ka tinnaraba
3. country in being pigs joining together

1. leishangba nongyai ohaoba pungbu
2. lairel marakta lam achaobada
3. pythons them among in country large in

1. puna ngalna nongshal o, haina tengthanei
2. chenduna leibabu khonglabana
3. running being though knowing by

1. poiroi tamthong mapungkoi lemthong
2. laishi lai thōl-la-badi nūmit
3. Divinity God praying sun

1. maphaipākpa pungda tengthabadi poiroi
2. nōngma chaoraktaba thā amada
3. Sun big growing not moon one in

1. asheiba wāngngam tengthaba pollem
2. sānglak-tabana sāng-lakte. Nūmit
3. high growing not high grow not. Sun

1. makhong leima likshishu Paima lilkoigi
2. ningthiba nūmit paiduna laishi
3. beautiful sun taking Divinity

1. poiroi leishei thon ahālbāmā wākmanārao
2. lai thōn narakpani nūmit yai
3. praying sun blessings

1. lemba maka lilou thoiba langlel tana
2. pūmnamak ki mapu oiba
3. all of their ancestor being

1. thon kumba pollem pinung manglababu
2. pūnsiba nang-gi natik arūba
3. long-lived you of your equal difficult

1. khayom leina thāna pollem pisakpa
2. ningthibabu yaona haiba ngamdre
3. beautiful up to to say cannot

1. palthon panung manglababu lonyom
2. nūmit sakpada thāba ngamlamde
3. sun singing in count cannot

1. wangngam lima thana paltham pasakpa
2. nūmit yaigi marū leipākki manam
3. Sun blessings of their source country of its smell

1. leirak khonglen maril tatlababu huirel
2. asida nūngsa sāba meini. Angālba
3. this in warmth making fire are. Bright

1. khomshilol tourang lomthana pural matangka
2. nūmit taipang-pānbagi pūnsigi
3. Sun world of longevity of

1. palbi youtampaina koakpui tingkhong
2. chen-chel oiriba yaigi marū
3. material (source) being blessings of their source

1. narababu leirak chenantana khongkhong
2. pūnsibagi mathoujālgi pūnsi
3. longevity of material longevity

1. pairam yaipung mingmanglababu yaoroi
2. thōujālbu phangjaningre laimaral
3. material get humbly desire is divine

1. satokpa tokmu meishangbu langpal
2. lal kubio aina ijabasi wā roubiganu
3. me by writing humbly blame not

1. shaoikoi leipungkoi chalaobana yā kanarababu
2. nanai angang apisak lousing
3. your slave child little intelligent

1. lamejāl chenna talna pungknangba chingya
2. pharak iba aina ijabane.
3. duly writing me by writing humbly is.

1. thelaming khemglababu shapu makhut

1. chumba lang heitel palbana shapu chelonehal

1. langhei yathangbiun chingyāthelming

1. manglababu chingyā chelnadana thelkhangbu

1. lamyaikei mingmanglababu oklel hum yania

1. lairel hum thimarababu lamyai chehatālnā

1. kaikhangbana tengthabadi yorinayai

1. Taodalbana karon muning mapuchaokapa

1. lachao lakte loidani thapung mapu shanglak

1. kapala shanglakte yoimayai Taodal chumba

1. sheichal ningthiba yoimayai tao haina teng

1. thamrakpa meine, yoimayai lairel shedababu

1. ma khommadalbu chimomduna tengthajarake

1. lairel shedabagi yoikhang mashanom

1. migthibabu namugamda tapta sua mangai

1. thonghe sheiomapu tha ngamde yoimayai

1. taodalba nongthil liklu yaiomba malem

1. manamshina nongshaha mime angalba sua

1. khommadal taipong pulshi chungchel kuina

1. yai lairel shedabagi maralkubu pulshi

1. marulkubu leiwainashi pithraipi ashembi

1. shem khutsha khongloubigunu nanai nao

1. ashisha lonshing matamlakpana ijabane.

NOTE.—The archaic version is reproduced without diacritical vowel marks or consonantal emendations. I do not know enough of the archaic language to venture on these tasks.—T.C.H.

INDEX.

Abdanta Prabhugi Palla, 70.
Achan khuba, 68.
—— *khulel*, 68.
Achramba, 68.
Achrōmba (*Achrōmbi*), 68; order of precedence, 72.
ADOPTION, 84 *et seq.*
Adultery, 91.
AFFINITIES, 10–13.
Agar, 29.
Agari Holdar, 71.
AGRICULTURE, 39–44, 86; implements, 42.
Ahaiba, 69.
Ahāllūp lākpa, 65.
AHĀLŪP (AHALLUP, AHARUP, AHULLOOP), 58; boat races, 52; Chirap, 65, 66; Lallup, 63.
Airaba, *Rajah*, 9.
Akhanba Hanjaba, 72.
—— *Hidang*, 72.
Akhōnba, 70.
Alcohol, manufacture, 32, 60; as marriage gift, 116; tabu, 47.
Amandar, 71.
—— *Major*, 71.
Ametpa, 69.
Ammonite, 102.
Anam Sang, 67.
ANCESTOR WORSHIP, 96, 99–103.
ANDRO, deities, 103; expedition against, 9; officials, 72; origin, 9.
Angōm, deities, 99–100; genealogy, 100, 183; marriage, 75; rebellions of, 153; structure, 73.
Angōm Hanba, 68.
Angōm Ningthou, 9; marriage, 76; status, 65; succession, 83.
Angōnjambam, 69.
Anik Loisang, 70.
ANIMALS, 2, 46; as food, 47; as sacrifice, 103, 109; worship of, 100–101.
ANIMISM, 95 *et seq.*
Anklets, 18.
ANTHROPOMETRICAL DATA, 3.
AO NAGA LANGUAGE, comparative structure, 163–170; comparative vocabularies, 158, 161.
Apaibi, 88.
Apampa, 68.
Apānbi, 76.
Apple, 40, 44.
Apricot, 40.
Arāmba, 20.
Arāngba (*Arongba*), 70; duties, 68.
Archery, 47; in folk-tale, 144.
ARCHITECTURE, 8, 25, 26.
Argus pheasant, 16
Armlet, 28.
ARMS. See WEAPONS.
ARMY, 58, 61, 93; regiments, 71.
ART, 29.
ARTS AND CRAFTS, 22–39.
Asālba, 90.
ASCENDING THE THRONE, ceremony, 125; costume worn, 6, 8.
Asin, 62.
Aton Puremba, 132, 135.
Atum, 74.
AWA PUREL (AWA PUREN, AYA PUREN), 59; functions, 61; status, 71.
Awondar, 71.
Ayapuren. See *Awa purel*.
AYŌKPA, 63, 64.

Babroobahan (*Bahrubahan*, *Bubra Baha*), *Rajah*, 5, 7.
Bāgh Māsh, 46.
BALLADS, 117; "*Nūmit kāppa*" translated, 125; idem in Meithei, 188–210.
Bamboo, 25.
Bamdiar, 71.
Bamjigi Palla, 70.

Banishment, 88.
Bao māsh, 45.
Barāk, river, 1.
Bazar, 18, 23.
Bebosta, 68.
Bed, 25, 27; in marriage procession, 115.
Bee, 47.
Beetroot, 40.
Bengal, 4.
Bengalis and Meitheis, compared, 4.
Betel-nut tree, 48.
BETROTHAL, 116, 138.
Bhadra, 62.
Bhandari, 70.
Bharat Shai, Rajah, 80.
Bhitna Tuli, 71.
Bijaya Garot, 61, 71.
Birds, 2.
BIRTH, CEREMONIES, 112; DEITIES, 97, 127.
Bishenpur, 102.
Bishnu Naha, 71.
—— *Saina* (*Soina*) *Ahal*, 71.
Black coss, 29.
Boats, 33, 52.
BOAT-RACES, 51–53; costume, 8, 16.
BODO, linguistic affinities, 11, 155 *et seq.*
Boldeb Seina, 69.
Boro Gayet, 72.
Bow and Arrow, 20; in Chronicles, 47; in folk-tale, 126, 144.
Bracelet, 18, 19.
Brahma, marriage ceremony, 115.
Brahmedev, 5.
BRAHMIN, 70; prohibition from Lamchel, 53; and Lallup, 60, 61, 63, 70; land tenure, 85; legal position, 88.
BREECH-LOADING GUN, 20.
Bribery, 24.
Bricks, 26.
Brindabon Chandro Pujari, 70.
BRITISH OCCUPATION, 11, 81, 82, 97.
BROWN, DR., on caste, 108; costume, 13; crime, 24; facial characteristics, 2; Gharib Newaz, 78; land tenure, 85; manufactures, 28; naming system, 112; origin of race, 7; ornaments, 18; salt, 33; silk, 30; superstitions, 120.
Bubra Baha. See *Babroobahan*.
BUDDHISM, 97.
Budhiraj, 9, 72.
Buffalo, 41.
Building, 25; superstitions, 122.
Bull in folk-tale, 143, 144.
BURMA, invasion of Manipur, 29; Meithei colonies in, 4; Meithei invasion of, 4, 58, 59; silk trade with Manipur, 31.
BURMESE LANGUAGE, affinities with Meithei, 11, 155; comparative structure, 163–170; comparative vocabularies, 157–162.
—— War, First, 19.
Butterfly, 121.

Cabbage, 40.
Cachar, Meithei settlements, 4, 23.
Camphor, 29.
CAPITAL PUNISHMENT, 88–89.
Card playing, 56.
Carpentry, 28.
Carrot, 40.
Cassay Horse, 19, 20.
Castanets, 57.
CASTE, 84; food and drink, 32, 47; and Lois, 10; marriage, 76; punishments involving loss of, 88; purificatory rites, 108; reed instruments, 57; silk manufacture, 30.
Catapult, 21.
Cattle theft, 24, 88.
Cavalry, 19.
Census of 1901, 2, 182.
Ceremonies, sacred, 103 *et seq.*; physical defects a disqualification, 83.
Chabon, 67.
Chadar, 14, 15.
CHĀHITABA, 104–107; sanctity of, 110.
CHAIREL (CHAIREN), 9; administration, etc., 60, 72; pottery manufacture, 32.
Chairong, 43.
Chakkon, 70.
Chakpa Laimaram, 72.
Chalamba (*Chalumba*) *Rajah*, dress reforms, 17; introduces surnames, 112.
Chandra Kirti Singh (*Nowchingleng Nougdren Khomba*), 81, 114; creates foreign minister, 59; and Hinduism, 95.
Changam Ningthou, 66.

Changning Kānbi, 149.
Chaobi Nongnāngma-chāk, 134.
Chaphu, 104.
Charairomba. See *Churairomba.*
Charang Pāt, 70.
CHENGLEI (CHENGLOI), administration, etc., 73; deity, 100; genealogy, 100, 184; marriage, 75.
Cheshire, 33.
Chest, 27.
Chikhong. See *Seekong.*
Children, 79; costume, 14, 15; food, 48; sepulture, 116.
Chin Hills, 1.
CHINESE, introduce colour stamping, 15; introduce dhotie, 17; introduce gunpowder, 21.
Chingā Makhā, hill, 124.
Chingkuba Akhuba, 133.
Chingku Tel haiba, Rajah, 132, 134.
Ching-ngai-rakpa, 72
Chingtung Komba (*Ching Thang Kōmba, Jaee Singh*), Rajah, 81; in ballads, 56; coinage, 37.
CHIRĀP, 59, 60; costume, 15; officials, 65, 66, 91.
CHIROUBA, 104.
Chitra Ketoo, 5
—— *Rat*, 5.
—— *Sarba*, 5.
—— *Vanoo*, 5.
Chitrabij (*Chitrabija*), 5.
Chitradhaja, 5.
Chitranggada, 5.
Chongkhanba, 67.
Choto Gayet, 72.
Chourjeet Singh (*Chourjit Singh*) *Rajah*, 81; coinage, 37.
"CHRONICLES OF THE STATE OF MANIPUR," brick walls, 26; costume, 17; deities, 97; games, 56; inheritance, 77 *et seq.*; irrigation, 42; Loi villages, 9; origin, 4, 5; religion, 102, 109; superstitions, 120–124; sepulture, 116; women, 75, 89.
Chudder. See *Chadar.*
Chundrakong, 33, 35.
Churairomba (*Charairomba*) *Rajah*, 78–80; coinage, 37.
Cigarette smoking, 48.
CLAN GODS, 98; see also DEITIES.
Clay, 28.
Clock, 29.
CLOTH MANUFACTURE, 27.
Cock fighting, 23.
Cohabitation, 115.
Coiffure, styles of, 3.
COINAGE, 36–39.
Coining, 24.
Colour stamping, 15.
COLQUHOUN, H. A., on adoption, 84 marriage, 115.
Conchshell, 57.
Copper coinage, 38.
Coronation Hall, architecture, 8; folk-tale, 122; see also Kangla.
Cossiahs, 10.
COSTUME, 13–18; boat-race, 8; and individuality, 3; Loi, 18; Panggan, 18; Captain Pemberton on, 6; Raja and coronation, 6, 8; festivals, 104.
Cotton, 28.
Counting, 105.
Cowry, 38–39.
CREATION, 5.
Cremation, 94, 116.
Crime, 24.
CROPS, 40–44; deities, 96, 103.

Dacca, 4.
Dal (*Dhal*), 40, 43.
Dam, 38.
Dammer, 29.
DANCES, DANCER, DANCING, 54; costume, 16; in folk-tale, 141; travelling, 23.
Dao, 19, 32, 39; in folk-tale, 111.
Dapar Jug, 5.
Dart, 20.
Days, superstitions, 120.
DEAD, DEATH, customs, 116; deities, 97, 127; omen, 121.
Debendro Singh (*Debindro Singh*) *Rajah*, 81, 123; wives, 76; and *Yim tinaba*, 64.
Debt, 89.
Decapitation, 89.
Deer, 2.
Defects, physical, 81, 83.
DEITIES, 96, 98 *et seq.*, 103.
DEMONOLOGY, 98, 120–124.
Design, in costume, 14, 15.
Dewan, 36; status, 61.
Dhal. See Dal.
Dhananjai, 56.
Dhobi, 69.
Dhotie (*Dhutie*), 14, 17.
DISTRIBUTION, geographical, 4.

Divorce, 91.
Dolai-roi (*Dularoi*), 68.
—— *Hanjaba*, 59; order of precedence, 72.
—— *Hidang*, 72.
Drawing, 29.
DREAMS, divine sanction in, 119, 131; interpretation of, 124.
DRESS. See COSTUME.
DRINK, 47.
DROUGHT, 107–108.
Drum, 55, 57.
Duhol, 70.
Duhon Loisang, 70.
Dulai-paba, 68.
Dulairoi Hanjaba. See *Dolairoi Hanjaba.*
—— *Hidang*. See *Dolairoi Hidang.*
Durga, 102; festival of, 49.
Dussera, 102.
Dyeing, 29.

Earring, 18, 19.
EARTH-GODDESS, 98, 125–129.
EARTHQUAKE, 35; animistic belief, 111, 120.
EAST INDIA COMPANY, 29, 38.
ECLIPSE, superstition, 121.
Economics, 22; and Lallūp, 58, 59.
Education, 24.
Eharoi Loi, 9.
Ekma Haodongla, 126–129.
Electro-plating, 29.
Elephant, 2; in folk-tale, 145.
Endren-Lakpa, 66.
Enoog Howba Chonoo, 5.
Exchange, 38.
Execution, 89.

Faichareng, 18.
Fanek, 14; Panggan, 18.
FAUNA, 12, 46.
Fayeng, 9; deity, 103.
Feida, 67.
Feiroijamba, 135–138.
FESTIVALS, 16, 49, 117.
FISH, FISHING, FISHERIES, 44–46, industry, 30, varieties, 45.
FIREARMS, 20.
Fireplace, 25.
FLORA, 1, 44.
FOLK-TALES AND LEGENDS, 5, 7, 120–124; "*Khamba and Thoibi*," 134–151; history of "*Moirang*," 130–134; "*Numit Kappa*," 125–129; "*Numit Kappa*," in *Meithei*, 188–210.
FOOD, 47.
FOOT HOCKEY, 49, 54.
FOOT RACE, 52–53; 141–142.
Frontal bone, 117.
Fruit, cultivation, 40–43, 44; as marriage gifts, 145, 146.
FURNITURE, HOUSEHOLD, 27.

Gambhir Singh (*Gumbeer Sing*) *Rajah*, 63, 81; end of dynasty foretold, 123; and Lallūp, 58; military levy, 93.
Gambling, 23, 56.
GAMES, 49–57; boat races, 8; National, 16.
Gandharva marriages, 115.
Gārisang, 68.
Geese, 2.
GENNA, 118, 119; marriage, 75; Nagas, 94; rain-compelling ceremonies, 108; and Rajah, 107, 124; warriors, 153.
Geometrical figures, 14.
Gharib Newaz (*Pamheiba*, *Moianba*, *Gurreeb Newaz*) *Rajah*, 18; and animism, 97, 98; coinage, 37; cremation, 116; Hinduism, 9, 95, 114; and Kokching, 9; Lallūp, 58; legends concerning, 78 *et seq.*; murder of, 80; and Nagas, 11; succession of, 78.
Ghurrah, 28.
Gifts, betrothal, 138; in law cases, 92; marriage, 115.
Gnā rao, 45.
—— *rel*, 46.
—— *tel*, 46.
Goallee, 45.
Gobinda (*Govindji*), 70, 99.
Goldsmith, 19, 22, 28, 30.
Gourosham. See *Guru Sham.*
GRAMMAR, MEITHEI, 171–180.
GRIERSON, DR., on language, 11; on linguistic affinities of Lois, 12.
Guava, 40.
Gulap machu dhoti, 15.
Gumbeer Sing. See *Gambhir Singh.*
Gunpowder, 21.
Gurreeb Newaz. See *Gharib Newaz.*
Guru (the Lord of the Universe), 100.

Guru Sham (*Gourosham, Gouroo Sham*) *Rajah*, and East India Company, 38; reason for joint rule, 83; reign, 80.

HABITAT, 1, 2.
*H*AIR-DRESSING, 3.
Hairok, 72.
Hameng-mitpa, 103.
Haojaopam, 70.
Haomacha, 70.
Haonu Changkanu, 126.
Haoramba-hal (*Haoram-hal*), 134.
Haoramningoi (*Haoram-yeima*), 134.
Haoram-thol Louthiba, 134.
Haoram-yeima. See *Haoramningoi*.
Hari Kirtan, 115.
Havildar, 71.
Head-dress, 17, 18.
HEAD-HUNTING, 94.
Head, sanctity of, 80.
Heijapot, 115.
HEIR, inheritance of property, 77; succession to titles, 78.
Hiang Loi Namoi Chaoba, 105.
HIDĀKPHĀNBA (HITĀKPHĀLBA HITĀKPHĀNBA), 58; boat-races, 52; duties, 64, 67.
Hidang, 66.
High treason, 89; in Chronicles, 93.
Hijaba bangmai, 68.
Hijarakpa, 72.
Hills, holy, 106, 107, 111; legends of, 124.
HILL TRIBES compared with Meithei, 5 *et seq.*; linguistic affinity with Meithei, 10–12.
Hinaoba, functions, 61; status, 72.
HINDUISM, 7, 95–97; ceremony of admission, 84; and Lois, 10, 74; result of, on Meithei, 5, 47.
Hiroi Lamgang, 33.
Hiruba, functions, 61; status, 72.
Hiruhinaoba, 67.
Hisang, 69.
Hitākphālba, *Hitākphānba*. See *Hidākphānba*.
Hiyāngthāng, 102.
Hockey, 49, 54.
HODGSON, B. H., 10.
Hogaibi, 26.
Holi, 103.
Honey, 48.
Horn, 57.
HOUSE, arrangement, 25, 146, 153; deities, 96, 98; furniture, 27; structure, 25; superstitions re building, 121.
Huidru Hanba, 66.
Hui-rai, 46.
Huirai Hanba, 66.
Huirai Hidang, 66.
Humai, 42.
Humai-roi, 68.
Hume's pheasant, 16.
HUNTING, 46, 47.

IMPHĀL, river, 9.
—— town, Bazars, 23; education, 24; population, 26; tumulus at, 118, 133.
IMPLEMENTS, 39 *et seq.*, 42.
IMPORTS, dried fish, 48; salt, 33.
IMŪNG LAI, 96; birth ceremony, 112; worship, 103.
Indian hemp, 48.
Indigo, 40.
Indoo Muni, 5.
Indra, 111.
INHERITANCE, 77–82.
Innaphi, 14, 115.
Irāk-Lakpa, 66.
IRON SMELTING, 9, 30, 31.
IRRIGATION, 40–42.
ISEISAKPAS, 55, 56, 117.
Iting, Lallūp, 72; origin of, 9.
Ivory, 29.
Iwang Fang Fang Ponglenhanba, King, 130, 131.

Jackfruit, 40.
Jaee Singh. See *Chingtung Komba*.
Jail, labour, 88; statistics, 23.
Jaisagun Hidang, 66.
—— *Lakpa*, 65.
Jamadar (*Jemadar*), 71.
Javelin throwing, 20, 51.
Jemadar. See *Jamadar*.
Jessami, 1.
JEWELRY, 18; manufacture, 28.
Jit Shah (*Shai*) *Rajah*, 80.
Jobista. See *Pākhangba*.
JOHNSTONE, MAJOR-GENERAL SIR JAMES, K.C.S.I., on brick-built walls, 26; on capital punishment, 89; on education, 24; on racial affinities, 8.
Jubraj, meaning, 65; puberty customs, 114; status, 59.

Ju-gi mairi dhoti, 15.
Jungle gods, worship of, 69, 96, 103.
Jute, 44.

Kabo Hanba, 68.
Kachari language, comparative structure, 163–170; comparative vocabularies, 158, 161.
Kachin language, affinities, 11, 156; comparative structure, 164–170; comparative vocabularies, 158–161.
Kahar, 84.
Kairungba (*Keirungba*), 68; status, 72.
Kairungba maroi, 67.
—— *yairek sang*, 67.
Kaithenmānbi, scapegoat ceremony at, 106, 111.
Kali Jug, 5.
Kallika Debi Palla, 70.
Kalye, 43.
Kameng, 9; administration, etc., 72; iron ore, 32.
Kameng chatpa dhoti, 15, 16, 17.
Kameng Kokching, 72.
Kammokha Debi, 70.
Kāng drūm, 50.
—— *hū*, 49.
Kangla architecture, 8; coronation rites, 108; erection of, 122.
Kangnao Tuli, 71.
Kangpōt, 42.
Kāng sū-na-ba, 55.
Kangsubi, 115.
Kang Tuli, 71.
Kao Taruk, 72.
Kaphum. See *Khūbum*.
Kasu, 74.
Kathē, 1.
Katnam, 92.
Katum, 65.
Kazi, 70.
Keeyamba Rajah. See *Kiamba Rajah*.
Kei, administration, etc., 70; duties, 63, 64; Lallup, 60; land tenure, 87.
Kei-roi thau, 64, 65.
Keirungba. See *Kairungba*.
Keirup, 46, 94.
Keisham, 69.
Kekere ke sanaba, 56.
Kekre Hanba, 66.
—— *Hidang*, 66.
Kess, 28.
Khūba, 97.
Khabam. See *Khabum*.
Khābam Sanglen, 61.
Khābanānba, administration, etc., 73; deities, 100; genealogy, 100, 184; marriage, 75.
Khabru, 103, 106.
Khabum (Kaphum), administration, etc., 63 *et seq.*; boat-races, 52; meaning, 58.
Khādarakpa, 142; status, 72.
Khāgenba (Khagi-yen-ba Khakamba) Rajah, 26; boat-races, 53; burial law, 116; Chinese, 15; coinage, 37; dress reforms, 17; gunpowder, 21; houses, 26; Lois, 9; polo, 49; Sena Kaithel, 23; table equipage, 30.
Khamba, 56, 117; in history of Moirang, 132, 133.
Khamba and Thoibi, folk tale, 134–154.
Khambi-rakpa, 72.
Khamdingou, 100.
Khāmi language, comparative structure, 164–170; comparative vocabularies, 159, 161.
Khamnu, 132, 133, 135–154.
Khangabōk, 72.
Khangjing sanaba, 57.
Khanton-Lakpa, 66.
Khasi, 10; belief in snake contrasted with that of Meitheis, 101.
Khessaree, 43.
Khetri Hanchaba, 66.
Khoi-haoba, 3.
Khongjai Lambus, 69.
Khōng kāngjei, 49.
Khoomon. See *Kumul*.
Khooi Ningon, *King*, 26.
Khoot naiba, 63.
Khowai Nongjengba, 126.
Khoyal lakpa, 72.
Khubeiseisakpa, 54.
Khudong, 70.
Khul Chaoba, *Rajah*, 9.
Khullakpa, 72; house, 8; status, 60, 66.
Khumal. See Kumul.
Khuman. See Kumul.
Khumanthem sagei, 68.
Khundang Hidang, 66.
Khundin, 62.
Khungoinaba, 88.

Khunjahanba, 60.
Khuraijam, 98.
Khurai-rakpa duties, 91; status, 65.
Khutheiba Loisang, 68.
Khutlai, 39.
Khuyal Leikhong, 131.
Kiambà (*Keeyamba*) *Rajah*, institutes Chāhitābas, 105; coinage, 37.
King cobra (*Ophiophagus elaps*), 2.
KINGSHIP, 78, 101, 106, 110, 118.
Kirtana, 70, 115.
Koibi Namthou, 47.
Koidè ngamba, 125–129.
Koirengba Rajah, 58.
Kokching (*Khul-len*), 9; administration, etc., 72.
—— *Khunao*, 72.
—— *Yairi*, 72.
Kōngūbam, 69.
Kōngjamba. See *Kongyamba*.
Kōngsang, 69.
Kōngyamba (*Kongjamba*), 138, 139.
Kōnsā Hanba, 66.
Kōnsam, 69, 106.
Konthounamba Sāphaba, 132.
Kookie. See *Kuki*.
Koomul. See *Kumul*.
Koorta, 14.
Korai, 36.
Kosshop Muni, 5.
Kothandor, 71.
Kotwāl, 59.
Koupooee, 6.
Kuarangba, 67.
Kubbo, 31.
Kubo Valley, 1, 148.
KUKI (Kookie), gunpowder manufacture, 21; habitat, 6; language, 6; succession to village offices, 84.
KUKI CHIN LANGUAGES, 11, 156.
Kula Chandra Singh, 82.
KUMUL (KOOMUL, KHOOMON, KHUMAL, KHUMAN) administration, etc., 72, 73; genealogy, 100, 185; genna, 118; habitat, 6; history, 5, 132; marriage, 75; religion, 99, 100, 108, 110.
Kunda Sang, 70.
Kupass, 29.
Kuru Khul, 72.
Kut, 71.
KWĀKTĀLBA, 103.

Lai, 102.
Lai bhandari, 70.
Laiching, 98.
Laifacheng, *Rajah*, 131.
Laifam. See *Laipham*.
LAI HARAOBA, 104, 117; costume worn, 16; in "Khamba and Thoibi," 138.
Laikai, 63.
Laikhong Siphai, 70.
Laikhu Hidang, 66.
—— *Rakpa*, 66.
Laimakhubi, 76.
Laima-nai, 67.
Laima-ren, 98, 99, 103.
Laima Semba, 67.
LAIPHAM (LAI PHUM, LAIFAM), (name of PANNA), administration, etc., 65, 66; boat-races, 52; Lallūp, 63.
Lai-pham, meaning of, 102.
Lairel, 2.
Lairema (*Lirema Hooidompokpi*, *Thōngnūk Lairemma*) in Numit Kappa, 125–129; worship of, 98.
Lairen hidang, 72.
—— *lakpa*, 67; status, 72.
Lairik Yengbam, 26; duties, 69; status, 66.
Lairik-yengba Hanchaba, 66.
Lai Sangkong, 79.
Laisangthem Lamabi, 98.
Laishing-choubi, 98.
Lake spirits, 96.
Lākpa, 60 *et seq.*
LĀLLŪP (LALLOOP), 58 *et seq.*; Brahmins, 61; definition, 31; exemption from, 53; land tenure, 85; Col. McCulloch on operation of, 22; military service and, 59; salt manufacture, 36; vernacular statement of, 62.
Lāllup chingba, 60.
LĀLMĪ (LALMEE) and Chirāp, 66; lāllūp, 63; organization, 61.
Lamchel (*Lumchel*), 52 *et seq.*, 141.
Lamkhang poak, 15; introduction of, 17.
LAM LAI, 96.
Lammi Loisang, 68.
Land, inheritance laws, 77.
LAND TENURE, 85 *et seq.*; and lāllūp, 65.
Langathen, 72.
Langōl, 42.
Langpon, 62.

LANGUAGE, affinities, 6, 10–13; comparative vocabularies, 155–162. dialect in songs, 117; tabus on, 118, 131.
Lao mi hidang, 61.
—— —— *rūkpa*, 61.
LAWS, 88–93, see Costume. Dress, Inheritance, Land, Marriage, etc.
Leather, 28.
Leikai Loisang, 68.
Leikeirakpa, 141.
Leima Nangban Chanu Meirapanjenlei, 130.
Leipareng, 115.
Leopard, 2, 46.
Lightning, folk tale, 111.
Liman Sang, 68.
Lime, 40.
Limestone 32.
Lingba, 41.
Lirema Hooidompokpi. See *Lairema*.
Lock-making, 29.
Loee. See *Loi*.
Loee-il, 63, 152.
Loeening, 43.
Logtūk Lake, fauna, 2; fishing, 45; origin of villages on, 9.
LOI (LUI, LOEE) administration, etc., 71; boat-making, 33; characteristics, 3; costume, 18; deities, 103; fishing, 46; foot-race, 53; Hinduism, 84; history, 8 *et seq.*; Lallūp, 60–63; language, 12, 13; marriage, 116; origin, 12, 65; pottery, 32, 39; silk, 27, 30; succession laws, 84; timber, 33; Yū manufacture, 32.
Loisang, 69.
Looang. See *Luang*.
Loukham, 69.
Loukhumta, 70.
Lourungsang, 67.
LUANG (LOOANG), administration, etc., 65; deities, 99 *et seq.*; genealogy, 100, 185; habitat, 5, 6; marriage, 75.
Luhup, 17.
LUI. See LOI.
Lumchel. See *Lamchel*.
Lūp-lakpa, 60, 66.
Luplengka, 25.
Lushai Hills, 1.
LUSHEI LANGUAGE, comparative structure, 164–170; comparative vocabularies, 159, 161.
MCCULLOCH, COLONEL, on agriculture, 40; art, 29; costume, 13; houses, 25; kāngsānaba, 55; Lāllūp, 62; land tenure, 86; Lois 30; maibis, 109; marriage, 115; naming system, 112; nomenclature, 1; original occupants, 5; law of property, 78; religion, 98 *et seq.*; slave system, 90; superstitions, 121.
Machi Manao, legend of, 124.
MCLENNAN, J. F., 12.
Madu Chandra, 81.
MAGIC, 107, 128.
Mahabali Thakur Palla, 70.
Mahabārat, 7.
Maharāni, 76.
Mahindrapahar, 7.
Mahindrapore, 7.
MAIBA, 95, 96, 106, 109, 110, 153; *lāl-lūp*, 69.
MAIBI, 109, 110, 131; *lāl-lūp*, 69.
Maifengba, 68.
Maikel (*Mekrimi*), 79; precedence of, 80; war-stone, 102.
Manang Usang, 70.
Mango, 40, 43.
Māngsōk, 146.
MANIPUR (MANNIPUR, MANIPORE, MUNNIPOR, KATHĒ, MEKLE, MOGLAI, MAHINDRAPORE, MAHINDRAPAHAR), administration, 58–72; agriculture, 39–44, 85; census, 2; chronicles, 4, and *passim*; coinage, 36–39; crime, 23, 88; economics, 21; education, 24; feasts and festivals, 16, 49 *et seq.*, 103 *et seq.*, 117; fishing, 44; flora and fauna, 1, 43, 44; hunting, 46; history, 78, 133; (see also special headings, *e.g.* Gharib Newaz, British occupation); land tenure, 85–87; laws, 88–93; manufactures, 27–36; military organization, 59, 61, 71, 93; minerals, 31; name, origin of; penal settlements, 4, 9, 22, 74; prison system, 23, 88; salt-wells, 33; slavery, 90; topography, 1. For religion, customs, etc., see Meithei.
MANIPURI. See MEITHEI.
MANNIPUR. See MANIPUR.
Mantri, 65, 72.
Mantri Sebok, 70.

MANUFACTURES, 27 *et seq.*
Mao, 1.
Maolong, 1.
Mapanthong, 70.
MARAM, 11.
Marangba, Rajah, 37.
Marjit Singh, 81.
Maribōkjagoi, 54.
Marichi Muni, 5.
MARRIAGE, 75, 92; Brahmins, 75; Loi, 74; Maram, 11; Nagas, 11, 76; rites, 115, 137; tabu, 153.
MARRIED WOMEN, coiffure, 3; status, 91.
Matchlock, 20.
Matriarchy, 101.
Mayang Hanba, 68.
—— *-sajik*, 69.
Medicine-man. See Maiba.
Meenai chanaba, 90.
MEITHEI (MANIPURI, MUNNIPORI, MOITAY), affinities, 4 *et seq.*, 10 *et seq.*; ancestor worship, 99–102; appearance, 2 *et seq.*; art, 29; caste, 30, 57, 84; character, 23, 94; clan organization, 73 *et seq.*; costume, 13–18; courage, 46; death, 116; deities, 95–99; domestic occupations, 22–24; folk tales, 56, 111, 117, 125, 132, 188; genna, 118; geographical distribution, 4; habitat, 1 *et seq.*; Hinduism, 46 *et seq.*, 95 *et seq.*; houses, 25–27; industries, 27 *et seq.*; jewelry, 18; lāllūp, 59; marriage, 75, 115; marriage with Nagas, 11; music, 57; name, derivation of, 10; origin, 5 *et seq.*; political organization, 59 *et seq.*; rites and ceremonies, 103; sports and pastimes, 16, 49–57, 103, 117; superstitions, 120–124; weapons, 19–21; women, see under Women.
MEITHEI LANGUAGE, 155–181; affinities, 10 *et seq.*; grammar, 171; "Numit kappa" in, 189.
MEITHEI LEIPAK, 1; submersion theory, 7.
Meilūn-sang, 69.
Meklē, 1.
Mekrimi. See *Maikel*.
Meng-khong ba, 103.
Mera, 62.
MILITARY ORGANIZATION, 58, 61, 70, 71.
Militia, 58, 59.
MINERALS, 31, 32.
Mi-ngonda nai-ba, 91.
MINSTRELSY, 55, 56, 117.
Moglai, 1.
Moianba. See *Gharib Newaz*.
MOIRANG, administration, 65, 72, 73; deities, 100; folk tales, 130–133, 135–154; genealogy, 100, 186; genna, 118, 119; habitat, 5, 6; history, 6, 59, 133; marriage, 75.
Moirang-khōng, battle of, 133.
Moitay, 10.
Mongeanba, 23, 124.
Moon, worship of, 111.
Moongh, 43.
MUHAMMEDANS. See PANGGANS.
Mukna Kanba, 70.
Mulberry tree, 44.
MUNNIPOR. See MANIPUR.
MUNNIPORIE. See MEITHEI.
Murder, 88, 89.
Murring, 6, 16.
Music, 55 *et seq.*
Mustard, 40.
Mutilation, 88.

Nadia, 4.
NAGA, administration, 60; chāhitāba, 106; cloth trade, 27; genna, 118; Gharib Newaz, 11, 79; Hinduism, 84; lāllūp, 60; linguistic affinities, 11, 156; marriage, 11, 76; and origin of Meithei, 6 *et seq.*; Moirang, 130; ordeal, 93; pottery, 33; succession to village offices, 84.
Nahūrakpa, 61; duties, 67; order of precedence, 72.
NAHARUP (NIHAROOP), administration, 65 *et seq.*; boat-races, 52; lāllup, 63; meaning, 58.
Nakap-lakpa, 66.
Nakappa Hidang, 66.
Nakon Hidang, 66.
Nambol, river, 53.
NAMING SYSTEM, 112 *et seq.*; pre-Hinduism, 135.
NĀMUNG-BA, 118, 119; meaning, 107; penalty for breach, 75; rain-compelling ceremonies, 108.
Nandeiba loisangba, 68.
Napit, 69.
Narayan, 5.
Natch Ghar, beams, 1; construction, 26.

NATURE WORSHIP, 95, 96, 111, 112; deities, 103; "Nūmit Kāppa," 125; rain-festivals, 107.
Nawa Tuli, 71.
Necklet, 18.
Ngangba. See *Khūbanūba*.
Ngangkharakpa, 72.
Ngangningsing, 100.
Ngang-ngourakpa, 72.
NIHABOOP, NIHABŪP. See NAHĀRŪP.
Ningail, 33 *et seq.*
Ningkham furi, 18.
NINGTHAJA (NINGTHOUJA), administration, etc., 73; deities, 99; genealogy, 5, 100, 182; marriage, 75; sacrifices, 109; tabu, 118.
Ningthau selba, 63.
Ningthem porohit, 68.
NINGTHOU, 60; status, 65, 72.
Ningthoukhong, 72.
Ningthou phisāba, 69.
Nōngbal Chaoba, 135.
—— *Kongyamba*. See *Kongyamba*.
Nongmai-Ching hill, 9; meaning, 7; rain-puja, 107.
Nongpōk Ningthou, 99, 100.
NŌNGSHĀ, 89; symbolism of, 102.
Nongthonba (*Nongtholba*), 65, 72.
Nōngthōn Hidang, 66.
Noongshaba, 98.
Noongtil Chaibee, 79.
Nose ornaments, 19.
Nowchingleng Nongdren Khomba. See *Chandra Kirti Singh*.
"NŪMIT KĀPPA," 56, 111; literal translation, 125 *et seq.*; Meithei version and translation, 188 *et seq.*
Nungaoyumthāngba, 100.
Nungbi, 74.
Nur Singh, 81.

Oak, 44.
OATH, 92, 137.
OCCUPATION, 22 *et seq.* See Manufactures, Fishing, Games, Internal Structure.
Oināmnōng, 71.
Okchinglakpa, 72.
OMEN, 105, 120 *et seq.*; marriage, 116.
ONEIROMANCY, 124; deities, 98; connection with genna, 119.
Onion, 43.
Ophiophagus ōelaps. See King cobra.
Opium, 40, 48.
Orange, 40, 43, 44.
ORDEAL, 93.
ORNAMENTS, 18.
ORIGIN, Lois, 8 *et seq.*; Meitheis, 5 *et seq.*; Panggans, 4.

Pagri, (*Puggree*) introduction, 17; laws, 14 *et seq.*
Pahila. See *Pihila*.
Paijasuba, 68.
Paikomba Rajah. See *Pikhomba*.
PAINTING, 29.
Paja, 83, 92.
—— *Hulbum*, 83.
PĀKHANGBA (The JOBISTA, PAKHUNGBA, PAKUNGBA), coinage, 37; genealogy, 5; Lois, 9; parricide legend, 5, 80; snake legend, 5, 101, 125; as tribal deity, 99 *et seq.*
Pākhan-lakpa, duties, 67; meaning, 60; order of precedence, 72.
Pākhanvāl, 145.
PĀKUNGBA. See PAKHANGBA.
Palla amanba, 70.
Palla-han, 70.
Palla nahā, 70.
Pallayeima, 70.
Pallum Hidang, 66.
—— *Puren*, 66.
Pamheiba. See *Gharib Newaz*.
Panam Ningthou, 103.
—— *semba*, 67.
PANGGAN, administration, 70; chāhitāba, 106; costume, 18; lal-lup, 60; origin, 4.
Panggan Mall, 70.
Pang phel, 41.
Panji Loisang, 69, 125.
PANNA (PUNNAH), administration, 65–67; definition, 52; lāllūp, 58–63; national sports, 49.
Pān sooparee, 48.
PANTHEISM, 111 *et seq.*
Panthoibi, in "Numit Kappa," 127, 128; worship of, 97, 99
Parenkoiba, 135.
PARRICIDE, 5, 80.
Pātcha Hanba, 72; duties, 68.
—— *Loisang*, 68.
Pāts, 45.
Pea, 40, 43.
Peach, 43.
PEEPA. See PIBA.

PEMBERTON, CAPTAIN, on agriculture, 39; iron smelting, 31; on origin of Meithei, 6.
Pena, 55, 56.
Penakhōngba, 69.
PENAL SETTLEMENTS, 9, 88.
Pepper, 43.
Phambankāba. See *Phumbānkāba*.
Phamen, 146.
Phammi Ahal, 67.
—— *Nahā*, 67.
Phamtokcha, 66.
Phangthou, 72.
Phao intōk, 42.
Phaorungba, 67.
Pheasant, 2, 16.
Phi-ge-napu dhoti, 15.
PHILOLOGICAL NOTES, 7, 16, 17, 26, 33, 39, 43, 46–49, 53, 64, 67–69, 73, 76, 80, 90–92, 98, 103, 104, 106, 109, 111–114, 119, 125, 131, 152–154.
Phoonan Saloomba, 85.
Phoongnai (*Phungnai*), 63, 64, 67.
—— *Sang lakpa*, 65.
Phourail, 43.
Phumbānkāba (*Phambān kāba*), 6, 125; costume worn, 8.
PIBA (PEEPA), 72, 73; functions, 110; lāllūp, 63; succession, 83.
Pigeon fighting, 56.
Pihila (*Pahila*), 71.
Pikhomba (*Paikomba*), *Rajah*, 17; coinage, 37; shooting prowess, 47.
Pineapple, 40, 43.
Plantain, 43.
Plough, 41.
Plum, 43.
Poiraiton, 100.
POLITICAL ORGANIZATION AND ADMINISTRATION, 58–72.
POLO, 49, 50; costume, 16; pony 49; stick, 49.
POLYGAMY, 76.
Pomegranate, 40.
PONG, Kingdom of, 114.
Pony, 49.
Poong hul, 41.
Potato, 40, 43.
Pōtsangba (*Pōtsungba*), administration, 67; boat-races, 52; duties, 64, 67; meaning, 58.
POTTERY INDUSTRY, 32, 33.
Prajapati, 115.
PRIESTHOOD, 95, 96, 131; functions, 109, 110; genna, 118.
PRIMOGENITURE, 75; kingship of clans, 78, 83; Nagas, 84.
Prison, statistics, 23; system, 88.
PROPERTY, Real and Personal, 77.
Puggree (*Pagri*), 14, 17.
Pukei, 70.
Pukhrumba, 65.
Pukhrun Hidang, 66.
Pukshore. 98.
PUNNĀH. See PANNA.
Punsiba, King, 134.
Purairōmba, 100, 103.
Puren (*Purel*), 66.
Purenba. See *Aton Puremba*.
Purree, 86.
Puthiba, 98.
Python, 2.

Quiron, 79.

Rabino Chandra, 81.
RACES, 51–54.
Radha Krishna, 17.
Radish, 40.
RAIN, deities, 96, 103; legend, 111; as omen, 121; pujas, 8, 107.
Rainbow, 121.
RAJAH, boat-races, 16, 52; chāhitaba, 107; genna, 118; installation of, 6, 8, 125; land tenure, 85–87; marriage, 76; name, assumption of, 114; rain-pujas, 107; salt-wells, 35; servants, 63 64, 67; snake-worship, 100; succession, 78 *et seq.*; tabu, 107, 110, 124.
Rajkumar, 15.
Rakshasa, 115.
Rāmbai, 20.
Rāmbai hūnba, 51.
RANEE (RĀNI), chahitāba, 107; costume, 6, 125; marriage, 76; servants, 67.
Ranee mash, 45.
RANGKHOL LANGUAGE, comparative structure, 164–170; comparative vocabularies, 159, 161.
Rās, 54.
Raspberry, 40.
Recidivism, 88
Reed instruments, 57.
Reed jungle, 25.
Regiment, 61, 71.

RELIGION, 94; ancestor worship, 99–103; deities 95-99; rites and ceremonies, 16, 103–109. See also nature-worship, priesthood, etc.
Rice, cultivation, 39 *et seq.*; cooking, 47; varieties, 43.
Riddles, 56.
Rikkhran, 107.
River-pools, legends of, 124; spirits, 96.
Roads, 34.
Romanando Singh, 133
Roof, 25.
Rook, 121.
Roul Loisang, 70.
Royal Family of Manipur. See Ningthaja.
Rubber, 1; cultivation, 44.
Runner, 15.
Rupee, 36, 38.
Russell's viper, 2.

Sacred thread, investiture with, 84, 114.
SACRIFICE, animal, 103; human, 108, and Ningthaja clan, 109.
Saddle, 28; polo, 49.
SAGAI. See SALEI.
Sa-gol (*Sa-kol*), 19.
Sagol Hanjaba, 59.
Sagonsang, 68, 70.
Sagonsem sagei, 68.
Sagontongba, 68.
Sajor, 71.
Salai Hanba, 68.
SALEI (SAGAI), 73, 182–187.
Sallungsang, 68.
SALT, 30, 33–36; imported from Cheshire, 33.
Salt-wells, 34–36; and lāl-lūp, 60.
Samlongpha, 97.
Sampati Rajbibaha, 115.
Sāmū Hanjaba, 59.
Sāmūsang, 68.
Sandal wood, 29.
Sandstone, 28.
Sangairen, 67.
Sangaisel paire, 121.
Sang-cha-loi, 69.
Sanggai sanglen, 70.
Sanggoiba Hanjaba, 67.
—— *Hidang*, 67.
Sangguba, 66, 67.
—— *Sanglakpa*, 66.
Sang-Kai punsiba, 8, 125.
Sanglakpa, 66.
Sanglen, 66, 67.
—— *Hidang*, 66.
—— *Lakpa*, 61, 65.
Sanglinba, 69.
Sangōm Loisang, 70.
Sanjem, 69.
Sanjoiba, 54.
Santhong Mari Mai Langjeng Langmei Thouba, 131.
Sapta pradakhsin, 115.
Sarangthem Lamabi, 98.
SCAPEGOAT CEREMONY, 106.
SCHOOLS, 24.
Sebok-pulla, 70.
—— *pukei*, 70.
Seekong (*Chikhong*), Khul Chaoba, 9; salt-wells, 33–35.
Sekmai. See *Sengmai*.
—— *Awang*, 72.
SEL, 30, 36 *et seq.*
Sellungba, duties, 68; order of precedence, 72.
Sellungba ahal, 67.
——, *naha*, 67.
Sena Kaithel, 18, 23.
Sena-Mehi, festival to, 104; in "Numit Kāppā," 125–129; worship of, 97 *et seq.*, 103.
Senapati, 59, 60; functions, 61, 72.
Sengmai (*Sekmai*), administration, 72; deities, 103; marriage, 116; situation, 9; stills, 32.
Sennakhal, 67.
Separation (marriage), 91.
Sepoy, land tenure, 85; military organization, 61.
Sept, 85.
SEPULTURE, 116.
Serao, 2.
SEVERALTY, 85, 87.
Shaborna Muni, 5.
Sham Shah (*Shai*), 80.
SHAN RACE, influence on Manipuri culture, 10; and religion, 97.
Shan, vel Syan, 10.
Shield, 20.
Shoe, 28.
Shuganu, officials, 72; origin, 9; pottery, 32.
SILK, 30.
Silkworm, 31.
SIN, TRANSFER OF, 101, 104 *et seq.*
Sing-lūp, 94.

Singpho, 32.
Singsu Hanba, 66.
—— *Hidang*, 66.
Singsuba Ahal, 67.
Sky god, 111.
SLAVE AND SLAVERY, desertion of, 23; lällüp, 60, 64, 65; two systems described, 90.
SNAKE, 2; worship of, 100, 110, 125.
Snipe, 2.
Soldier, cavalry, 19; equipment, 28; lalmi, 61; Bijaya Garot, 71.
SONGS, 55, 56.
Sooprabahoo, 5.
Sorarel, 111.
Spear, 20.
Spirit industry, 23, 30, 60.
Spirits, 96; see RELIGION.
Sport, 2, 46.
SPORTS AND PASTIMES, 16, 49–57, 103, 117.
STATE OFFICIALS, 59 *et seq*.
Sticks, omens and calculations by, 105; tabu, 150.
STONES, deity, 98, 99; superstitions, 121; forecast from, 125; worship, 102.
Strawberry, 40.
Subedar (*Subadar*), 71.
Sugarcane, 40, 43.
SUMPTUARY LAWS, 13 *et seq*., 39.
SUN GOD, in "Nūmit Kāppa," 125–129; legends, 111; worship, 97, 103.
Sungsa roi, 63.
SUPERSTITIONS, 120–124.
Sur Chandra Singh, Rajah, 81, 82.
Surja, 5.
Surreng, 45.
Surrong Koibee, 46.
Survey, Land, 86.
Susakameng, inhabitants, 9; officials, 72.
Sylhet, colonies, 4, 23.

TABU, 118–119; marriage, 75; rain ceremonies, 108; rajah, 107, 124; sticks, 150.
TAI RACES, 10.
Taibangbānbagi mapu, 100.
Taibongkhaiba, 98.
Taibong Khōmbi, 98.
Takhen Hanba, 68.
Takhen pungaiba, 69.
Tampāk mayum, 70.
Tangal, 79.
Tāngjing, 72.
Tangkhul, 74.
Tānglei, 2.
Tanning, 28.
Taohuirenga, 126–129.
TATTOOING, 18.
Tax, land, 85–87.
Tea, 1, 44.
Teak, 1.
Teal, 2.
Telhaiba, 131.
Telloi Hanjaba, 61.
—— *Hidang*, 61.
TEMPLE, COL. SIR RICHARD, on currency, 38.
Temple, 26.
Tengkhul Loisang, 69.
Tengkul, 63, 64.
Tensu-Hanba, 66.
THĀDO folk tale, 111.
—— language, comparative structure, 164; comparative vocabularies, 159, 162.
Thāngā, lällüp, 71; Moirang conquers, 131; origin, 9.
Thāngaren, 100.
Thāngchao, 43.
Thānggang saba, 68.
Thānggārakpa, 72.
Thānggol, 43.
Thāngja pānnaba, 68.
Thāngjam, 106.
Thāngjing, 128, 130, 134.
Thāngloihaiba, 135.
Thāngsu-Hanba, 66.
Thaurichingba, 57.
THEFT, laws, 88; statistics, 24.
THIBETAN LANGUAGE, affinities, 10, 155; comparative structure, 163, 170; comparative vocabularies, 157–162.
Thingnung, 70.
Thobal, 41.
Thoibee (*Thoibi Laima*), 56, 133, 134 *et seq*.
Thonglen, 135, 140.
Thong-loi-sang, 67.
Thongnak Lairemma. *See Lairema*.
Thouban-tong, 69.
Thūmjao Rūngba, 60, 67, 72.
Thunder, 111.
TIBETO-BURMAN LANGUAGES, 10.
Tiger, 2, 46, 135.

Tilak, 84.
Til haiba, 47, 131.
Tilli-loi-sang, 69.
Time, reckoning of, 105.
Tingri, 70.
Title, 59 *et seq.*
Tobacco, 40, 43, 48.
Toe-ring, 18.
Toosook, 79.
Tōp garde, 92.
Tōp Tuli, 71.
Tossing the caber, 51.
Tourongbam, 69.
TRADITIONS. See Khāgenba, Origin, Pākhangba, Pamheiba.
Travelling and superstitions, 120.
TREASON, comparative statistics, 23; punishment, 89; example of trial of, in Chronicles, 93.
TRIBAL DEITIES, 99 *et seq.*
Truthfulness, 23.
Tuli-Han, 71.
Tuli Nahā, 71.
——, *Yaima*, 71.
Turnip, 40.

Ukai anālba, 42.
U-kai kāppa, 144, 152.
Ukai samjet, 42.
UMANG LAI, 96; feast, 69; worship, 103.
Umbrellas, use of, 39.
Umu Hidang, 66.
Umu Khullakpa, 66.
United Provinces, India, Meithei settlements in, 4.
Urakonthouba, 132, 133.
Urungba Loisang, 68.
Usāba, 68.
UTENSILS, household, 39.
U-Thlen, 101.
Utōng chāk, 48.

VAISHNAVISM, 96, 104. See also Hinduism.
Vampire, 96.
Vanda caerulea, 16.
Vapeea, 46.
VERELST, GOVERNOR, 29.
VILLAGES, administration, 60, 61, 71 *et seq.*; origin of administration, 131; described, 26; Keis, 70; land tenure, 85–87; Loi, 9, 32 *et seq.*; 71 *et seq.*; succession to offices, 83.

WADDELL, LL.D., C.B., C.I.E., COLONEL L. A., 3.
Waihaiba, 98.
Waikōng, 33, 35.
Wākching, 13, 70.
Wall, 26.
Wānching, 13.
Wāngbon Ningthoukhong, 70.
Wāngkhai Hidang, 66
——, *rakpa*, duties, 91; status, 65.
Wangmanai, 68.
Wangpurel, 98.
Wāritābas, 56, 117.
War stone, 102, 103.
WATT, K.C.I.E., SIR GEORGE, 44.
Wax, 29.
Wazir, 75.
WEAPONS, 19 *et seq.*
WEAVING, 23, 27, 28.
Wheat, 43, 44.
White fowl, in "Nūmit Kāppa," 128.
Widow, 77.
Wild duck, 2.
WOMEN, appearance, 2; coiffure, 3; coinage, 38; costume, 13 *et seq.*; dancing, 16, 17, 22, 54; divorce, 91; economic position, 22; education, 24; fishing, 45; jewelry, 19; Law Courts, 83, 92; laws, 77, 91; marriage, 75, 115; pastimes, 16, 55 *et seq.*; pottery, 32; as priestess, 101, 109, 110; punishment, 88, 89; rain-compelling ceremony, 108; tabu, 102, 153; weaving, 22, 27; status as wives, 91.
Wood turning, 28.
Woodcock, 2.
WRESTLER, WRESTLING, 54; costume, 16; in "Khamba and Thoibi," 137–141; pagri, 15.

Yairibok Ningthounai Kei, 70.
Yaithibi, 70.
Yakhong Lai, 131.
Yandabo, Treaty of, 58, 59, 81.
Yaosurakpa, 72.
Yaphi ahal, 67.
—— *Naha*, 67.
Yaripōk, 9.
—— *Chāba*, 70.
Yathang thaba, 115.
Yeina phak, 43.

Yek, 85.
Yentik, 43.
Yim Chau, 6.
Yim tinaba, 64.
Yoithongnai, 134.
Yōt, 43.
Yū (*Zū*), manufacture, 32, 60; as marriage gift, 116.
Yumjilloi, 68.
YUMNĀK, 73, 85; lists, 182–187.
Yumnam, 98.
Yumthai Lai, 98, 99.
Yūpalpa, 60, 72.

Zū. See *Yū*.

THE END.

PRINTED BY WILLIAM CLOWES AND SONS, LIMITED, LONDON AND BECCLES.